KT-482-857

POLITICS AND POWER

With

Withdrawn

SKILLS-BASED SOCIOLOGY

Series Editors: Tony Lawson and Tim Heaton

The *Skills-based Sociology* series is designed to cover all the key concepts, issues and debates in Sociology. The books take a critical look at contemporary developments in sociological knowledge as well as essential social theories. Each title examines a key topic area within sociology, offering relevant examples and student-focused pedagogical features to aid learning and develop essential study skills.

Published

THEORY AND METHOD (*second edition*)
Mel Churton and Anne Brown

RELIGION AND BELIEF
Joan Garrod and Marsha Jones

CULTURE AND IDENTITY
Warren Kidd

POLITICS AND POWER
Warren Kidd, Karen Legge and Philippe Harari

STRATIFICATION AND DIFFERENCE
Mark Kirby

CRIME AND DEVIANCE (*second edition*)
Tony Lawson and Tim Heaton

EDUCATION AND TRAINING (*second edition*)
Tony Lawson, Tim Heaton and Anne Brown

HEALTH AND ILLNESS
Michael Senior and Bruce Viveash

Forthcoming

THE MEDIA (*second edition*)
Marsha Jones, Emma Jones and Andy Jones

THE FAMILY (*second edition*)
Liz Steel, Warren Kidd and Anne Brown

Skills-based Sociology
Series Standing Order ISBN 0–333–69350–7
(*outside North America only*)

You can receive future titles in this series as they are published. To place a standing order please contact your bookseller or, in the case of difficulty, write to us at the address below with your name and address, the title of the series and the ISBN quoted above.

Customer Service Department, Macmillan Distribution Ltd, Houndmills, Basingstoke, Hampshire RG21 6XS, England

Politics and Power

Warren Kidd

Karen Legge

and

Philippe Harari

palgrave
macmillan

First published 2010 by
PALGRAVE MACMILLAN

Palgrave Macmillan in the UK is an imprint of Macmillan Publishers Limited, registered in England, company number 785998, of Houndmills, Basingstoke, Hampshire RG21 6XS.

Palgrave Macmillan in the US is a division of St Martin's Press LLC, 175 Fifth Avenue, New York, NY 10010.

Palgrave Macmillan is the global academic imprint of the above companies and has companies and representatives throughout the world.

Palgrave® and Macmillan® are registered trademarks in the United States, the United Kingdom, Europe and other countries.

ISBN 978–0–333–96889–5

This book is printed on paper suitable for recycling and made from fully managed and sustained forest sources. Logging, pulping and manufacturing processes are expected to conform to the environmental regulations of the country of origin.

A catalogue record for this book is available from the British Library.

A catalog record for this book is available from the Library of Congress.

10   9   8   7   6   5   4   3   2   1
19   18   17   16   15   14   13   12   11   10

Printed in Great Britain by
CPI Antony Rowe, Chippenham and Eastbourne

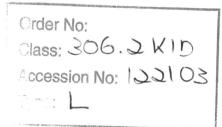

Contents

Chapter 1

Introduction

THE PHILOSOPHY BEHIND THE BOOK

This book is part of the Skills-based Sociology series – a series that seeks to provide theoretical and research up-dates in important sociology topic areas. This series also develops students' understanding of these topic areas by providing detailed and student-centred activities to work through.

This book takes an important feature of contemporary sociological debate and discussion – *politics* and, more generally, sociological ideas of *power* – and shows how these ideas have changed as society itself has developed. The book does not present a chronological 'history of ideas' of sociological interpretations of the role of power in society. It takes the ideas of classical sociologists and maps out how they have been developed, reinterpreted and evaluated in the light of changes in society. It focuses on post-Second World War developments and, in particular, on more recent changes in the social, economic, cultural and political landscapes that make up the contemporary United Kingdom.

WHAT IS THE ROLE OF POLITICAL ISSUES WITHIN SOCIOLOGY?

This book will suggest that political issues are fundamental to sociology – we cannot have sociological debates and especially sociological theories without giving consideration to issues that are political in nature – even if we do not always use this word in an overt fashion. In sociological language, the word *politics* and its related concept of *power* mean very particular things, which may be slightly different from what these words might mean in everyday language and in other subjects.

As sociologists, we must make a key distinction between:

- **Power** – getting one's own way in society – being able to do what one wishes, and have others do what you wish;
- **Politics** – the battles or struggles for power between different groups, and even individuals.

Issues of power are essential if we are to understand how society works and, therefore, they are essential to understanding sociology. We will take up this theme in more detail in Chapters 2 and 3, where we look at the different theories sociologists have on the nature of power and its role in society.

THE FEATURES OF THE BOOK

Like all editions in the Skills-based Sociology series, this book is intended to educate and inform, as well as to help students to pass examinations. Although we are interested in up-dating the sociology of politics, we are also mindful that due attention must be paid to more classical ideas, especially those of the so-called 'founders' of sociology, even though they wrote such a long time ago. These ideas are the legacy and inheritance of modern-day sociology. Although we should be open to being critical of such thinking if we feel it is 'out-dated' in any way, we must also see how sociological ideas have flowed out from these original conceptualizations of the nature of power and politics.

For most assessments, students will be examined on their:

- knowledge
- understanding
- application
- analysis
- interpretation
- evaluation

In order to help readers to develop the above skills, this text provides exercises in each chapter. Each exercise identifies the particular skill or skills that they seek to help you to develop: the symbol **K** is used for the skill of knowledge; **U** is used to stand for understanding; **A** is used for application; **I** for interpretation; **An** for analysis; and, finally, **E** stands for evaluation.

At the end of each chapter there is a list of important terms, a summary of the chapter content and a 'Critical Thinking' section. Taken together, it is hoped that these will help you to engage with the text, and to reflect on some of the important issues.

CONTENT OF THE BOOK

We recommend that after this chapter, whatever else you do, you read Chapters 2, 3 and 4 before any others. These chapters will introduce you to the key ideas, themes and debates in political sociology and will introduce many of the theories needed to understand what sociology has to say. Chapter 2, specifically, looks at the related ideas of power and politics and how these are vital to all sociology. Chapters 3 and 4 provide an overview of various sociological theories and interpretations of what power is like and how it is used in society. Chapter 3 looks at the ideas on power and politics of the classical sociologists who are seen to have founded the discipline of sociology that we recognize today, while Chapter 4 looks at a brief history of sociological ideas on power from the founders to the modern day. Chapter 5 continues looking at how sociological theories have changed over time and discusses more contemporary theories of power.

Chapters 6 through to 9 each take a key theme in sociological debates on the role of power in society, and use the theories introduced in Chapters 2–5 to understand these debates. They are, in chapter order:

▪ (Chapter 6) The political landscape of modern UK society and the ideologies or political views that different political parties have.
▪ (Chapter 7) Looking at how and why people in the UK vote as they do.
▪ (Chapter 8) Sociological debates on and interpretations over the nature of the state in the UK.
▪ (Chapter 9) Looking at issues of globalization and nationalization and how they have shaped modern-day societies. Plus, understanding the role played by people in trying to achieve political change – through the joining of pressure groups, new social movements or through revolution and protest.

Chapter 2

Introducing the Nature of Power and Politics in Everyday Life

By the end of this chapter you should be able to:

- recognize the difference between the sociological use of the terms power and politics
- understand the difficulties in defining the word power clearly and universally
- appreciate the different ways in which sociologists have thought about the role of power in society

INTRODUCTION

We will start this book with a statement that summarizes how we see the role of political sociology within sociology as a whole:

All aspects of social life are based upon power, and therefore all aspects of sociological study draw from themes within political sociology.

This is a bold statement, but such is the importance of power and politics in everyday life, it is necessary to understand its importance to sociology as well. If you want a general introduction to how different sociologists see the world around them, looking at political sociology would be a good choice to make.

As suggested in Chapter 1, it is important to draw a distinction between the concept of power and that of politics:

Power is about getting what you want, and politics is about how and why different groups struggle to get what they want.

There might be various ways in which this struggle takes place, and even various groups who are involved in it. However, one thing is sure: all sociological theories have a view on this aspect of society. Deciding which one might be the most realistic, however, is a far from easy task, given the diverse natures of both sociological thinking and society itself – and the many varied relationships between the different groups that make society what it is.

TRYING TO DEFINE POWER AND POLITICS

At its most simple, power means the ability to do what you want – to be successful in your goals. This is a useful definition, but it is by no means a universal one. Although most sociologists would agree that this is broadly what the term means, quite how individuals or groups might go about it causes great disagreement and debate. Carry out Exercise 2.1 to begin to explore the exercise of power in your own life.

Exercise 2.1

1. Think about different ways in which you exercise power, and in which power is exercised over you. Make a list of as many people, organizations etc. as you can under the following headings:

   ○ Those who exercise power over me
   ○ Those over whom I exercise power

You may like to use the following questions to help you with your list. All of these are important questions in any consideration of power.

1. Does power exist at an individual or a group level?
2. What groups have more power than other groups?
3. Why do powerful groups have power? (What is their basis for having power?)
4. For how long have they had this power?
5. How do they use this power? (Who benefits?)

There may be no agreed answers to these questions (although there is agreement that we should ask these questions).

2. Look at your two lists, and for each point think about where the source of the power lies (for example, age, the law, gender, work status etc.). You should copy and use the following grid:

Those who exercise power over me	Those over whom I exercise power	Source of power

It is one thing to say that power means 'to do what you want', but in asking how this is possible we can see that the idea of power is quite abstract and difficult to measure, since it may not be easy to see the actual working of power in society. Sociology seeks, then,

1. to try and define the concept of power carefully;
2. to develop ways to measure power;
3. to suggest ways that power might be more fairly divided (although again, what is and is not considered to be fair might also depend on how you see the world).

As Iain MacKenzie says,

> Everyone has a sense of what it means to be powerful or powerless. We say people are powerful when they can wield influence over others ... [and] the powerless, whom we typically think of as the majority of any society, are those without ... just as 'cold' is defined as the absence of 'heat', so powerlessness is defined as the absence of power. This implies that we know what power is and that we can unproblematically describe and categorise its various manifestations. However, the whole drift of contemporary social and political theory is in the other direction. Power is an 'essentially contested concept'. (Ashe *et al.*, 1999, p. 69)

As we can see, the fact that ideas of power are *contested* – not agreed upon – is at odds with how we might think about power as ordinary members of a society, going about our day-to-day business. The fact that sociologists believe the meaning of power is unclear is even more important, because only by arguing and debating about it might we think about it in fresh and interesting ways.

Marxist sociologists Westergaard and Resler (1976) have also identified the problems that sociologists have when beginning to think about power in society: 'Power . . . is a rather exclusive phenomenon. Its effects are tangible. But power as such is something of an abstraction . . . and just because it is not hard and fact, there is no simple and agreed definition of what it is' (p. 142).

In trying to think about power – what it is and what it does – MacKenzie identifies five areas or levels in society that we might try and think about:

1. *Power and agency* (individuals) – how much say do ordinary people have over their actions on a day-to-day basis? How much agency (or freedom/free will) do they have?
2. *Power and structure* (society) – how rooted and integral are power relationships within the overall make-up of society as a whole? To what extent does society as a thing weigh down upon individuals – regulating their decisions, actions and options?
3. *Power and domination* – what happens if people step out of line? How are they punished? Is it the case that some groups benefit from the punishing of others?
4. *Power and empowerment* – should we see power as a tool to use against others or as a way to make decisions about and for ourselves? Is it, in MacKenzie's words a question of power over *what others do* or is it power to do something *for ourselves*?
5. *Power and identity* – how does having power, struggling for power or being the objects of someone else's power make us who we are? What is the relationship between power and how we come to see ourselves in society – our identity?

ⒶⓊ

Exercise 2.2

Give examples of each area of power that MacKenzie outlines above. For instance, an individual who decides to give up cigarettes and succeeds in doing so has a high level of agency. However, if the person feels obliged to give up smoking because of social disapproval, then that is an example of 'power and structure'. Similarly, a sweatshop worker in India may feel she has very little agency because she is forced to work long hours in poor conditions out of economic necessity. In addition, her behaviour may also be regulated by society because she is female. The owner of the sweatshop may appoint one of the workers as an overseer, with the authority to punish other workers if they are late or are working too slowly. This individual now has power over others and, because they are now earning a little more, they also have the power to do more for themselves. Finally, people's position in the power hierarchy is often closely linked to their identity. People tend to say 'I am the boss' rather than 'my job is to be the boss'.

Steven Lukes (1974), whose radical theory of power has been important in sociological debates on the nature of power (see Chapter 3), identifies two ways that sociologists think about power and its role in society:

1. either power is gained through battle, struggle and the possible resistance from others;
2. or, power is the outcome of agreement – it is not held by some over and at the expense of, others who have none of it.

These two views on power go to the very heart of all sociological theories, and are related to the fundamental sociological question – are societies in harmony or are they in conflict (and if so, between whom)?

Using the 'sociological imagination' to think about power

A very useful idea, for the sociologist and student of sociology alike, is that of a 'sociological imagination' and it is this that we need to develop in order to think about power and politics in a detailed way. This imagination refers to the fact that, when thinking about how society operates, we need, as sociologists, to try and distance ourselves from what we think about society as members of it. We need to use theories, look at history and conduct research – to provide the evidence – before we can begin to relate our understanding to our own personal experiences. This sociological imagination means that if we, as sociologists, see power in the same common-sense way that we use the term as social actors, then we will miss the point. The point is that power is not clear, not easy and not agreed upon. But, by understanding this, we can think more clearly about *why* power is not clear: we can begin to look in a detailed way at power, to tease out its very essence more closely. This will enable sociologists to expose power's workings in society, in a way that as members of such a society they might take for granted or misunderstand.

The idea of a sociological imagination has been developed from the ideas of American sociologist C. Wright Mills (1959) in his book of the same name. In terms of thinking about power, Mills, elsewhere, says:

> Power has to do with whatever decisions men [*sic*] make about the arrangements under which they live, and about the events which make up the history of their times. Events that are beyond human decision do happen; social arrangements do change without benefit of explicit decision. But in so far as such decisions are made, the problem of who is involved in making them is the basic problem of power. In so far as they could be made but are not, the problem becomes who fails to make them? (Mills, 1963, p. 236)

What this means is that it is important to see society as a complex web of decision making. There are a whole range of individuals, groups and organizations struggling to make decisions, to have influence and to get their own way. Even when things appear to happen without reason, those who have power may have either decided to let these things happen or they may have failed to do prevent them happening. Either way, the fact that the powerful can influence the shape of society, and do so on other occasions of their choosing, means they must be able to manipulate massive resources of power. The rest of us, us 'ordinary social actors' – the most we are likely to be able to do is to maybe influence the shape, direction and course of our own life and actions and make our own decisions. Even then, this may only be within a framework handed down by others.

Is power a large-scale or small-scale phenomenon?

Issues of power are, thus, related to issues of freedom and independence. How much freedom I have to do as I wish (to make my own choices) is probably a good indicator of how much power I have. This assumes, of course, that the things I think I wish to do have not been manipulated by someone else without my knowledge of this manipulation. For example, it can be argued that advertizing works in this way. I may go to a shop and buy a particular item in the firm belief that I have chosen to do so out of my own free will, whereas I have been, in effect, persuaded to buy that item by a television advert I watched the night before. It can be hard to tell whether our actions genuinely reflect free choices.

The sociologist Zygmunt Bauman (1990) suggests we should always think of power and choice as being related. The amount of choice I have is dependent upon the amount of power I have to be able to make a choice that is of my own choosing, not someone else's. For example, Bauman asks us to consider the vital question 'Why do I do what I do?'. Bauman says that the answer to this question is often *not* 'Because I felt like it' (although it may seem like this at the time), but in fact, it is usually 'Because society says so'. It is custom or habit to do so, as taught to us through our socialization into our society.

For example, all our seemingly individual choices can be seen to relate to the cause-and-effect of much wider, social-wide forces:

Why do I rush when late for classes?	*Because my teachers will tell me off.*
Why do I wear these trousers?	*Because they are fashionable.*
Why am I reading this book?	*Because I want to pass my examinations.*

Take this last example and let us think about the role of power and choice in society – at both large-scale and small-scale levels. You are reading this book to pass your examinations. However, this reading might be set as personal work and you might get in trouble if you don't do it. So, how much say do you really have over this? You might choose not to do it, but if so, you cannot choose to be or not to be punished for it – someone else decides your fate for you. Your choices have consequences that are controlled by someone else. Why are you bothering to pass your examinations? Did you choose to take sociology – or was this choice constrained by your parents or your teachers? Are you really choosing to continue with your studies, or is it the case that other people have suggested that you ought to, and you don't really feel that you have the option not to, given the importance society places on education? Who was it that decided that education was a good thing for society? What groups have the power to decide what subjects you can and cannot be taught?

As we can see, we may be able to make choices, but those with real power are those who get to shape the exact choices on offer at any given time, and who also get to say what consequences the wrong choice will have.

This means that power exists on both large-scale and small-scale levels. For example:

Small scale

1. Individuals can pick and choose what they do on a day-to-day basis.
2. Individuals can try and get their own way over other individuals.
3. Individuals can refuse to do something, or try and resist having something done to them.

Large scale

1. Governments decide what individuals can or cannot legally do.
2. Governments can decide how and why individuals can be punished for what they do that is wrong.
3. Society teaches you what is customary (through the process of socialization) and some groups might benefit from this more than others.
4. Some groups shape what is considered to be customary in the first place.
5. Power can be exercised internationally, such as the intervention by Western troops in Afghanistan.

Exercise 2.3

Give a real-world example of each of the small-scale and large-scale forms of power listed above, other than the one used in point 5.

Keith Dowding (1996) suggests that in order to analyse power and how it works we need to move beyond a simple distinction between *elite theories* and *democratic theories*. An elite is a select group of people who consider themselves superior in some way to the mass of the population and who adopt the right to rule over others. Elite theorists tend to think of power as something that is wielded by a few people in their own interests whereas democratic theorists tend to see power as belonging to everyone and being used collectively for the benefit of society. Instead, Dowding suggests that we should look at:

1. Individual action: for example, the decision of a mother whether or not to breastfeed her newborn baby.
2. Group action: the decision whether to breastfeed will be strongly influenced by the social group of the mother and by the opportunities, or lack of them, for breastfeeding.
3. The actions performed by organizations: companies that manufacture powdered baby milk can attempt to persuade mothers not to breastfeed; other organizations may try to persuade mothers that 'breast is best'.
4. The incentives (motivations) that direct human action in the very first place: the mother will be motivated by the desire to have a healthy child, but also by wanting to be seen to be a good mother, whatever that involves.

Ⓤ①
Exercise 2.4

Think about what Dowding is suggesting. Give examples of the way power is used in Dowding's four categories.

	Example
Individual action	
Group action	
Actions performed by organizations	
Incentives that direct human actions	

Dowding says that we must recognize that people's desires, goals and subsequent actions are not just individual motivations but are structured and influenced by the sorts of relationships they have with groups of others, and with the organizations they belong to and those they would like to belong to. Dowding also notes that whereas those who have power tend to want it, they may not have been especially successful in actually trying to get it. Having power may be the result of luck as well as desire and calculation and we should separate these types of power from each other, in order to study power in greater detail.

Understanding power as the 'freedom to choose to act'

For many sociologists, power is a feature hidden behind every choice that we make or think we make and therefore it is an ever present feature of society, no matter who we are, who we are with and what we are doing. Power is both macro and micro, and if you have it, it frees you to act as you wish – power is something that you can use it for your own benefit.

As Bauman points out:

Power is, indeed, best understood as the ability to act – both in the sense of choosing freely the ends of any action and of commanding the means which make such ends realistic. Power is an enabling capacity. The more power people have, the wider is their range of choice, the larger the amount of decisions they can see as realistic, the broader the scope of outcomes they may realistically pursue while being reasonably certain that they would get what they want. Being less powerful, or powerless, means it is necessary to moderate one's dreams, or to abandon attempts to reach one's aims due to the absence of necessary resources. (Bauman, 1990, p. 113)

TWO VIEWS OF POWER

To take our initial discussion of the nature of power further, we shall now consider the views of two very influential thinkers who have both tried to define what power is, how it works and who benefits from it:

1. Thomas Hobbes
2. Steven Lukes

These ideas on power represent a very early classical view on power – provided by the ideas of Hobbes – and a more up-to-date view of power – as seen in the writings of Lukes. Together, these will illustrate how sociologists think about power in society. Both of these views have been adopted, developed and adapted by many sociologists and form the basis of many of the newer sociological ideas on power to be discussed in Chapter 3 in more detail.

Thomas Hobbes: natural and instrumental types of power

Political thinker and philosopher Thomas Hobbes, in his book *Leviathan*, written in the middle of the seventeenth century, makes a distinction between natural and instrumental types of power. This is considered by many to be one of the earliest attempts to think about power in any detailed or ordered way.

- Natural power comes *before* instrumental power, and refers to the sort of power that allows someone to dominate someone else – physically or mentally/intellectually. So, for example, having the gift of the gab is a form of natural power. Again, in this view, Hobbes sees power as being able to exercise your own will.
- Secondly, there is instrumental power, which refers to any more power you develop or build upon, as a result of already having natural power – in other words, how you might continue to acquire even more power once you have started. For example, an individual may be naturally articulate, but they can gain further power by being trained in the use of rhetoric (see Exercise 2.5).

MacKenzie (2005) suggests that because it describes power as something that allows people to dominate others, there are three important aspects to this early definition of power that are worth thinking about:

1. Power can be *individualistic* – it can be held by individual people and everyone has the ability to have it.
2. Power is about having the *potential* or the ability to choose or get that which you wish for – power is about being able to have the freedom to do as you wish, to be able to fulfil your dreams and desires unhindered.
3. Finally, power is *relative* – this means that if you have it, you only have it because someone else does not: your power is gained through someone else's powerlessness.

Exercise 2.5

Make a list of all the examples of natural power that you can think of. For each example, describe how it could be enhanced, resulting in instrumental power.

Steven Lukes: the three dimensions of power

Like Hobbes, Lukes seeks to understand the nature of power in society by thinking about the ways that people and groups are able to get their own way, and therefore the ways they are able to get other people to do as they wish. Lukes identifies three levels or, as he calls them, dimensions of power as a feature of every society. However, Lukes warns against sociological theories that only take into account the first or second levels, and ignore the important third and hidden level of power. This is a criticism he uses against pluralist and pluralist-influenced theories of power (see Chapter 3).

Lukes makes a distinction between:

- Dimension one – power as decision-making.
- Dimension two – power as non-decision-making.
- Dimension three – power as shaping the decisions of others.

Making decisions, dimension one, is the most basic, simple and visible form of power, since we can see decisions being made or, at least, we can see the outcomes and consequences of such decisions. We can then try and figure out who was in a position to make or influence the decision and who benefited from the decision – and were they the same group of people? An example of this is where a Principal of a college decides to ban all drinks from classrooms in an attempt to create a more formal and disciplined atmosphere during lessons. The second dimension needs more explaining – what is a non-decision and how do you (not) make it? This refers to the way in which some decisions aren't actual decisions that are thought about, planned, discussed and then decided upon. Instead, some courses of action seem so utterly *obvious* to a powerful group that they don't actually make a decision. They just do what they want to do, and don't think or question it since it seems so obvious that this would be the only possible or desirable way of doing things in the first place. An example of this is where a college decides to introduce a strict regime to improve punctuality and attendance, without considering whether it is educationally beneficial for students to be made to turn up to all lessons on time rather than be given greater control over their learning.

Lukes describes the third dimension of power as the most powerful and also the most worrying of all, due to its hidden nature – and the fact that by shaping the decisions of others you are controlling what others think and what they think they think! Some would argue that an example of this is the way that schoolchildren are brainwashed over the years into accepting the authority of their teachers so that they do not even question being told to do things that may not be in their best interests.

> Is it not the supreme and most insidious exercise of power to prevent people, to whatever degree, from having grievances by shaping their perceptions, cognitions and preferences in such a way that they accept their role in the existing order of things . . . ? (Lukes, 1974, p. 24)

This shaping of decisions is very similar to classical sociologist Weber's notion of trying to win the hearts and minds of those you wish to have power over. If you can get people to think that your rule and their interests are the same – when they are not – you are more likely to get them to do as you wish (see Chapter 3). Equally, if you can convince people that what you want them to do is in fact exactly what they themselves would wish to do, they will do it all the more readily and come to see this situation as normal, as natural and, most worrying of all, as beyond question. This is also similar to the neo-Marxist idea of hegemony as developed by Italian thinker Gramsci (see Chapter 4).

CONTEMPORARY RETHINKING ON THE NATURE OF POLITICS IN SOCIETY

Keith Dowding notes that there are two main ways of thinking about power:

- power to do something
- power over someone or something

These two are interrelated, yet it is also useful to think about them separately since they can be quite different. To have power over others seems to suggest that you have the ability to control some people in society. To have power to do something might mean that you are able to help some people – yet, at the end of the day, you are still in control in deciding to help others in the first place (do Exercise 2.6 to explore this distinction more deeply). Finally, Dowding usefully notes that power is a dispositional concept. By this he means that to have power is not the same thing as using power: it is power *to do*, rather than always power *to have done* something. For example, some feminists argue that all men, regardless of their own feelings and beliefs, have power over women because they have the potential to commit sexual assaults, and that, consequently, relations between the sexes can never be truly equal. So, although an individual man may never choose to wield this power, the mere fact that our patriarchal society provides him with the potential to wield it gives him power over the women he meets. Others would argue that, in order for a man to have real power over the women he meets in this context, he needs to have actually wielded this power.

(E)

Exercise 2.6

Do you agree that merely having the potential to exert power over others is bound to affect the relationship you have with them, or do you believe that this only happens if you actually act to exert that power? For example, can people in positions of power in society ever form successful interpersonal relationships with the people over whom they have power? Some would argue that bosses should not have relationships with employees, teachers with students (even if above the age of consent) and therapists with clients etc.

Write a paragraph on your opinions about this issue, including an example from your own life.

Have we lost politics?

Zygmunt Bauman (1999) suggests that politics is something very different from what it once was. He notes that there is an almost contradictory attitude to politics and to shaping decisions in the contemporary world:

- On the one hand, it seems that most people in the West are happy with what they see as the democratic nature of their society – major protest does not happen very often.
- Yet, on the other hand, most people seem to consider that nothing can be changed about the present society and that it would be pointless to try to make change happen.

As Bauman himself notes:

> How these two beliefs can be held at the same time would be a mystery to any person trained in logical thinking. If freedom has been won, how does it come about that human ability to imagine a better world and to do something to make it better was not among the trophies of victory? And what sort of freedom is it that discourages imagination and tolerates the impotence of free people in matters which concern them all? (Bauman, 1999, p. 1)

For Bauman, modern day society has lost the ability to translate private worries into public issues. What he means by this is that although many people in society have their concerns, fears, aspirations and expectations, the activities of those elected to rule and the sorts of issues they make public seem a different world away from what people themselves think about. In a sense, we have lost politics, since we have lost a society were people are interested in politics in the sense of what rulers do for, to and over them.

Bauman is quite critical of this sort of society – one where individualism has replaced collective political action and debate. Instead, he suggests, people do still have their worries and concerns but feel there is no point in voicing them (explore your own opinions of this issue in Exercise 2.7). Meanwhile, governments make people happy by allowing them to spend their money on more and more commodities as a source of freedom – as Bauman puts it, the removal of limits (the creation of a freedom) to accumulate even more junk as source of satisfaction and as a means by which ordinary people can feel they have some sort of power. This view is very similar to the ideas held by Marxists on politics (see Chapter 3), but the idea that we have lost interest in political action in contemporary times is a common theme of a much newer political sociology.

Exercise 2.7

As a class or in small groups consider recent political and economic events. Think of some examples of inactivity over issues that should perhaps concern us all.

Do you agree with Bauman's assertion that we tend not to translate *private worries* into *public issues?* Give reasons for your answer.

In echoing the ideas of Bauman, that politics for some is seen to have come to an end, Andrew Gamble (2000) suggests that:

> Politics was once regarded as an activity which could give human societies control over their fate. There is now a deep pessimism about the ability of human beings to control anything very much, least of all through politics. This new fatalism about the human condition claims we are living through a major watershed in human affairs . . . Its most characteristic expression is the endless discourses on endism . . . the end of authority, the end of the public domain, the end of politics itself – all have been proclaimed in recent years. (Gamble, 2000, p. ix)

Exercise 2.8

1. Using Gamble's quote above, copy and complete the following grid:

Things over which I have control	Things over which I have little or no control

2. Compare your lists with other members of your class. How do your lists differ, and in what ways are they similar? In the light of what you have read in this chapter, what does this tell you about your own attitudes and values?

We are often told by the media, by some sociologists and by some politicians themselves that politics is at an end – and that this is our fate. Since we live in a so-called advanced globalized world, the older political conflicts between classes, extremes of political views and between different parts of the globe are at an end. As a result, the more similar societies and political parties become. For some, this sameness of politics is a good thing, showing just how advanced society is becoming since we now all agree on what the best course of action is. For others, it is a source of concern since the more same we are told we are becoming, the less opportunity there is for critical thought and open, free debate.

For those who are glad that politics has come – or is coming – to an end, politics is seen, according to Gamble, to be something based upon greed, corruption and waste. The activities of politicians and political parties are seen to be based upon self-interest and the end of this sort of politics will mean that people start to get what they need, rather than those in power doing what they want. On the other hand, for others, the end of politics means that, as political parties seem to get increasingly similar as time goes on (see Chapter 5), choice disappears. This end of politics leads to the lack of political choice and an increase in corruption and greed, since parties can do what they wish as there is no choice between them. In both cases, value-judgements are being used rather than evidence.

The media often lead the way in declaring the end of politics – using lack of voting at general elections as evidence of the growing mistrust ordinary people have with politics and politicians.

Exercise 2.9

Work in groups to design a questionnaire to test the assertions of Bauman and Gamble.

You could make this as elaborate or as simple as time allows. For example, you could design a questionnaire to find out about the attitudes of your peers to political ideas and action, and collect data from this group alone; or you could compare this group with the ideas and attitudes of a different age group.

Gamble – like Bauman above – suggests that we need not fear the so-called end of politics, nor write politics off as left over from a bygone age. Politics is seen to have a great deal to offer, but this clearly depends upon how the notion of politics is defined in the first place. For Gamble and Bauman, politics is not simply deciding who will run the government, or who has control over public affairs, or even how we reach compromises with others in our public and our private lives. They argue that politics is everywhere; wherever people associate with each other, conflict is inevitable, and power helps to decide who gets their way in the end. We need to face the world rather than to give in to claims of the end of politics. This is not our fate, but the inability for people to become involved in the process of decision-making will increase the more people give up and accept what they are told – that politics has nothing to do with their lives. Instead, for Gamble and Bauman, politics should be seen as bound up with the ordinary lives of ordinary people – ordinary decisions that people make over their lives are themselves political since they involve desires, wishes, fears and the opportunity to improve on what they already have. These *are* political concerns since they are based upon decision making and the desire to obtain resources in society that might make one's life more desirable and comfortable.

Understanding the new political sociology

For some modern day sociologists, definitions of power have changed within sociology so much that it is now possible to identify a new political sociology quite different in focus from the older, more classical sociological studies (as we will see in Chapter 3). This change in sociological ways of looking at politics is often seen to have changed in line with how politics is seen by members of society, especially in the light of the claims to an end of politics that are being discussed in the media at present. Kate Nash (2000) defines the old and the new sociologies of politics as follows:

The old sociology of politics looks at:

- the role of the state in decision-making;
- the role of class in the political struggle between groups;
- power within nation states.

The new sociology of politics, however, looks at:

- defining power in the broadest sense possible;
- politics after class;
- power between nation states rather than within nation states.

Nash refers to this new sociology of politics as being concerned with cultural politics. This means that modern day sociologists of power seek to see power in everyday life, rather than just as something done by governments, trade unions and political parties. We chart the development of this change or rethink from the old sociology of power (in Chapter 3) to the new sociologies of power in Chapter 4.

CONCLUSION

As we can see, sociological discussion of power starts with the realization that the idea of power is a complex, often invisible and difficult idea to define and measure directly. However, it is an important feature of all societies and all social relationships. The analysis of power – and the struggles between groups for power (what we call politics) – is central to sociological debate and to all sociological theorizing. It is to these theories we now turn in Chapter 3 by initially looking at the ideas of those thinkers considered to be the founders of modern day sociology.

Exam focus

For the following question, identify the material from this chapter that you could use in a response.

> Identify and describe *two* different sociological definitions of power. Which do you find the most convincing and why?

Carry out an audit of the question before you try and answer it. In an audit you should ask yourself the following questions:

a) What is the question asking me to do in terms of the skills I have to demonstrate? (Hint: there are *three* skills contained within the wording of the question.)
b) What is the subject matter of the question? (Hint: you need to recognize the numerical limitation in the question, as well as the content.)

Important concepts

- power and ... agency, structure, domination, empowerment, identity
- sociological imagination • freedom, choice and independence
- elite versus democratic theories of power • Hobbes: natural and instrumental power • Lukes: the three dimensions of power • power as a dispositional concept • Bauman: private worries and public issues
- the end of politics • the new sociology of politics: cultural politics

---

Summary points

- Power is difficult to define because it is quite abstract and difficult to measure. Also, different people have different views of what power is. Sociology seeks to:

  - try and define the concept of power carefully;
  - develop ways to measure power;
  - suggest ways that power might be more fairly divided.

- Power operates at different levels within society, and sociologists argue whether:

  - power is gained through battle, struggle and possible resistance from others (the elitist model), or
  - power is the outcome of agreement (the democratic model).

- Zygmunt Bauman suggests that power and choice are related. However, Dowding argues that people's desires and goals are not just individual motivations but are structured and influenced by the sorts of relationships they have with groups of others, and with the organizations.

- Thomas Hobbes makes a distinction between natural and instrumental types of power.

- Steven Lukes seeks to understand the nature of power in society by thinking about the ways that people and groups are able to get their own way, and identifies three dimensions of power:

  - Dimension one – power as decision-making;
  - Dimension two – power as non-decision-making;
  - Dimension three – power as shaping the decisions of others.

- Dowding notes that there are two main ways of thinking about power: power to do something and power over someone or something. He also argues that power is a dispositional concept; having power is not the same thing as using power.

- Bauman argues that modern day society has lost the ability to translate private worries into public issues. This means the end of politics because we have lost a society in which people are interested in what rulers do for, to and over them.

- However, others argue that politics is not simply deciding who will run the government or who has control over public affairs. Wherever people associate with each other conflict is inevitable, and power helps to decide who gets their way in the end.
- The old sociology of politics looked at:
  - the role of the state in decision-making;
  - the role of class in the political struggle between groups;
  - power within nation-states.

The new sociology of politics, however, looks at:

- defining power in the broadest sense possible;
- politics after class;
- power between nation-states rather than within nation states.

Critical thinking

1. Is power in our society concentrated in the hands of a minority?
2. Describe, with examples, the difference between natural and instrumental forms of power.
3. Describe the distinctions among Steven Lukes three dimensions of power.
4. Do you agree with Bauman that, in modern society, individualism has replaced collective political action and debate?
5. Is politics at an end?

Chapter 3

Classical Views on Power and Politics

By the end of this chapter you should:

- understand the origins of sociology and the contributions made by Comte
- be familiar with the classical/founding ideas of Marx, Durkheim and Weber on the nature of power and politics
- understand the personal political views of the founders themselves
- be able to compare and contrast the ideas of Marx, Durkheim and Weber
- be able to evaluate the ideas of Marx, Durkheim and Weber
- be able to apply the ideas of Marx, Durkheim and Weber to power in modern day society

INTRODUCTION

Auguste Comte (1798–1857) is generally considered to be the founder of modern-day sociology. He is generally seen to have created the term, at a time when many other philosophers and economists were also trying to develop a new science of society that would help to make sense of the industrial changes in Europe. These early sociologists (although not everyone would have recognized this term, or even used it in the same way) were concerned to discover the underlying laws of society – the hidden movements and currents behind all human social behaviour. They were interested in developing a way of seeing into the very heart of human social life and discovering the essential forces behind all that humans do. Their aim was to use these discoveries to try and predict the shape of things to come: to understand what the implications of industrialization were for the European societies involved.

The modern social science of sociology that we recognize today owes a great deal to the insights of three key thinkers in particular – known, collectively, as the founders:

1. German political philosopher and economist Karl Marx (1818–1883).
2. French sociologist Emile Durkheim (1858–1917).
3. German social historian Max Weber (1864–1920).

When first developed, this science of society met with a mixed reaction from philosophers and scientists. It was many different things to different people – controversial and a lesser form of knowledge to some, but for others it was welcomed as the greatest science of all. It should come as no surprise that these founders themselves did not agree on what sociology was and how it should develop as a study of society. Marx even rejected the term, associating the word sociology with the ideas of Comte and Spencer, both of whom he thought were justifying ruling-class elites, rather than trying to overthrow them!

A central debate in early sociology was about how power was organized in society – and, for those at the time, how it should be organized in their future (our past and present). Early sociology was always concerned, therefore, with issues of politics, and all early sociological theorizing helped to shape what we have called in this book modern day political sociology.

THE ROLE OF EARLY SOCIOLOGY IN POLITICAL CHANGE

What all the early founding thinkers and theorists shared was a commitment to the following views:

1. They were all interested in developing a way of seeing how society worked as a whole (although Weber also wished to look at individual action).
2. A belief in social progress – that societies were moving through history in particular directions.
3. That societies have evolved throughout history.
4. That sociology could help to shape the future directions society took.
5. A commitment to science as a form of knowledge (although all three meant very different things by this).

And, for our purposes in this chapter:

1. A commitment to the analysis of power and power relationships in society.

2. A personal commitment to political views and causes and, in some cases (most notably Marx), a commitment to taking part in actual political action.

It is important to see the concerns of Marx, Durkheim and Weber within the context of the societies in which they themselves lived. The origins of an industrial society brought with them mixed reactions from those involved at the time – intellectuals, philosophers, scientists and ordinary social members. For example:

1. fear of an uncertain future;
2. celebration of the rise of science and technology;
3. a sense of society progressing towards some greater social 'good';
4. a sense of the past having been lost;
5. a sense of previous traditions being revised and modernized;
6. impatience for the new 'brighter' future.

Exercise 3.1

Using the birth and death dates of these three key sociologists (spanning 1818–1920) list some of the social and political events and conditions that would have led to the six types of reactions listed above. For example, the First World War saw the decline of Edwardian social structure and led to uncertainty about the future of Europe; technological advances in transport and communication would have changed people's perception of the world and of the future. Use the internet for your research, along with texts from your college library.

1. Fear of an uncertain future	
2. The rise of science and technology	
3. Progressing towards greater social good	
4. The past having been lost	
5. Traditions being revised	
6. Impatience for the new future	

These early sociologists all had a sense of change, but whereas some were optimistic about the new path society was heading along, others were highly pessimistic, fearing what the future might offer. Sociology was needed, therefore, to help explain this unknown – and to help to inform politicians and rulers with their decision-making. Early sociology was not happy to simply explain and understand social change and the nature of politics, it wished to influence the political decision-making process and thereby affect the future of society.

The sociologist as political ruler

Comte described his sociology as both a philosophy and a polity. He means by this:

1. Sociology as philosophy – a way to interpret, understand and explain social change using scientific methods.
2. Sociology as polity – a way to make sets of recommendations to rulers to help them to guide society into the new future, along the best path for social change available.

These ideas of Comte's were very similar to the recommendations made by the ancient Greek philosopher Plato, who spoke of the philosopher-king. This concept suggests that those who best understood the nature of society through their intellectual work were ultimately the most suitable to rule such a society, since they had insight that others lacked.

Modern-day sociologist Krishan Kumar (1978) notes that the emergence of sociology as a way of thinking about society was the end result of a historical process that had risen hand in hand with the forces of industrialization itself. This process was the movement away from religious and superstitious thinking towards thinking based upon future-looking change where humans became masters of their own social and historical destinies. It was in this intellectual climate that the origins of sociology could flourish and it was this climate that sociology contributed to. Sociology developed the idea that science was a tool for humans to use to shape their own political destinies, rather than leaving it to chance, or to rulers who lacked foresight, or to the whims of superstitious thinking. Early sociological ideas were as much concerned with the society of the future as they were with the society of their present. It was as much political futurology as it was present sociology.

As Kumar observes:

> In a sense it was illogical to try to determine the happy end-point of this progression [of industrialisation]; but the attraction to do so proved irresistible. However dimly perceived, the future was seen in terms of the triumph of some existing quality or principle deemed to be of supreme worth... it might be reason, science or liberty. But whatever it was... the end, the future, became the vantage point, from which to view the present and past stages of mankind... the future was the guiding thread. (Kumar, 1978, pp. 13–14)

This thinking – that sociology can help politics to shape the 'correct' directions for future social change – can be seen in the claims of Comte, when he writes:

> The aim of every science is foresight. For the laws established by observation of phenomena are generally employed to foresee their succession. All men, however little advanced, make true predictions, which are always based on the same principle, the knowledge of the future from the past... the foresight of the astronomer who predicts with complete precision the state of the solar system many years in advance is absolutely the same in kind as that of the savage who predicts the next sunrise. The only difference lies in the extent of their knowledge... it is quite in accordance with the nature of the human mind that observation of the past should unveil the future in politics, as it does in astronomy, physics, chemistry... the determination of the future must even be regarded as the direct aim of political science. (Comte, 1822, cited in Kumar, 1978, p. 25)

You can establish your own thoughts on this issue by carrying out Exercise 3.2.

Ⓔ

Exercise 3.2

Astronomy, physics and chemistry are physical sciences that describe a world controlled by reliable laws of cause and effect. To what extent do you believe that it is possible to discover laws that govern human behaviour? Is it possible to predict what will happen to society in the same way that it is possible to predict the movement of the planets in the solar system?

The sociologist as political revolutionary

Karl Marx's particular political views were different to Comte's. He suggests (originally in 1845) that, 'The philosophers have only interpreted the world in various ways; the point is to change it' (Marx, 1963, p. 84). For Marx, Comte's claim that the sociologist can help the rulers to make political decisions makes such sociologists just as much an enemy of the people as the corrupt rulers in the first place. Marx's own political ideas and philosophical theorizing led him to advocate a total transformation of society – a revolution, a total change in how society works. Like Comte, Marx wished to use his scientific insight to imagine what this perfect future might be like, but he wanted political action, not simply making suggestions for rulers to follow if they wished.

Marx also noted:

> Men make their own history, but they do not make it just as they please; they do not make it under circumstances chosen by themselves, but under circumstances directly found, given and transmitted from the past. The tradition of all the dead generations weighs like a nightmare on the brain of the living. (Marx, 1954, originally 1852, p. 10)

For Marx, political science or philosophy should aim to show people the true nature of the conditions under which they live – exploitation by a ruling class. It should help them to organize themselves together to make their own history, rather than be tied down to tradition and customs which ultimately enslave them into the routines that lead to political domination by those who rule. Marx believes that his ideas are also scientific, and he claims that he has 'done for politics what Darwin did for biology' – namely, he has discovered the laws of politics that underpin the future evolution of all societies in history. These laws are drawn from his belief that all societies are based on the political domination of one class against those who work for them. '[Darwin's work] . . . serves me as a natural scientific basis for the class-struggle in history' (Marx, cited in Beer, 1985).

Ⓘ Ⓐn

Exercise 3.3

Do you agree with Marx that all political struggle is based on class conflict? Consider whether the political struggles listed below have anything to do with class. If you believe that they all do, can you think of examples of political struggles that have entirely other origins?

- a gay rights protest;
- a Reclaim the Night march;
- a community in Brazil campaigning against local deforestation;
- Palestinians protesting against the actions of the Israeli government;
- Japanese environmentalists attempting to stop the hunting of whales;
- the democracy movement in Zimbabwe;
- the wages for housework campaign;
- the Rwandan war;
- anti-abortion campaigns in the USA.

Equally, Fredrick Engels – Marx's friend and intellectual companion, said at Marx's funeral: *'Just as Darwin discovered the law of development of organic nature, so Marx discovered the law of development of human history'* (Engels, cited in Kumar, 1978).

Although they are based on different images of the role of the political sociologist in society, both Comte and Marx share one very important idea in common: the belief that sociology has a great deal to offer society and that through understanding society using sociological ideas we can shape the nature of politics, and in turn the future direction that society can take. Interestingly enough, both Comte and Marx were committed to what could variously be called socialism, communism or even revolutionary socialism.

Classical sociology and socialism

Traditionally, classical sociology and the ideas of the founders themselves have been characterized in the following way: Comte and Durkheim have been seen as theorists of consensus whereas Marx and Weber have been characterized as theorists of conflict. Whereas Durkheim looked at the need to integrate social members into a harmonious and collective culture, Marx and Weber identify how ruling groups use their power to control others in society. Although this distinction is quite useful to help us understand the basic ideas of these classical sociologists, we should also see their ideas as having similarity as well as difference. All the classical founders have what we call today a highly modernist image of society and of sociology – they are all interested in large-scale generalization and in looking at the future direction and shape that social change would take. They also tend to see change as progression (in other words as a march of progress) and in some cases as following inevitable rules. (These ideas have been criticised lately by sociologists describing themselves as postmodernists.)

In recent years, for many modern day sociologists, it is a key misunderstanding of classical sociological theory to see Comte and his student Durkheim as right wing, standing for everything opposite to Marx and the left-wing conflict sociologists. Writers such as Pearce (1989) and Gane (1992) have spoken of a radical Durkheimianism – the idea that Durkheim has been misunderstood and mistakenly associated with the ideas of what we call functionalism due to the ways in which he was translated, interpreted and used, by thinkers such as Talcott Parsons. The alternative interpretation of thinkers such as Comte and Durkheim is to see them as much more concerned with equality, social justice and inequality than sociology might have thought before. Comte himself wrote a great deal about the merits of socialism among the workers in France – the idea that collective action was important for those disadvantaged in society in order for them to acquire a fair share in the benefits of society. Comte's warning about socialism, however, was that it would have a tendency to suppress individuality and was rather unrealistic. Interestingly enough, Marx himself often doubted the potential success of some left-wing workers' movements.

Comte wrote of the problems of equality in society and also claimed that his new science of society – positive sociology – had a key focus upon looking at how property was distributed in society. He criticizes the notion that people who own property have the absolute right to do what they like with that property. Rather, owning property is a social act and brings responsibilities on the owner. In fact, it was Comte who coined the word altruism to refer to what he believed to be a moral obligation of individuals to serve others and place their interests above one's own. He also believed that society has a right to exert control over property owners who abuse their right to own property. For example, someone who buys a listed building is not permitted to make whatever modifications they wish, even though they own the property.

This view puts the sociological ideas of Comte in contrast to many of the observations made by Marx on communism and other radical thinkers and philosophers of the time. Comte is not arguing in favour of the collectivization of private property, but rather that the state has the right to take top-down measures to ensure that property owners act in a morally responsible way.

Durkheim wrote much more critically of socialism, but, like Comte and to a certain extent Marx, he drew an important distinction between communism and socialism. For Durkheim, communist ideas had (at his time of writing – the late 1800s) a long history of intellectual thought, whereas socialism specifically, was a more recent social phenomenon and itself a product of the industrial age. Durkheim felt that socialism was not an actual solution to the problems of inequality in an industrial society, but was an indicator that such problems did exist. Durkheim believed that socialist beliefs and the rise of workers' socialist movements were an expression of the sickness of society due to changes in the way labour and the economy were organized in an industrial society. For Durkheim, the rise of these beliefs was interesting material for sociological analysis in their own right. They were social facts like suicide or new forms of economic organization that sociologists should study in a scientific way: to try and understand why they rose to importance and what their existence means for the nature of society, and the future directions change might take.

Durkheim says:

> It is interesting to study socialism...one can hope that it will aid us in understanding the social conditions which have given rise to it. For precisely because it derives from certain conditions, socialism manifests and expresses them in its own way, and thereby gives us another means of analysing them. It is certainly not that socialism reflects them accurately. Quite the contrary, for the reasons given above. We can be certain that it unknowingly distorts them and gives us only an unfaithful impression, just as a sick man faultily interprets the feelings that he experiences, and most often attributes them to a cause which is not the true one. But these feelings, such as they are, have an intrinsic interest, and the clinician notes them with care and takes great account of them. (Durkheim, originally published in 1928, cited in Giddens, 1972)

For Durkheim, socialist ideas (or any political ideas within society) were not necessarily true representations of the way society was, but they were facts that could be studied in order for the scientific sociologist to see what society is like. Durkheim believed that no social ideas rise by mistake – they all exist for a reason – and that we can see what society is like (the causes of the beliefs) by treating them as symptoms of social conditions, not as solutions to these conditions.

This is a different approach to politics than that taken by Marx and Comte. Durkheim arguably saw himself much more as the *detached* scientist, looking into the laws of society. Both Marx and Comte saw themselves as scientists trying to understand and then *change* society for the better, each in their own way.

Having said this, Durkheim looked towards the role of a centralized state to take the lead in social change and to make sure that the social ills that created socialism were combated. Durkheim himself noted that great inequalities between the rich and the poor in society would be negative for the collective health of the whole system, and as a result the state should take responsibility for collective social welfare. Too much inequality was seen by Durkheim to lead to instability – it was a form of social sickness – what he called anomie; it led to a state of normlessness during which society would be vulnerable and unable to organize correctly. Again, this is a social policy that today we associate with thinkers on the left – in particular modern day socialist ideas: Durkheim seems to advocate a policy of the redistribution of welfare – an approach similar to the welfare state of today.

For Durkheim, freedom and justice in the industrial age were initially unstable. Society itself was anomic (sick due to the withering away of stable norms) due to the insecurities that great social change caused. The rise of industrialization was potentially a massive social problem as the stability of society becomes weakened due to population migration, the rise of new roles and new working conditions. After the transition in the division of labour from pre-industrial societies where everyone did all jobs equally, to industrialized economies where individuals develop occupational specialisms, society would need to find new ways to integrate these different individuals with one another. However, Durkheim argued that this specialization would in the long term create more order and stability. Even stronger moral bonds would be created, because mutual dependence would be needed and individuals would come to rely on one another.

(K)(U)

Exercise 3.4

Using your knowledge of the process of industrialization, and your notes and textbooks on this area, outline sociological ideas that might tie in with Durkheim's ideas about the possible weakening of social ties, and the eventual strengthening of those ties. Use the grid below to record your responses.

	Weakens social ties because ...	Eventually strengthens social ties because ...
Centralization of ownership		
Migration to towns		
Specialization of occupation		
Other factors (specify)		

The job of politics in the industrial age, for Durkheim, was to prevent individuality from weakening collective bonds. It was important to develop a strong centralized state governing all, under the same laws, rights and obligations. Durkheim felt that the moral society was one where the state regulated individualism yet allowed individuals to make contracts with one another, in order to bond individuals together with mutual ties of interdependence and cooperation.

Although they are different in content, the ideas of Comte, Durkheim and Marx were all themselves products of their times. Just as Durkheim suggested that we see ideas in society as symptoms of the nature of those societies, we can see sociological ideas on the nature of politics as symptoms of the state of the society in which they developed. In the case of the early classical sociologists, all their ideas on politics and the nature of power can be seen to be products of the change towards industrialization – what we call today the rise of 'modernity'.

The founders' image of modernity

The founders' views of politics during the time they lived – the rise of the industrial era – is today seen to be very much a product of their times – the products of modernity. The intellectual climate of those times was one based upon a belief in science as an ultimate form of knowledge – as a tool that humans could use to manipulate nature and society around them, to take control and have power over their own environmental and social destinies. The *zeitgeist* or spirit of the times of this early modernity was one where industrialization was seen as the most significant development in society, and the end of the march of social history. All social history was seen to culminate in this development. In other words, the society lived in by the founders was seen as the ultimate development of human life.

This early era of modernity characterized itself as a new, better and more rational society than that before it. The ideas of the founders – Comte, Durkheim, Marx and Weber – took this modern society and tried to analyse it. They were interested in:

1. How this new (more modern) society developed?
2. Why it developed first in Europe?
3. Where this society would develop in the future?

This industrial society was seen as the model by which to judge all other societies. Politics and power in this new age were seen to play a highly significant role in the structure, management and mastery of the new age by human beings: before industrialization humans were seen to be powerless and at the whim of nature, luck and superstition. After industrialization, with the rise of science, technology and the rational/scientific mind, humans were able to shape society into their preferred image.

Both Marx and Comte wished to contribute to this shaping process: to have their images of modernity used as the blueprint by which to judge, mould and direct future social change. A new group of leaders rose to positions of key social significance, taking over from those who had their power in religion and tradition. The new leaders for the new industrial age were those in positions of power from business, trade, science and government. It was these groups that the founders were interested in studying and, in some senses, it was their mastery over industrial society that Marx and others like him wished for themselves. They wanted to be the ones pulling the strings, directing the shape of things to come (Exercise 3.5 builds on this viewpoint).

Exercise 3.5

Modernists believed that rational human beings would be able to use advances in science and technology to manipulate nature and society around them and to take control and have power over their own environmental and social destinies. In recent years, issues such as climate change, conflict and poverty seem to indicate that we are less in control of our physical and social environments than ever.

1. List other issues that seem to contradict the optimistic predictions of modernity.
2. Why do you think that the enormous technological advances we have witnessed in recent years have not led to a perfect world?

PROBLEMS WITH THE INDUSTRIAL AGE: CLASS AND POWER INEQUALITY

The key feature of power in society according to Marx is that of class and the conflict produced between the different classes by their different interests. These different interests lead to inequality where one class rules over the other and as a result there is struggle, resulting in revolution and social transformation. Again, like the other founders, this was a very modernist image of power since it suggested that there are invisible laws that govern how societies operate and what direction future change would take. The mechanisms of class conflict were also seen to be global – they were universal laws and offered a universal path for all social development. This image of social change is called teleological. It is based upon the assumption that social change moves forward along a straight line in a clear direction and that this direction is a progression from previous stages in social history.

Marx opened his *Communist Manifesto* written with Engels in 1848. The first chapter is entitled 'Bourgeois and Proletarians' and opens with the statement: *'The history of all hitherto existing society is the history of class struggles.'* Marx goes on to describe a new form of class oppression in the new industrial capitalist society:

> The modern bourgeois society that has sprouted from the ruins of feudal society has not done away with class antagonisms. It has but established new classes, new conditions of oppression, new forms of struggle in place of the old ones. Our epoch, the epoch of the bourgeoisie, possesses, however, this distinctive feature: it has simplified the class antagonisms. Society as a whole is more and more splitting up into two great hostile camps, into two great classes directly facing each other: bourgeoisie and proletariat.

Class then, was the dynamic, the force that moves society onwards. For Marx, class was the most important feature of society – it was the very inner workings of all societies as a whole, it was the basis of all history and therefore of all power. In the industrial age, class power was based not upon slavery or upon land ownership, but rather upon the ownership of the means of production – all that was needed to make the products of the economy, in total. Under a capitalist form of economic organization, these means of production (factories, land, capital, machinery, etc.) were owned by the bourgeoisie – the ruling class – and this was the source of their power. In such a society, there were only two classes according to Marx, those who owned the means of production and those who did not: the ruling bourgeoisie and the workers, the proletariat.

Exercise 3.6

Are Marx's ideas as relevant today as they were 100 years ago? If you believe that the world is still divided 'into two great classes directly facing each other: bourgeoisie and proletariat', provide evidence for your opinion. If not, explain what has changed.

For Marx, economic ownership gave so much power that it enabled these capitalists to determine the actions of everything and everyone else in society – governments and the state included. In the *Communist Manifesto* he writes: 'The executive of the modern state is but a committee for managing the common affairs of the whole bourgeoisie' (Marx and Engels, 1848). In other words all members of society, including the government, the army, the judiciary and other state institutions, were like puppets in the hands of those who controlled how the economy was organized. Marx's legacy is enormous, not just in society but in many academic subjects, and has led to many newer versions of his original ideas – referred to collectively as neo-Marxism (see Chapter 4 for a fuller discussion).

Max Weber: power, authority and domination

Some of the ideas of Hobbes (see Chapter 2) are very similar to the ideas on power held by founder Max Weber (1968), originally writing at the start of the nineteenth century, but the most important influence on the ideas of Weber is arguably the work of Marx.

Weber's sociology as a whole, and his views on power in particular, are based upon a rejection of the narrowness of Marx's image of class and class conflict. Although, like Marx, Weber was interested in the role of conflict and inequality in society, Weber extended his analysis to look at sources of power that were not based upon economic ownership alone. Weber made an important distinction between authority and coercion – both types of power (what Weber calls in German *Macht*), since they allowed a ruler or ruling group to get their own way, potentially at the expense of someone else:

1. *Authority* – means to be seen to have the right to rule, by those that you rule over. If you rule by authority your power is seen as right, just or fitting. Those who are powerless feel you have the right to have your power over them. This is also referred to as being legitimate power.
2. *Coercion* – means to rule through violence, force or the threat of violence. This is illegitimate power since you are not seen to have the moral right to rule, yet you dominate over all others, forcing them into submission. This type of power tends not to last as long as authority, since you are forcing people to obey your wishes rather than getting them to believe in your right as a justifiable ruler. (Exercise 3.7 will help you to develop your understanding of this distinction.)

Weber noted that both are really forms of domination since, although they might feel different to those involved, they end up with the same result – one dominant group gets what it wants at the expense of others. If authority failed at any time, Weber noted that ruling groups always have coercion to fall back on, since behind all authority lies coercion. This is echoed in the famous quotation and saying 'Within the velvet glove there lies a fist of steel.'

ⒾⒶ

Exercise 3.7

Copy and fill in the following grid, giving as many examples as you can of *coercion* and *authority* in contemporary society. Which have lasted, which have been short-lived? A couple of examples are shown in the table below.

Examples of 'authority':	Lasting or short-lived?
Classroom control that teachers have over their students	Lasting

Examples of 'coercion':	Lasting or short-lived?
Blackmailing someone into doing something	Short-lived

The ideal type of authority

Weber extended his analysis to include the construction of an ideal type of authority. An ideal type is an analytical tool often used by Weber and involves the creation of a list of ideal features of any given aspect of social reality. This ideal list is then compared to every society to be studied in turn, and acts as a starting point for analysis. In some circumstances and in some historical periods, different characteristics of the ideal type would be more or less a match, compared to other times.

For Weber, power that is authoritative comes in three forms:

1. rational-legal authority – just power based upon laws and legal procedures;
2. traditional authority – just power based upon tradition, custom and legacy;
3. charismatic authority – just power based upon the special qualities held by the ruler or ruling group as people.

Exercise 3.8

Think of some examples of each of these types of authority. An illustration has been given to you for each type. Try to think of as many other examples as you can. Of course, there will be an overlap between the types of authority in any particular case. For example, the boss in an office has rational-legal authority because they have been legitimately appointed as line-manager to the staff, they have traditional authority because staff may be reluctant to challenge a hierarchy that has existed for years and they may have charismatic authority if staff respect them as a good leader.

Rational-legal authority:

• the police: their power is located in law and is therefore seen as fair

---

Traditional authority:

• the father in a family: his power results from the rest of the family not challenging a historical situation

---

Charismatic authority:

- the captain of a sports team: here power comes from the rest of the team respecting the captain's leadership qualities

---

Weber suggested that power that is based in authority allows the ruler or ruling group to win the hearts and minds of the people – to make themselves seem to have the natural and unquestionable right to rule, since they are seen to be the most suitable. At the end of the day, however, for Weber, as for Hobbes, ' "power" [is] the chance of a man or a number of men to realise their own will in a social action even against the resistance of others who are participating in the action' (Weber, 1968, p. 926).

Class, status and party – three sources of power

On the subject of the sources of power inequality, Weber said, 'Power is the probability that one actor within a social relationship will be in a position to carry out his own will despite resistance, regardless of the basis on which this probability rests' (Weber, 1968, p. 53). In terms of exactly what this 'basis' by which power is obtained by a ruling group might be, Weber noted that, ' "Classes", "status groups" and "parties" are phenomena of the distribution of power within a community' (Weber, 1948, p. 181). This claim puts the ideas of Weber and his followers in opposition to a great deal of traditional Marxist thinking which identified class alone as a basis for one group to have power over another.

Weber's distinction of these three types of power rested upon the following definitions:

1. *Class* – Marx believed that there were two classes in society: the bourgeoisie, who owned the means of production, and the proletariat, who sold their labour to the bourgeoisie. For Weber, class is connected to the distribution of power, and as there are various ways that power can be exercised, it is not sufficient to focus entirely on ownership of the means of production. Like Marx, Weber believed that class is rooted in economics,

but his idea of class is much more diverse than that of Marx. For example, he considered groups such as financiers, debtors and professional groups such as lawyers or doctors to be different classes. Weber felt that people of the same class had similar life chances, but that these were not simply a factor of whether they were capitalists or workers. A range of different economic factors contribute to an individual's life chances. One such factor, for example, is the relationship of the individual to a particular market. Weber would distinguish between a factory owner (a member of the ownership class) and a banker (a member of the commercial class), whereas Marx would classify them both as bourgeoisie.

2. *Status* – Weber was also looked at more subjective ways in which power might be held and measured – not just property ownership. Status refers to how an individual or group is viewed and valued by others in society. It is referred to by Weber as *social esteem* or *social honour*. Some groups may enjoy more privilege than others since in the eyes of society they are seen to have special characteristics that afford them more honour than others. Status groups seek what Weber calls social closure – total power and influence over a specific aspect of society. For example, the British Medical Association (BMA) has social closure over the legal and therefore acceptable and legitimate practice of medicine in our society: this is a massive source of power.

3. *Party* – by this term Weber means not what we call political parties, but any *organization devoted to obtaining power for its members*.

Ⓤⓘ

Exercise 3.9

Draw a spider diagram that illustrates each of these three types of power.

Party:

Class:

Status:

Compare your diagram with others in your class. Amalgamate your ideas and discuss any that are contentious. It may be that some of them overlap.

Weber noted that these three sources of power overlap with each other. Thus a party may also be a status group and may seek to own property (class).

For Weber these three forms of power and social inequality addup together to give an individual a location in the strata of society – into the hierarchy of power in a society. Thus, this power location is unique since one's life chances might differ, but it is also a shared or group location – shared with others who have a similar *marketable value*: groups made up of individuals who are able to manipulate similar sources of and amounts of power.

THE DARK SIDE OF MODERNIST POLITICS

The process of industrialization – the shift from tradition to what was considered at the time to be the modern – was a shift in awareness of those in society themselves: a move from looking back to the past to looking towards the future. For many, such as the founders of sociology, the future had already arrived. This future was based upon new technologies, new ways of organizing production and new ways of having and using power.

This modern future, this new society, was not without its critics, and not without its problems. Industrialization was such a massive social change that, like all disruptions to the stable fabric of social life, it caused great tension, concern and anxiety.

1. For *Marx*, economic life in industrial capitalism was based upon the exploitation of the working class by the ruling class – those who owned the ways goods were produced. *Class conflict* was seen as the force behind all social change, and in this new modern age, capitalism as a form of economic organization was seen to strip the masses of their dignity and humanity. Marx painted a bleak short-term future for the masses under capitalist control; a future that would eventually end with revolution and a more equitable form of economic organization called

communism – the communal/shared ownership and organization of the economy.

2. *Weber*, perhaps the most pessimistic and disillusioned of all the founders of modernity, wrote of what he called the iron cage of bureaucracy. This was the idea that power would become located with those who had their authority based in law, and that, as a result, society would become trapped by rules and regulations. People would lose spontaneity, follow the rules, blindly accept the correct ways of doing things, and be unable to break free from the regulations laid down by those in power.

3. *Weber* also spoke of the process of disenchantment where the scientific mind took over from the mind of traditional societies where the world and events in the world were understood through reference to magic, superstition and chance. Weber felt it was a shame, in some senses, that science had come to totally dominate society and the minds of those in society. He believed a certain innocence of thinking had been lost, and replaced with a worldview based upon calculation, looking at the ends and goals and looking at efficiency. In terms of politics, this new modernist worldview, this new scientific mind, was seen to result in calculation, manipulation and ruthlessness of those in power in the name of scientific reason – a very powerful basis upon which to exercise domination over others.

4. *Durkheim*, like Marx and Comte, was largely positive regarding the rise of this new scientific age, but, like Marx, was worried about the transition from the traditions of the past to the new modern world. Durkheim was concerned about the *problems of integration*, given that as society changed, so too would the normal way of doing things. This *anomie* would result in problems of order for society – problems that political leaders and the state would need to solve, before the new industrial age could progress.

ⓀⓊ

Exercise 3.10

In this chapter a number of important concepts have been used, some of which are listed below. Using your own understanding and/or a sociology dictionary, explain the meaning of each of these concepts:

- sociology as science
- bourgeoisie
- proletariat
- modernity

- life-chances
- social closure
- anomie

Exercise 3.11

To check your understanding, or as a revision exercise, copy and use the following table to outline the differences and similarities between the three main classical approaches to power and politics:

	Main ideas on the nature of power	Similarities to ...	Differences from ...	Applications to contemporary society
Durkheim	• • • •			
Marx	• • • •			
Weber	• • • •			

CONCLUSION

The legacy of the founders' ideas for modern day sociology is enormous and the debt modern day thinkers and new theories owe to these original ideas is considerable. All modern day thinkers and theorists feel the need to still debate with the ghosts of the founders – to use their insights and to apply them to the social conditions of the times. This is true of all sociological interests, but of power and politics in particular, since so many of the founders' ideas were concerned with identifying who has power and how they use it. In Chapter 5 we will take the ideas of the founders and apply them to more modern day sociological theories on power.

Exam focus

'Weber's most important contribution to the study of politics is the distinction he makes between class, status and party.'
  Examine this view.

Write a response to this position, taking note of the following description of what a high-mark answer is likely to do.

Top-mark answer

To achieve the highest mark, the answer must specifically address the idea of most important contribution. In assessing whether the distinction between class, status and power is his most important contribution, an answer at the top level will consider other contributions that Weber made and come to a conclusion whether they are as important, more important or less important than the distinction. Judgement will be made on the basis of the evidence included in the response. A focus on the sociology of politics is also required at this level, and candidates who offer an assessment of Weber's contribution to sociology in general will not grade as highly as those who focus on the sociology of politics. Evaluation will therefore be explicit and evidence applied to the specific question set. The most likely contender for an alternative 'most important contribution' is Weber's ideal types of authority, although others may appear and this is not a necessary element for the answer to reach the highest grades.

Important concepts

- sociology as philosophy vs sociology as polity • socialism and communism • radical Durkheimianism • the zeitgeist of modernity • teleological social change • power as authority or coercion • Weber's ideal type of authority • rational-legal, traditional and charismatic authority • Weber's sources of power: class, status and party • problems with modernist politics: class conflict, the iron cage of bureaucracy, disenchantment and problems of integration.

Summary points

- *Auguste Comte* (1798–1857) is generally considered to be the founder of modern-day sociology: a new science of society that would help to make sense of the industrial changes in Europe. Comte described his sociology as both a philosophy and a polity.

- The modern social science of sociology owes a great deal to the insights of three key thinkers in particular – known, collectively, as the founders: *Karl Marx* (1818–1883), *Emile Durkheim* (1858–1917) and *Max Weber* (1864–1920). All three shared a commitment to the analysis of power and power relationships in society and to political views and causes.

- The emergence of sociology as a way of thinking about society was the end result of a historical process that had risen hand in hand with the forces of industrialization itself. Sociology developed the idea that science was a tool for humans to use to shape their own political destinies, rather than leaving it to chance, or to rulers who lacked foresight, or to the whims of superstitious thinking.

- For Marx, Comte's claim that the sociologist can help the rulers to make political decisions makes such sociologists just as much an enemy of the people as the corrupt rulers in the first place. Marx advocated a total transformation of society. Like Comte, Marx wished to use his scientific insight to imagine what this perfect future might be like, but he wanted political action, not simply making suggestions for rulers to follow if they wished.

- Comte and Durkheim have been seen as theorists of consensus, whereas Marx and Weber have been characterized as theorists of conflict. However, some writers argue that Durkheim has been mistakenly associated with the ideas of functionalism due to the ways in which he was translated, interpreted and used. The alternative interpretation of Comte and Durkheim is to see them as much more concerned with equality, social justice and inequality.

- The founders' views of politics are very much the products of their times – the products of modernity. The industrial society was seen as the model by which to judge all other societies. After industrialization, with the rise of science, technology and the rational/scientific mind, humans were able to shape society into their preferred image.

- For Marx, class was the most important feature of society – it was the basis of all history and therefore of all power. In the industrial age, class power was based not upon slavery or upon land ownership, but rather upon the ownership of the means of production.

- Like Marx, Weber was interested in the role of conflict and inequality in society, but he extended his analysis to look at sources of power that were not based upon economic ownership alone, and made an important distinction between authority and coercion. For Weber, power that is authoritative comes in three forms: rational-legal, traditional and charismatic, and can be based on class, status or party.

- Modern society, however, was not without its problems. Industrialization was such a massive social change that, like all disruptions to the stable fabric of social life, it caused great tension, concern and anxiety.

Critical thinking

1. What did the three founders believe was the role of sociology in society?
2. Comte and Durkheim have been seen as theorists of consensus, whereas Marx and Weber have been characterized as theorists of conflict. Which of these theoretical positions do you agree with and why?
3. Was Karl Marx a scientist?
4. In what ways did Weber disagree with Marx?

Chapter 4

Theories on the Nature and Distribution of Power

By the end of this chapter you should:

- understand how contemporary theories of power have developed from those of the classical sociologists of the past
- understand how theories of power have changed over time
- be able to compare and contrast theories together
- be able to evaluate theories of power

INTRODUCTION

The discipline of sociology is heavily indebted to the classical ideas of thinkers such as Marx, Durkheim and Weber (see Chapter 3). From these, we have gained varied definitions of power and different images of how the political process operates in society. The job of modern day sociology is to evaluate and update sociological theorizing on power, in the light of changes that have taken place in the contemporary world. Some changes serve to support the original ideas of the founders, while others suggest we need to be selective about which bits of the classical sociological legacy to adopt and which to drop. For some sociologists, the contemporary world has changed so much that we cannot use much of classical sociology to explain the present.

It is impossible to ignore the legacy of classical sociologists, and contemporary theories do use some classical themes about power and politics. For example, sociologists still think in the following ways about power; that we need to:

- define power as a form of domination of one group over another (Marx and Weber)
- look at the role played by the community in making decisions in society (Durkheim)
- look at the ways in which power operates at structural and at individual levels (Weber)
- identify the existence of a ruling class who use power in their own interests (Marx)
- identify the existence of a ruling elite, who manipulate more types of power than simply that of economic ownership (Weber)

These observations have come to shape most debates within sociology and the theories of power that have developed within sociology often take these issues as their starting point. This chapter will review sociological ideas on power since the classical theorists, through to the present time. Theoretical views on the role of the state, and the power it has in society, will be discussed in Chapter 8.

A HISTORY OF IDEAS

We can identify the following key time periods for sociological theorizing, although some ideas and thinkers transcend historical time periods and others seemingly disappear, only to become more popular at a later date:

- *The industrial revolution, or modernity* – mid-1800s–1920 (death of Weber)
- *Pre-Second World War* – 1920s–1940s
- *Post-Second World War* – 1950s–1970s
- *Growth of the late industrial age* (characterized by economic booms and slumps, and the transformation of production to consumption)– 1970s–1980s
- *The rise of late-, advanced-, reflexive- or post-modernity* – 1990s to present

Exercise 4.1

For each of the periods suggested in the text, identify an event or series of events from anywhere in the world that affected society in a significant way during that time, and may have given rise to a change in theories about society. You may try doing an historical search on the internet. Record your events and their effects in a table.

Across these periods, we can identify a number of key developments that have affected sociological thinking:

- A growing concern with the death of class as a form of identity.
- The rise of globalization (and people's awareness of it).
- The seeming decline of mass class-based revolution.
- The rise of the media and communications industries.
- The growth of transnational corporations exercising massive economic power.
- A decline in global conflict and a rise in localized conflict, often based upon identity or ethnicity.

Exercise 4.2

Think of a specific example to illustrate each of the following sociologically important developments. You could do this as a class exercise or in groups. Use a newspaper archive if you have access to one on the internet. Try to include at least one international example.

Development	Example
The death of class	
The rise of globalization	
The decline of mass class-based revolution	
Developments in media and communications	
Increasing economic power of corporations	
Rise of localized conflict compared to global	

Across these different times, we can also identify a number of trends in sociological thought in general and sociological thinking about politics in particular:

- The rise of multiple sociological theories (see Churton and Brown, 2009).
- Attempts to combine structural and action theories together.
- A growing concern with non-class forms of stratification (see Kirby, 1999).
- The rise of theories that treat individuals as knowledgeable actors.
- A growing awareness of lifestyle as a key aspect of how individuals think about themselves.
- A concern with power as an individual phenomenon, rather than something exclusively exercised by groups.

The 'new sociology of politics'

Present day sociological theorizing on the nature of power and politics has been described by some as a 'new sociology of politics' since it is very different from the views of the founders (see Chapter 2). For example, modern day views of power focus upon:

- micro levels of power struggle, such as language or interpersonal interaction
- lifestyle forms of political struggle, such as sexuality and ethnicity (see Kirby, 1999)
- cultural politics based upon small groups' attempts to take control of areas of social life, such as scientists exercising power over definitions of truth
- the impact that globalization has had on different societies
- an apparent rise in apathy towards politics in Western democracies (see Chapter 5)
- the power of the media as an instrument of control and persuasion (see Jones and Jones, 1999)
- the increasing uncertainty experienced by people towards once dominant political ideas (see Chapter 6)
- the absence of class as a motivating force behind political action
- the rise of political movements based upon lifestyle and cultural politics, such as environmentalism, that seem to have taken over from traditional class-based politics
- the decline of class as a source of voting behaviour.

Although some modern day thinking on power has moved away from the founders, it is still useful to review the older material. It is only by understanding the intellectual history behind these more contemporary ideas that we can better understand them. Equally, for every sociologist committed to removing the classical sociologists from today's sociological analysis, there is another sociologist keen to retain sociology's classical legacy.

Ways of thinking about sociological views on power

There are two key ways to start thinking about sociological views on the nature of power and its role in society:

- chronologically – in order of time
- thematically – by common ideas and issues raised

In terms of their rough chronological development, we have seen the rise of the following theories:

- classical elite theories
- interpretative sociologies
- functionalism – as developed by Talcott Parsons
- pluralist theories
- a return to interpretative sociologies
- neo-Marxism
- theories of elite rule influenced by both neo-Marxism and Weberian sociology – also referred to as radical elite theories
- various neo-pluralisms
- feminist theories
- New Right thinking
- postmodern and poststructural thinking

In terms of the themes, issues and common ideas expressed by this great variety of theories we can identify two opposing observations about society:

- *Power in society is democratic* – a view held by functionalism, pluralism, neo-pluralism and the New Right.
- *Power in society is undemocratic* – a view held by classical elite theories, neo-Marxists, Weberian-influenced theories of elite rule, feminist thinking, some postmodern and some poststructural thinking.

Steven Lukes (1974) has outlined this distinction:

> conceptions of power may be divided into two very broad categories. On the one hand, there are those theories which are asymmetrical and tend to involve (actual or potential) conflict and resistance. Such conceptions appear to presuppose a view of social or political relations as competitive and inherently conflictual... on the other hand, there are those conceptions which do not imply that some gain at others' expense but rather that all may gain: power is a collective capacity or achievement. Such conceptions appear to rest on a view of social or political relations as at least potentially harmonious and communal. (Lukes, 1974, p. 636)

Interestingly enough, of those theories that argue that power is **not** used in a democratic way, we can make a further distinction between:

- *theories that believe power should be democratic* – neo-Marxism, Weberian-influenced theories of elite rule, feminist thinking, some post-modern and some poststructural thinking; and
- *theories that believe power cannot and should not be democratic* – classical elite theories.

Exercise 4.3 will help you to explore these differences in your own society.

Exercise 4.3

Think about the culture and society in which you live. In small groups brainstorm examples of ways in which you think society is not (but should be) democratic, and examples of areas of social life where society cannot (and perhaps should not) be democratic. For example, you may believe that schools should be run more democratically than most of them currently are, but that you cannot run an army unit democratically.

Write your examples in the table below. Is one of your lists longer than the other? Why is this? Compare your ideas with those of other groups. Do you think that students living in other societies around the world would come up with similar lists? If not, why not?

Examples of areas in which there should be more democracy than there currently is	Examples of areas in which power cannot and should not be organized democratically

The theories that concentrate upon the small-scale or micro levels of society – individual meaning, motivation and interaction – often do not easily fit into the above categories because they do not look at society on a large scale. Instead, they concern themselves with how power might operate between small groups of people in everyday life. We call these theories interpretative theories, since they are concerned with understanding how individuals themselves make sense or interpret society around them. These theories are very different to the ideas of more structural theories, such as functionalism and traditional Marxism, which look at the overall pattern of how society as a whole is made up.

We shall now look at these different sociological theories in turn. Finally, we shall discuss interpretative sociological theories, along with the recent ideas from postmodernism and poststructuralism, by looking at sociological theories that seek to understand how power works in everyday life, on the small-scale level. Contemporary theories of power that seek to understand the role played by power in everyday life will be discussed in Chapter 5.

THEORIES OF DEMOCRACY IN SOCIETY

Theories of democracy in society tend to be more positive about the role of power in society and about the position and activities of the powerful themselves. Both functionalism and various pluralist theories agree that there is a *shared* aspect to decision-making which means that the *whole community* gets to have their say, and both theories believe that rulers operate in the interests of *everyone*, in a fair and *representative* fashion. The key difference between functionalist and pluralist theories is that pluralist theories look more at the role played by conflict and compromise than functionalists do.

Functionalism

For Talcott Parsons (1960; 1967), power is something that is generated by the community and used for the good of the community. Parsons himself is critical of more left-wing theories (see Chapter 5) since he believes that they concentrate too much upon how leaders and rulers use power for their own ends, whereas Parsons believes that power is based upon mutual agreement and collective decision-making. He says:

> Power is a generalized facility or resource in the society. It has to be divided or allocated, but it also has to be produced and it has collective as well as distributive functions. It is the capacity to mobilize the resources of the society for the attainment of goals for which a general 'public' commitment has been made, or may be made. (Parsons, 1960, p. 221)

For Parsons, power is not fixed somewhere in society – it is not held by a group or person and kept by them. Power is more fluid. It is seen to flow from group to group, from decision to decision. Elected leaders in industrial Western democracies are caretakers of power – they manipulate the power given to them by the community. Therefore, power can be seen to have flowed from the community to the elected leader, for the uses that everyone has agreed it can be put to. This idea has been influenced by the general functionalist idea of value consensus – the belief that people in society have a collective outlook on the goals of their society, and all work towards these common, shared goals.

Guy Rocher (1974) has suggested that we can identify five key elements of Parsons' view on power:

- Power operates within the actions and interactions between people, groups and the whole community: it is a variable-sum force – it is not held somewhere fixed. People in positions of authority manipulate the power entrusted to them and redistribute it through their actions. They do not hang onto it and store it up for the benefit only of themselves.
- Power is like money – it is symbolic in nature: it is not an actual thing despite the fact that it flows around the whole of society. Instead, it is a form of exchange – the community decides who is allowed to draw from the reservoir of power that is communally owned.
- There is not a fixed amount of power, but the size of power available for leaders varies and, on some occasions, more power might be made for

circulation. Again, this image is very much like money in economics – there can be rises or slumps in the amount of power on offer.

■ Power is the means by which collective goals can be achieved by those elected to stand for the whole community. But, each new elected leadership needs to prove to the community its effectiveness in achieving the collective goals. A leadership needs to be seen to be able to distribute and use collective power in the easiest and most profitable fashion for everyone or they will not be re-elected.

■ Parsons sees power as different from authority. Power refers to the ability to use resources to achieve collective goals – power is about doing and achieving. Authority is the social status that gives groups and individuals the right to use power – and along with this right are a series of agreed rules made by the community about how those with power should act. Authority is a code for those who have power, as well as the legitimate right to use the community's power for the good of the community.

Exercise 4.4

Using Rocher's five key elements, give examples of how Parsons' views on power might be translated into examples in contemporary society. You can do this as a class activity, as individuals or in groups. Use the following grid if you want to:

Parsons' functionalist view of power:

It is a variable sum	
Power is like money (symbolic) – a form of exchange	
There is no fixed amount	
Power is the means by which collective goals can be achieved	
Power is different from authority	

This is very different from the Marxist position on power that says that a narrow ruling group – those who own and control the economy – hold power for themselves and use it to further their own interests, at the expense of everyone else's.

Iain MacKenzie (in Ashe *et al.*, 1999) suggests that we might best think about Parsons' image of power as power *to* rather than the more Marxist position that sees power as power over. For Parsons, power is the ability given by the group to individuals to act on their behalf and to enhance their lives in an agreed way.

A key theme which runs throughout Parsons' image of power is the comparison with economics, or, in particular, how money as a symbolic exchange flows throughout society. For example, some people in society lend money, others might borrow money. Those who deposit their money in a bank expect the bank to look after their money, using it to further their own interests – using it to pay them interest so they can have more money. This, according to Parsons, is how power also flows through Western democratic societies – power is both lent and borrowed. It is lent by the majority to the elected leaders to use it in the interests of all – a similar image of power to that of pluralism.

Pluralism

As the name might suggest, the pluralist image of power believes that there are many sources of power in society – a wide range (a 'plurality') of groups that influence decision-making. The pluralist view, held by thinkers such as Robert A. Dahl (1961), sees power as a flowing commodity – something that changes over time, reflects the will of the people and changes in line with how this will might change over time. In his book *Who Governs?*, Dahl looked at the decision-making processes in a society – and tried to investigate if a narrow ruling elite has the ability to make decisions, or if the community as a whole has access to this decision-making process. For Dahl, every community contains a wide variety of localized decision-making groups, all of which compete with each other to get their opinions and interests across. This localized competition is reflected across the wider picture of society as a whole, with different groups involved in struggles for power that can only be settled by decision-making that is based upon compromise.

Here we see the key difference between the functionalist view (held by Parsons) and the pluralist view (held by Dahl and others):

- *Functionalism* – looks at the collective decisions of the whole community: the collective goals that have been decided through a process of value consensus.
- *Pluralism* – looks at competition and compromise within consensus. For pluralists there is a general collective agreement regarding the goals of society and how the democratic process should work, but within this agreement there are lots of disagreements over the precise direction society should move in to achieve the goals. Thus, we have competition between

different groups with their own interests and then a process of compromise and negotiation to achieve a collectively agreed result. Everyone gets their interests represented, but not necessarily all the time.

Marsh (1983) notes, when describing the key features of pluralism, or, as he calls it, classical pluralism:

> In the classical pluralist position power is seen as diffuse rather than concentrated. Society is viewed as consisting of a large number of groups, representing all the significant, different interests of the population, who compete with one another for influence over government. This competition occurs within a consensus about the 'rules of the game'. (Marsh, 1983, p. 10)

The plurality of groups struggling for power might include:

- government
- opposition government
- disagreements within political parties of MPs on the same side
- local community/neighbourhood groups
- religious leaders
- localized religious groups
- media
- pressure groups (see Chapter 7)
- trade unions
- professional associations
- government regulating bodies
- business leaders

Exercise 4.5

Use newspaper archives on the Internet (or a range of current newspapers) to carry out a piece of research to look for an issue – at an international or national level, or in your local area – where a number of groups (such as those in the text) are competing for power. Try to find an example where there are competing interests at stake. Write in your own words what the dispute is about. Which groups are the most influential in resolving the dispute and why?

The situation of conflict within an overall consensus is fair since everyone gets their say, and all voices are represented. This in turn is seen to enable those in positions of government – elected leaders – to listen to the wishes of the people and to respond accordingly. Within this pluralist model of power is also an assumption of what it means to be human in society. Pluralists tend to see individuals as knowledgeable – much more so than more structural theories such as Marxism that tend to see people as cultural robots who are oppressed by ideology and unable to think for themselves (see Chapter 3). For the pluralist, people are able to assess society, make their own minds up about the future directions they wish their leaders to take, and are active in trying to get their voice heard.

Criticisms of pluralism

There are two key and related criticisms of pluralism in the sociological literature. First, pluralism only looks at decision-making and ignores other facets or faces of power. Marxists Westergaard and Resler (1976) condemn as simplistic the pluralist focus on decisions that can be seen as simplistic, missing the true nature of power – that which shapes society and goes unseen and therefore unquestioned. As they note, '[Pluralists] . . . studiously avert their gaze from questions that do matter. Because they then see nothing, they draw the conclusion that there is nothing to see' (Westergaard and Resler, 1976, p. 245).

Floyd Hunter (1953) – who might be described, like C. Wright Mills (see page 9), as a radical elite theorist – suggests that Dahl's book, *Who Governs?*, ignores the ability of unelected and unrepresentative elites to control community decisions, and to take these decisions out of the hands of the community itself. In his own book *Community Power Structure*, Hunter carried out a study of an American city with a population of about half a million during the early 1950s. He found that the decisions that were taken reflected only a minority of community interests and many decisions took place without any real involvement by groups others than those of the elites themselves.

Neo-pluralism

Some thinkers have criticised the classical pluralist notion of a democratic compromise between a plurality of localized power sources, arguing instead that some groups are far more powerful than others. They argue that to compare the amounts of power groups have as being in some way equal to each other is to miss the full picture: decision-making is easier for some groups than for others.

▦   This observation has led some to reject pluralism totally, arguing that society is not democratic since some voices are more powerful than others. This is seen in the thinking of Hunter (1953) and Wright Mills (1956) – described as Radical Elite theorists since they identify the existence of a ruling elite that has more access to decision-making than all other groups. This type of thinking is very similar to Marxist or Weberian notions of power, since power is seen to be held by a ruling group – or, in Weber's case, a collection of elite groups – who use it for their own ends.

▦   The second response, from writers such as Richardson and Jordan (1979) is to identify an elite pluralist position, an updated version of classical pluralism, more familiar in the writings of Dahl. There are a variety of updated pluralist-influenced theories in contemporary sociology.

Elite pluralism

The neo-pluralist elite pluralist position of Richardson and Jordan suggests that some groups are listened to by governments more than others and that, between them, this core of respectable groups (as defined by the government in question) represent an elite group themselves. Power and decision-making are still plural, but not as equal nor as plural as Dahl's ideas might suggest. For example, groups working in the interests of business might be able to influence government opinion more than environmental groups, since business groups may be able to exercise more power.

This observation has led Grant (1985) to draw a distinction between:

▦   insider groups, and
▦   outsider groups.

The insider groups are more powerful, since they are more listened to by governments. (A fuller discussion of the role of pressure groups in the political process is continued in Chapter 7.)

Fragmented elites

Marsh (1983) talks of a fragmentation of those who seek to influence opinion and decision-making. By this he means that decision-making involves some groups more than others, but there is no real coherence or stability to those who collectively might make up an elite group. Writers like Wrights Mills suggest that business, military and political elites all combine together to shape how society operates, especially in the USA, where Mills was writing. For Marsh, the connections between the elite groups are less strong – they are *fragmented*. These elite groups shift positions of power from time to time, due in part to the fact that governments and ruling political parties themselves contain internal conflict, with some leaders, MPs and state departments favouring certain groups, and others favouring other groups. These groups do not combine together, but are a series of elite groups often opposed to each other – yet all are listened to more than the outsider groups who tend to be ignored or criticized in public debate.

Veto-group elites

To continue the analysis of which groups have more power than others, Lindblom (1977) coined the phrase veto groups to refer to the situation whereby some groups – in particular business-based groups – have a veto over the decisions made by government. In other words, these groups can apply pressure so that some potential decisions made by governments are blocked or thrown out (or vetoed), since these groups are defined as the real experts in their chosen field. They are more expert than the government, who defers to their superior knowledge, thus giving these groups a great deal of power, with little representation of the interests of the voting majority. An example might be the banking elite in the USA and Western capitalist societies, which, until the credit crunch of 2009, were deferred to by governments as experts in economic matters. Develop your understanding of these aspects of interest groups through doing Exercise 4.6.

Ⓤ Ⓐ

Exercise 4.6

1. *Elite pluralists* suggest that a number of insider groups combine to form a powerful elite. List examples of powerful insider groups that exist in the world today.
2. Theorists who believe in *fragmented elites* suggest that there can be conflict between insider groups within the elite. Which of the groups you listed in question 1 would be in conflict with each other?
3. *Veto groups* have the power to block important decisions. Give examples of groups that exist in the world today that have this power.

THEORIES OF INEQUALITY AND UNFAIRNESS IN SOCIETY

Whereas functionalist and classical pluralist theories emphasize the agreed or shared nature of power, other theorists have taken a more critical stance, looking at the inequality of power and some people's lack of opportunity to participate in the decision-making process. These theories share with neo-pluralism the belief that some groups have more power than others, but, unlike the various types of neo-pluralism, these theories are much more critical of the inequalities that they see in society. The only exception to this – the first theory to be discussed here – is what is called the classical elite model, which considers inequality to be natural and desirable.

Classical elite theories

Classical elite theories identify the existence of a narrow ruling elite and the absence of democracy in society. This is a right-wing elite theory. This position, called classical elite theory, is associated with three Italian thinkers:

- Niccolo Machiavelli (1469–1527)
- Vilfredo Pareto (1849–1923)
- Gaetano Mosca (1858–1941)

Despite the considerable time period between Machiavelli, Pareto and Mosca, their ideas have a great deal in common. The key assumption of their work is the belief that the people should not be left to control how society works since they are not the best people to do so!

For Machiavelli, in his classic book *The Prince*, a distinction can be made between two types of ruler – those who rule through legal means, and those whose rule is based upon violence. He compared the cunning rulers to the fox and the violent rulers to the lion, since they control society based upon strength. Pareto adopts the same analogy as Machiavelli, but points out that power between these two types of elites – the foxes and the lions – circulates between the two. In other words, elite rule is based upon a circulation of elites – a process of constant change between the lions, back to the foxes and to the lions again. This is because although some elites are able to take control of society due to their cunning (the foxes), they often lack the physical strength to keep rule in times of competition. Instead, strong elites take their place (the lions), but also are unable to hold on to power since violence in controlling society is not as long-lasting as being seen to have the legal right to rule. This circulation between the two types of elites continues in contemporary societies.

Mosca, like Pareto, believed that elite rule was normal and natural in human societies (as with animal societies), as only the strong would be able to lead. In some respects, this is similar to some functionalist thinking on inequality, since those who lead are also seen as the most suited to do so. The difference is that Parsons places much greater emphasis upon the democratic and representative nature of this rule than Machiavelli or Pareto.

(K)(U)

Exercise 4.7

Although it could be argued that contemporary Britain is not a good example of foxes and lions alternating in power, there are countries in the world where this kind of power could be said to be exercised. Research or mindmap some examples (perhaps in Europe, Africa or Latin America) where these types of rule existed in recent history, or still exist in society today.

Traditional Marxism and neo-Marxism

The ideas of Pareto and Mosca on elite rule tend to concentrate upon the personal qualities of the elites themselves – some are able to have power due to their intellectual cunning, others due to their strength, or willingness to threaten and use violence. The Marxist analysis of elite rule, however, is concerned with the structural nature of power. What this means is that power does not come from an individual's personality or personal characteristics, but from their location in the class structure of society.

Traditional Marxism

For Marx, as discussed in Chapter 3, power is based upon the ownership of the means of production. This means that those who have power in society are not so much a ruling *elite*, but rather, a ruling *class*, since their power is based upon economic ownership: the control of the *means of production*.

Marxist ideas are highly critical of other sociological positions such as functionalism, pluralism and the classical elite theories, as discussed previously. Modern day Marxist thinkers make a number of key observations about the nature of power, in relation to other theories:

- Pressure groups are ineffective in changing decision-making since they target decisions made by the government, but not by the ruling class;
- Business groups are more powerful than others, but again, it is not the case that their power is simply based upon being an insider group for

the elected government to favour – business owners are those with the *real* power;

▪ A global ruling class can be identified – those who own the global means of production – through transnational corporations that operate outside and over the decisions made by separate governments.

Neo-Marxism

As we have seen, many theories undergo change over time, leading to what are called new or neo versions of the original theory. There are many different versions of neo-Marxist thinking and a great deal is written about the role of the state in modern society by these newer variations (see Chapter 8 for a fuller discussion). The key elements to all neo-Marxist thinking about power are the following observations:

▪ Owing some debt to Weber as well as to Marx, some neo-Marxists empha-sise the varied nature of the power sources used by the ruling class. It is not just the ownership of the means of production but the control of cap-ital, technology and a workforce that gives a ruling class its power. This reflects a change in emphasis from ownership to control, due to the rise of share-holding and the rise of global companies.

▪ Some neo-Marxists speak not of a ruling class but of a power bloc made up of the state, owners of capital and controllers of labour – the rise of a new managerial class who have some limited power over the workforce. They have more power than the masses, but not as much as the owners of companies themselves.

▪ The state is not seen necessarily as the direct puppet of the owners of the means of production. Instead, it can sometimes have a degree of rela-tive autonomy making its own decisions that might directly contradict the interests of capital.

▪ Ruling class power is maintained through *hegemony* rather than through *ideology*. This means that working-class groups in society can sometimes see through ideology and can develop an awareness of class inequality in society, but might end up resigned to such inequality, feeling powerless, and accepting capitalist rule as inevitable even if not desirable.

This general neo-Marxist approach agrees with the classical version of Marx-ism that power is undemocratic and unfair. It also agrees that those elected to rule in the interests of those who voted them into power are actually unable to manipulate true power since it comes from a very different source: not the ballot box, but the class structure of society. Like classical Marxists, neo-Marxists see inequality and the uneven distribution of power as continuing as long as the class system continues.

Unlike classical Marxists, neo-Marxists see the nature of power as having changed over time, since the class system itself has changed. These changes to class relations are due to:

- The rise of share-holding as a form of economic ownership.
- The separation of ownership and control.
- The rise of a managerial class with some limited power over the workforce.
- The increased (relative) autonomy of the state from capital.
- The rise of global capital markets.
- The creation of transnational companies and the global nature of capitalist power.

In some respects, the newer versions of Marxism are often seen to be indebted to Weber, since Weber places much more of an emphasis upon an elite rule composed of more than simply economic ownership. Weber looks not just at class, but also at status and party (see Chapter 3).

Radical elite theory

The ideas of C. Wright Mills (1956) share a great deal in common with contemporary neo-Marxist ideas, and both are direct criticisms of the pluralist arguments within the writings of Robert A Dahl. Wright Mills suggests that a narrow ruling elite make the decisions in society and that other groups have little if any potential to influence these decisions. Wright Mills also points out that decisions made benefit those who have power and enable them to continue their dominance of society, and to further their power in the future.

Wright Mills describes these powerful people as follows:

> some men come to occupy positions in American society from which they can look down upon, so to speak, and by their decisions affect, the everyday worlds of ordinary men and women. They are not made by their jobs; they set up and break down jobs for thousands of others; they are not confined by simple family responsibilities; they can escape. They may live in many hotels and houses, but they are bound by no community. They need not

merely 'meet the demands of the day and hour'; in some part, they create these demands, and cause others to meet them. (Mills, 1956, p. 3)

There is an element of Weberian thinking in the ideas that form the basis of this radical elite theory. For example, Wright Mills makes the following distinction between authority and coercion in much the same way as Weber (see Chapter 3):

> in the last resort, coercion is the 'final' form of power. But then, we are by no means constantly at the last resort. Authority (power that is justified by the beliefs of the voluntarily obedient) and manipulation (power that is wielded unbeknown to the powerless) must also be considered, along with coercion. (Mills, 1963, p. 236)

For Wright Mills, like Weber before him, power is about getting people to do what you want them to do. In defining what power is, Wright Mills says: '*By the powerful we mean, of course, those who are able to realise their will, even if others resist it*' (Mills, 1956, p. 9).

The power elite

Unlike Marxists, Wright Mills identifies three elite groups in American society (but his work is seen to apply to Western societies in general) – what he refers to collectively as the power elite. These groups are:

- military leaders
- political leaders
- business leaders

Like the idea of fragmented elites, there is a degree of fluidity between these groups – one may be dominant over the other two at different times. However, there is more coherence about the power elite than in the fragmented elite model since they are seen to know each other and to share a similar social status, class position and to socialize together: they share a common cultural background.

> The conception of the power elite and of its unity rests upon the corresponding developments and the coincidence of interest among economic,

political and military organisations. It also rests upon the similarity of origin and outlook, and the social and personal intermingling of the top circles from each of these dominant hierarchies. This conjunction of institutional and psychological forces, in turn, is revealed by the heavy personnel traffic within and between the big three institutional orders, as well as by the rise of go-betweens. (Mills, 1956, p. 292)

Wright Mills separates his ideas from that of Marx and that of Dahl by suggesting that the ideas of capital totally ruling society or political rulers representing the common will, are both rather simplistic ideas. Instead, he notes the following points:

> The simple Marxian view makes the big economic man the real holder of power; the simple liberal view makes the big political man the chief of the power system; and there are some who would view the warlords as virtual dictators. Each of these is an oversimplified view. It is to avoid them that we use the term 'power elite' rather than, for example, 'ruling class'. (Mills, 1956, p. 27)

Dimensions of power

Marxist, neo-Marxist and radical elite theories are highly critical of what they see as the unrealistic or simplistic view of power held by pluralist thinkers. Steven Lukes (Chapter 2) describes three dimensions of power:

- decision-making
- non-decision making
- shaping the decisions of others

Pluralist thinkers are seen to rely too much on the first dimension – they only really look at decision-making, the sort of power that can be seen in society. However, the major contribution made by the more radical theories is to point out that power is often an invisible yet still real and influential process.

Like Marxist thinkers, Wright Mills notes that people can have power over a person, even if they are not aware of it. For example:

- Marxists talk of ideology hiding class inequality and making the decisions taken in society that benefit the ruling class seem natural.

- Neo-Marxists talk of 'hegemony' whereby the masses in society might see through inequality, but still feel constrained or powerless to change society in any way.
- Steven Lukes (see Chapter 2) identifies what he calls the third dimension of power as shaping the decisions of others – where rulers control the activities of the ruled, who are unaware that they are being dominated and having their behaviour shaped.
- Wright Mills suggests that the masses are manipulated, unbeknown to them.

Exercise 4.8

Lukes' first dimension of power can be used by pluralists and elite theorists to describe the activities of those with power. As the text suggests, Lukes' other two dimensions of power are not used by classical pluralists. However, different elite theorists use these other dimensions to describe the activities of those with power. Copy out and fill in the following grid. Give examples of the activities of groups that fit in this model.

Lukes	Pluralists	Neo-pluralists	Classical elite theories	Marxism/ neo-Marxism	Radical elite theories
Decision-making					
Non-decision-making					
Shaping decisions of others					

Wright Mills notes, like Lukes, that power is also seen in what leaders and elites choose *not* to do (and in what they choose to *ignore*), as well as what they decide to actually do – these are the second and third dimensions of power, ignored by pluralist analysis.

> The power elite … are in positions to make decisions having major consequences. Whether they do or do not make such decisions is less important than the fact that they do occupy such pivotal positions: their failure to

act, their failure to make decisions, is itself an act that is often of greater consequence than the decisions they do make. (Mills, 1956, pp. 3–4)

Ⓚ

Exercise 4.9

Use the following grid as a revision of key theorists and their ideas on power:

	Key thinkers	Key ideas
Functionalism		
Pluralism		
Neo-pluralism		
Classical elite theories		
Marxism/neo-Marxism		
Radical elite theory		

CONCLUSION

The reason why so many theories and thinkers disagree is due to the different (and often contradictory) images, definitions and measurements that they use. For example:

- Parsons sees power as the ability to do the collective good: to carry out agreed action.
- Marx and Weber see power as the ability to dictate the actions of others: to have power over the lives of others in some way.
- Dahl and pluralists look only at power as the ability to make decisions.
- Lukes and Wright Mills are concerned with power as an ability to direct the outcome of society in both seen and unseen ways; to have both power over others and to have power to do as you wish.

Michael Mann (1986) has identified four sources of power, drawing on the ideas of the sociologists above:

- economic
- military

- political
- ideological

Mann suggests that these sources of power can be separate and no one source dominates. In looking at power, Mann identifies two key aspects:

- the power that some people have and use over others – to get them to do what they wish
- the power that groups have when joined together – power from collective action

For Mann, power based upon cooperation between groups is the most powerful sort of power in society. It is based upon organisation and it usually involves the adding together of more than one source of power in order for everyone involved to increase their sum total of power. This means that, as power is combined together, the more power is generated as a result.

This distinction between power to and power over is a useful way to think about various sociological theories and will be applied to more contemporary theories on power (in Chapter 5) – theories that build on the legacy of ideas and observations made by the theories in this chapter. These contemporary ideas represent what we called a new sociology of politics at the start of this chapter.

Exam focus

The issue of the distribution and nature of power in contemporary societies is an important focus in examinations in the sociology of politics. It is one of the key controversies between sociologists of power and is therefore often asked about in examinations in a variety of ways. The central thing to bear in mind is that you must tailor your response to answer the specific question asked and not just write down the same answer for any question about the nature and distribution of power. For example, consider the following question:

'Modern democracies are open societies, where power is dispersed among many different groups.'
  To what extent does the evidence support this view about the nature and distribution of power in modern democracies?

It is relatively easy to interpret the main approach to power that the question is asking about. If you have already thought of pluralism, then well done! Having established this, the temptation could be to write down everything you know about pluralism and then, to evaluate the proposition, write down all you know about elite theory, and then come to a conclusion. However, the question is asking for a specific slant on pluralism. You will need to define what is meant by an open society and also the dispersal of power. But the key thing to recognize is that you have to evaluate how far the *evidence* supports this view. Although you will have to include the familiar arguments between pluralists and elitists, the focus has to be on studies that have carried out empirical research on this issue and use that evidence to come to an evaluation of the proposition.

Important concepts

- the Industrial Revolution • pre- and post-Second World War
- the late industrial age • postmodernity • • the death of class
- globalization • the new sociology of politics • functionalism
- pluralism • neo-pluralism • elite pluralism • fragmented elites
- veto-group elites • classical elite theories • traditional Marxism
- neo-Marxism • radical elite theory • the power elite

Summary points

- It is possible to identify a number of key historical developments that have affected sociological thinking.
- Present day sociological theorizing on the nature of power and politics has been described by some as a new sociology of politics since it is very different from the views of the founders.
- Sociological views on the nature of power and its role in society can be studied chronologically or thematically, by dividing theories into those that believe that power is democratic and those that consider it to be undemocratic. Theories that argue that power is not democratic can further be divided into those that believe it should not be democratic and those that believe it should.
- *Functionalism* believes that power is something that is generated by the community and used for the good of the community.
- *Pluralism* believes that there are many sources of power in society and that power is something that changes over time in line with the will of the people.
- *Neo-pluralism* criticises the classical pluralist notion of a democratic compromise between a plurality of localized power sources, arguing that some groups are far more powerful than others. *Elite pluralists* suggest that some groups are listened to by governments more than others, and that this core of respectable groups represent an elite group themselves.

- *Classical elite theories* identify the existence of a narrow ruling elite and the absence of democracy in society. This is a right-wing elite theory because it argues that such elites are natural among humans and beneficial to society.
- *Traditional Marxism* is highly critical of functionalism, pluralism and the classical elite theories and argues that those who have power in society are not so much a ruling *elite* but a ruling *class*, since their power is based upon the control of the *means of production*.
- *Neo-Marxists* agree with the view of traditional Marxism that power is undemocratic and unfair, and that those elected to rule are actually unable to manipulate true power since it does not come from the ballot box, but the class structure of society. Unlike traditional Marxists, neo-Marxists see the nature of power as having changed over time, since the class system itself has changed.
- *Radical elite theory* suggests that a narrow ruling elite make the decisions in society and that other groups have little if any potential to influence these decisions which are made to benefit those who have power and enable them to continue their dominance of society. Unlike Marx, this theory believes that there are three sources of power in society: military leaders, political leaders and business leaders.

Critical thinking

1. What is meant by the new sociology of politics?
2. Outline the difference between functionalism and pluralism.
3. Do all elite theorists disapprove of elites?
4. How has Marx's view that those who have power in society are those that control of the means of production been criticized?

Chapter 5

A New Sociology of Politics for a New World?

By the end of this chapter you should:

- understand the contribution to political sociology played by interpretative forms of sociology
- be able to apply sociological ideas on power to small-scale social situations
- understand the diverse nature of feminist views on power and politics
- understand the differences between the ideas of modernism and post-modernism
- understand how sociological ideas have changed over time
- be able to apply the ideas of postmodernism to issues of power in society

INTRODUCTION

In previous chapters we have outlined a change or transformation in political sociology in recent years. With the rise of newer theories and with the continued analysis of modern day life, some sociologists have tried to reject much of what has gone before in terms of sociological theorizing. Others have tried to incorporate the old sociology of politics into a new sociology of politics.

Many of these debates within sociology are concerned with two key questions for political sociology:

1. What is the significance of class in the contemporary world?
2. Do structures still constrain human action?

We can explain these key questions as follows:

- *What is the significance of class in the contemporary world?* – Many sociologists suggest that *either* the nature of class has changed, *or* that class is no longer important to society. These thinkers have suggested that class is no longer the source of voting behaviour and no longer a key source of social identity. If this is the case (and not all sociologists subscribe to this view) then class no longer offers a meaningful basis for political action. Some thinkers argue that class has been replaced by newer forms of political identification, such as sexuality or lifestyle, whereas other thinkers feel that with the death of class there is nothing left that can be used as the basis for political action and that therefore the death of class leads to the end of the political in general (see Chapter 6). These debates and issues have led to the introduction of ideas of postmodernity into sociology – ideas we will discuss later in this chapter.
- *Do structures still constrain human action?* – With the rise of more micro or interpretative sociologies, some sociologists have moved away from structural theories that see human action as constrained by impersonal wider social forces towards an image of humanity as creative and free. These theories have existed for a long time in sociology (since Weber himself (see Chapter 3) discussed the importance of meaning and the role of human action in creating society). However, with the rise of various types of interpretative sociologies from the 1930s through to the 1980s, more and more thinkers have come to reject the view that humans are necessarily the puppets of structures bearing down upon them. These insights have proven highly influential for some modern day theorists who look at the opportunities for human action and for the creation of self-identity through lifestyle.

These two key sociological themes – class and action – have led many sociologists to turn away from looking at politics and power on a large scale, towards looking at these in everyday life itself.

THEORIES OF POWER IN EVERYDAY LIFE

Since the words power and politics are difficult to define, a simple definition sometimes is needed. Provisionally, we have used the word *power* to mean getting your own way and the word *politics* to mean struggling for power. This means that issues of power and politics are not just macro phenomena, but might also exist at smaller-scale, micro levels.

Day-to-day life might involve struggling with others for power. From the primary school child interacting with the school bully, the housewife feeling constrained by a dominant husband, the patient in a hospital feeling that choices over his life are in the hands of others who clearly know better, through to the single parent arguing with a representative from the social services about benefits – power inequalities, and therefore power struggles, are all around. How could it be otherwise? Every time we enter into interpersonnel interaction with others, do we do so for the good of the other or for what we want to get out of the situation? Although this is a profound philosophical question it illustrates our point well: politics is not just the remit of politicians, and power does not just rest with those elected through the ballot box or with those who are military or economic elites. Clearly there are many different types of power – but it is all power nonetheless. Some may even say that the large-scale forms of power are more important or more significant that the small-scale versions, but power struggles are still a feature of everyday life.

Even those who claim that politics means nothing to them may well talk about the frustration they feel with political elites who seem too detached from their own daily lives, or with a general feeling that voting might not change anything. Whether interested or not, all of our life is affected by struggles for power (see Exercise 5.1 to explore power in your own life).

For example, those who claim not be interested in politics in any way, will find that:

■ someone else decides how much pay they receive for their work;
■ a government decides how much tax they should pay;
■ a government decides what laws will exist and what might happen to them if they get caught breaking them.

All these situations are part of ordinary life, but they are also the consequence of decisions made by political elites.

Equally, for those who might say that they are interested in politics, they might:

■ join a political party;
■ join a pressure group and read its literature;
■ demonstrate;
■ go on strike for more pay or better working conditions;
■ discuss politics with friends and try and persuade them to think as they do, and perhaps change their voting behaviour in some way.

Some of our daily lives might be influenced by the practices of others at a large-scale level (government), but equally, some of our small-scale daily activities might in turn affect the bigger picture.

Many sociologists go further and question whether the behaviours listed above are any more political than certain everyday behaviours, such as:

1. teachers correcting students on the proper way to speak in lessons;
2. parents arguing with a teenage son who has just announced that he is homosexual;
3. doctors telling a teenager girl that she can not go on the pill since she should not be thinking about having sex at the age of 14;
4. a teenager being attacked by others for looking differently and for perhaps dressing according to the rulers of a different youth subculture;
5. a neighbour criticizing another for not recycling their glass and paper;

Exercise 5.1

Draw a spider diagram with yourself in the middle, and put on it examples of the way in which power is exerted upon you, and the way in which you exert power. Compare your spider diagram with your neighbour's – in what ways are your diagrams the same, and in what ways are they different? Why do you think this is? What key changes in your demographics would result in a different diagram?

The new sociology of politics differs from the old in that it does not just look at:

- class
- large-scale decision-making
- the activities of elites and elite groups
- structural constraints

Instead, it is concerned with power and politics within:

- language
- interaction
- lifestyle choice
- sexuality

- environmental risk and harm
- identity – especially gender and ethnic identities

INTERPRETATIVE SOCIOLOGIES

An early attempt to look at the role played by power in everyday life is provided by those sociological theories that we can describe as being interpretative or as interactionism. The key ideas of this type of sociology are:

1. Humans are active and creative – they manipulate symbols to help them make sense of their interaction with others.
2. The reality of society does not exist somehow above individuals, but society is simply made up of interaction itself. It does not exist as a thing in its own right.
3. Humans have meanings and motives behind the actions they perform in society – these meanings help their interactions make sense and therefore create reality for those involved.
4. Culture teaches us the norms and values of society – and, in particular, language – and it sets the framework within which our behaviour can take place: cultural agreement defines what is considered to be normal in a society.
5. Culture is the active creation of humans themselves.
6. Humans have a self-image that is of central importance in interaction: they are thinking creatures, able to think about who they are and who they might wish to be, how they act and how they should act. Humans are also not just reflexive about their own actions, but also think about what the action of others might mean.

This is a very different image of humans and their role in society from the more structural theories such as Marxism or functionalism that tend to see humans as the products of things done to them by society. For example, Marx, in his discussions of ideological control, and Durkheim, in his discussion of how the individual is bonded to the group by the collective consensus (see Chapter 3), both seem to suggest that humans are at the mercy of wider social forces controlling them. For interpretative sociologies humans are creative. They create through their actions and interactions with others the reality of society.

Power and impression management

A key thinker in this interpretative perspective is American Erving Goffman (1969) who contributes what he describes as a dramaturgical perspective or analogy to help us to think about how people interact with each other. For Goffman, human action can be compared to the theatre or to acting. In fact, he calls humans social actors since he sees them as playing parts in society. We can extend this analogy further:

- *We act out parts* – People act differently with different people, i.e. you can be a son, a best friend, a lover etc.
- *We can follow scripts* – we know that some things are acceptable to say in some situations and not in others; we learn that some language automatically follows others in a pre-scripted way. For example, if a friend asks 'How are you?', even if you are unwell, do you still say 'Okay. How are you?', since the words used do not actually mean 'How are you feeling?' but 'Hello'? The pre-scripted element to this interaction means that a request for information on health is really a pre-learnt form of normal greeting.
- *We take on roles* – we are expected to be a different person depending upon the role we adopt and the situation we are in. A teacher talking to students in a classroom by standing at the front and telling them off for talking is not the same role as the same person talking with friends once work is over, on the bus going home: both forms of interaction would look very out of place and very abnormal if swapped around.
- *We give performances* – we think about how other people might see us – and what they might want from us – and we adapt our behaviour accordingly. Goffman calls this 'impression management', since we can calculatingly try to give people the impression we want of us. This might apply if we go for a job interview or maybe meet our partner's family for the first time etc.

Within his ideas on impression management, Goffman's work contains a theory about power on micro levels – power as exercised in everyday life. We get the impression from his work that humans are thinking and calculating – we weigh up situations and then try and turn them to our advantage. For example, we have the impression of humans having constant internal dialogues (conversations) with themselves, constantly assessing the situation, trying to figure out what type of performance to act out. These internal dialogues might go as follows:

- What do they think of me?
- What do I think of them?

- What do they want me to think about them?
- What do I want them to think about me?
- What happens if I act in this way? Do they change their impression of me?
- What should I say in order to make sure they think about me what I want them to?
- Why are they acting as they are now? What do they want from me?
- What do I want from them?

Goffman says that individuals have power in an interaction if they are able to take *control of the definition of the social situation*. In other words, if you are able to make people think what you want them to think about you, and get them to act as you wish, rather than you acting as they might wish you do (assuming that these are not the same). This means that interactional encounters where we calculate the impression we give are political. *They are struggles for power.*

Exercise 5.2

Describe (or even act out!) a situation where the questions in the list above might apply. Think particularly of situations where power (perhaps in unequal measure) is an issue. An obvious example of such a situation is going for a job interview, but others might include a conversation in which one person is trying to break off a relationship with another, or in which parents a trying to persuade their child to stay on at college etc.

Goffman's ideas on interaction and impression management have been used by some to explain why some people might join political movements. Goffman, in his book *Frame Analysis* (1974), suggests that when humans seek to understand, make sense and give meaning to their experience and day-to-day encounters with others, they undertake the process of framing. What this means is that they draw upon categories, rules and sets of previous experiences and try to categorize what they perceive to be happening according to this previous experience and knowledge they have of society. They try to classify their experience in order to understand it. This act of classification is called framing.

McAllister Groves (1995) suggests that framing might help explain how and why people join political movements. Such movements might offer pre-arranged frames that an individual joining the group can use and adopt in order to make sense of the world.

Labelling

An extension of the interpretative analysis of power looks at how our image of our self as a person might be shaped by others. This is known as the process of labelling. From Goffman's ideas on impression management we have an idea of humans as creative and free, engaged in struggles for meaning. However, in some cases meaning might be imposed by a more powerful group, and might shape and define how the individual comes to see themselves over time.

Howard Becker (1963) has suggested that powerful groups might seek to label as deviant those whose behaviour might cause them problems – might not fit in with the rules they wish for society. By making some groups seem illegitimate in this way, the powerful also seek to control and define the social situation, by having their definitions accepted by the majority as the right way to view reality.

In this view, Becker suggests that there is no such thing as deviance because deviance simply refers to behaviour that has been defined as deviant. It is therefore not the action as such, but the label that makes the deviance real in the eyes of society and therefore wrong (see Lawson and Heaton, 2009, and Exercise 5.3).

As Becker famously states, 'Social groups create deviance by making rules whose infraction constitutes deviance, and by applying those rules to particular people and labelling them as outsiders' (Becker, 1963, p. 9).

Exercise 5.3

Think of situations in which you, or someone you know, have been treated as deviant. For each situation, try to answer the following questions:

1. What specific aspect of your behaviour led to you being treated as deviant?
2. What was the social rule that you broke by behaving in this way?
3. How is the rule expressed/transmitted?
4. Who, if anyone, gains from the application of this rule?
5. How did you feel about being labelled as an outsider and what, if anything, did you do about it?

Some Marxist-influenced sociologists have noted that this idea – that the powerful are able to define what other people think in society – is shared by Marx himself. Marx noted, 'The ideas of the ruling class are in every epoch the ruling ideas, i.e., the class which is the ruling material force of society, is at the same time its ruling intellectual force' (Marx and Engels, 1976).

From this we see the combination of interpretative (micro) sociology and structural Marxist sociology (macro) into what is now called neo-Marxism. This looks at power in everyday life, but also relates this everyday life to how society is patterned and to how the class system creates inequalities of power. For example, Stanley Cohen (2002) suggests that working-class attempts to struggle against the inequalities of power they experience in a capitalist society often become the target of 'moral panics'. These are attempts to label some groups as deviant and to shape how they might be seen by society in general: labelled as a problem for normal or decent society to solve.

> More moral panics will be generated and other, as yet nameless folk devils will be created. This is not because such developments have an inexorable inner logic, but because our society as present structured will continue to generate problems for some of its members – like working-class adolescents – and then condemn whatever solution these groups find. (Cohen, 2002, p. i)

For Cohen and others, this labelling process is a powerful form of *social control*. It makes the activities and views (or ideology) of the powerful seem to be natural and thus accepted without question (test out similar situations in your own life through Exercise 5.4).

Exercise 5.4

Can you think of situations where you accept the activities of the powerful without question? Identify who the powerful are, what you accept and why? Use the following grid to help you:

Powerful group	Ideology/view/ activity	Why do you follow it?	Whose interests does it serve?

FEMINISMS AND POWER IN SOCIETY

The inclusion of the many varieties of feminist sociology under the general category of theories that look at everyday life might need some explaining. Their inclusion denotes the change that feminist thinking has undergone through internal debates between different sorts of feminists and the influence that feminism has had on wider sociology in general.

Although seemingly structural, since it looks at the existence of *patriarchy* (male dominance) in society as a whole, much feminist thinking has tried to:

1. look at the lives of ordinary women in everyday social situations
2. look at how male power extends to the use of interpersonal forms of domination such as violence
3. look at how day-to-day language often contains many gendered assumptions about men and women
4. help to improve the lives of women engaged in small-scale political struggles against gender inequality

Much feminist thinking might therefore be structural in the sense that theoretically it identifies wide-scale patterns of inequality across the whole of society, but it often adopts more interpretive or micro research methods. A great deal of feminist research seeks to understand how gender inequalities of power affect women's lives at a level of ordinary action. This occurs for the following reasons:

1. Unlike any other theory, feminism is both an intellectual exercise and a practical activity. The feminist project seeks real change in society and therefore studies small-scale groups and behaviour in order to help effect change.
2. Some feminists often feel that for women to seek power, they must first understand themselves and how their role and position in society is psychologically different from that of men. Thus, feminist sociologists seek small-scale research in order to explore the meaning of femininity and to explore women's daily lives on a personal and intimate level.
3. Much feminist thought is anti-science. This is because science is seen as a male ideology – a means by which men dominate society and define female knowledge as less valuable than male rational scientific knowledge. Many feminists see positivist research methods (that try to be scientific) as little more than research as rape since they use people for their own interests and then cast them aside once the research is over, not trying to help them

to change their lives in any way. Many feminists wish for a feminist-only form of research and knowledge that seeks to help those it studies in an intimate way. Exercise 5.5 offers you some scenarios to think about male and female power relationships.

Exercise 5.5

Using the following extracts, write a short paragraph describing the inequalities of power that exist in each extract:

A: Domestic violence

A police officer pleaded guilty to a misconduct charge today following an independent inquiry into the fatal stabbing of a mother of three...Expected to last for up to five days, the hearing represents the first use by the Independent Police Complaints Commission (IPCC) of powers allowing it to order forces to hold such hearings in public. The move follows an IPCC investigation last year which concluded that Ms Lynch, 24, a mother of three, was 'grievously ill-served by a succession of officers, staff and their supervisors' who failed to ask questions, listen properly or follow policies in relation to domestic violence. In what the inquiry called a 'tragedy unfolding in slow motion' Ms Lynch was stabbed to death by her estranged partner Percy Wright on February 3, 2005, two days after she reported an incident in which he had come to her home, smashed the front room window and threatened to cut her throat. The inquiry found that despite repeated calls to police from Ms Lynch and her family, police failed to record the initial incident as a crime and did not arrest Wright at that time. (*Guardian Unlimited*, Monday, 5 November 2007)

B: Prostitution

This is a side of life the Burmese military junta might prefer you did not see: girls who appear to be 13 and 14 years old paraded in front of customers at a nightclub where a beauty contest thinly veils child prostitution. Tottering in stiletto heels and miniskirts, young teenage girls criss-crossed the dance-floor as part of a nightly 'modelling' show at the Asia Entertainment City nightclub on a recent evening in Rangoon....Watching these young entertainers of the 'Cherry-Sexy Girls' model groups were a few male customers, and a far larger crowd of Burmese sex workers, mostly in their late teens and early 20s, who sat at low tables in the darkness of the club. Escorting several girls to a nearby table of young men, a waiter said the show was not so much modelling as marketing. 'All the models are available,' the waiter said, adding that the youngest girls ask $100 (£48.50) to spend a night with a customer, while the older girls and young women in the audience could be bargained down for a lot less. Prostitution, particularly involving children, is a serious crime in military-ruled Burma, but girls taken from the club would have no problem with the authorities, the waiter assured the company, but did not explain why not. It would seem that prostitution is one of the few things the Burmese military, fresh from its recent crushing of pro-democracy demonstrations by Buddhist monks, is still willing to tolerate. (*Guardian*, Tuesday, 30 October 2007)

C: Women and work

Black and Asian women are facing significantly greater employment barriers than white women and are 'missing' from almost one third of workplaces even in areas with high ethnic minority populations, according to a new report. A study published today by the Equal Opportunities Commission finds that Pakistani, Bangladeshi and black Caribbean women find it harder than white counterparts to get a job or win promotion, and are more likely to be segregated in certain types of work despite having good qualifications. Such barriers are to blame rather than family or cultural resistance to women working, the report says ... The report, Moving On Up: Ethnic Minority Women at Work, argues that a 'fundamental shift' is needed if black and Asian women are to be given a chance to get better jobs. ... EOC chair Jenny Watson said: 'Young Pakistani, Bangladeshi and black Caribbean women are ambitious and equipped for work, but they are still suffering even greater penalties at work than white women. Time after time women told us about the "unwritten rules" in their workplace, hidden barriers that prevent them from realising these ambitions. Without tackling these unwritten rules, change will never come ... .' Katherine Rake, director of the Fawcett Society, said: 'Today's report fundamentally challenges the myth that it is family and culture that are holding ethnic minority women back in the workplace. Discrimination through outdated generalisations and inaccurate stereotypes are the real culprits.' ... CBI deputy director-general John Cridland said employers were keen to employ more women from ethnic minorities, but needed better guidance to support them. (*Guardian*, Thursday, 15 March 2007)

We can identify a wide range of different types of feminist theories, which see power and its operation in society in slightly different ways. A great deal of recent feminist thinking, has been highly critical of male power within sociology itself. This is known as the 'malestream criticism' – the idea that sociology has been 'By men, for men and about men' – as defined by Abbott and Wallace (1997). Traditionally, sociology has been concerned with class and, as a result, gender inequality has often been *invisible* to sociological study. For example, we all know of the founding fathers – but, what of the founding mothers, and the insights of early feminist thinking and how it might have shaped sociology? There is little in the textbooks.

The personal is political

The rise of feminist thinking in sociology – and of feminist views on power in particular – has led to the re-assessment of the importance of class in sociology and in society. The introduction of gender and sexuality as forms of power inequality has opened up sociological thinking on power to include a wide range of political expression and not just to concentrate upon class. Equally, some feminist thinking has urged women to see how their everyday lives are political in the sense that many women struggle everyday with sexual politics. As some feminists have argued, the personal is political, and, in this statement, we are once more led to consider the role of power in everyday life.

As Abbott and Wallace (1991) argue:

> Feminists have pointed out that the personal is political – i.e. that it is active agents who 'do the oppressing' and that it is necessary to give credence to women's concrete experiences of oppression – ones occurring in personal everyday events – as well as those at the collective and the institutional level. We need to recognize that men and women, oppressors and oppressed, confront one another in their everyday lives, in the home, at school, at work, in the courts and so on. (Abbott and Wallace, 1991, p. xiii).

Old and new feminist views on power

Most varieties of feminist thinking share the following essential arguments:

- Society is male-dominated ('patriarchal').
- Women's oppression often is 'invisible' since it occurs in 'private' institutions such as the family etc.
- For most feminists male power is not the product of biology – it is created through tradition and through 'common-sense thought' (some feminists would disagree, looking at male power as based in the male physiology and the use of violence – carry out Exercise 5.6 to lay bare your own thoughts on these matters).
- Common-sense thought and dominant ways of thinking are usually male sources of knowledge and thus contribute to male power.
- The psychological experience of belonging to society is different for men and women – because of the different power inequalities they experience in every aspect of society.

As Abbott and Wallace (1991) note:

> In the classical discussions, power is more often seen as a product of public institutions such as the state and the economy rather than of private institutions such as the family and interpersonal relations. Yet if we are considering gender and power, our attention is directed towards these more 'private' institutions, and their relations to the more public institutions of power. (Abbott and Wallace, 1991, p. xi)

and, in discussing reasons for male power:

> Why do men hold power? We reject the explanation that is simply because they are physically stronger. Rather, we need to look at how power enables men to define situations, to define what is 'real' – even within sociology, so that patriarchal power is not even seen as a main issue. The ways in which women are defined away or portrayed in particular ways through legal or medical discourse are examples of the diffusion of power which we need to unravel: for example...the ways in which they are defined in terms of their bodies or their sexuality, and the ways in which the skills which they possess are not considered to be of any importance. (Abbott and Wallace, 1991, p. xii)

(A)(An)

Exercise 5.6

List as many ways in which you think that men may be traditionally seen to be holding power over women within the private institutions of family and interpersonal relationships. For example:

- Men may have tended to bring more money into the household, and could claim that this gives them certain rights in the home;
-
-

Traditional feminist discussions of the nature of power in society sought to identify the following unequal power relations between men and women:

1. Inequality in *domestic labour* (housework and childcare) performed by men and women (see Steele and Kidd, 2000);

2. Male *violence* – rape and domestic violence (see Lawson and Heaton, 2009);
3. Unequal representation in the *media* of male and female bodies (see Jones and Jones, 1999);
4. Unequal *socialization* of children into traditional gender roles – often through the use of gendered play and toys;
5. The unequal access to *employment* for men and women.

Much contemporary feminist thought has contributed to the new sociology of politics by looking at the following issues of power:

1. how female sexuality is defined by male-dominated media products – both in pornography and in mainstream media products;
2. how female bodies are limited and controlled more and in different ways to male bodies by the medical profession;
3. how an ideology of the family exists in the welfare services and among political and religious leaders that makes it seem natural for women to wish to care for children;
4. how an ideology of pro-natalism also exists in society that makes it seem a biological fact that women who do not have children are not 'whole or full women'.

Abbott and Wallace illustrate how these forms of gendered inequality and gender power relations operate in everyday life:

> Women are controlled by lack of access to economic resources and to positions of formal power, but also in a range of other ways which involve sexuality – the ways in which they are defined as sexual beings and, deriving from these, the ways in which they are the victims of sexual abuse. Sexuality emerges repeatedly as the instrument by which power over women is maintained and exercised because it serves to define them in particular ways. (Abbott and Wallace, 1991, p. xii)

Exercise 5.7

Identify the kind of power relationships that are expressed in the following examples.

*   a cleaner
*   an athlete
*   a pole-dancer

- a housewife and mother
- a body-builder
- a nursery nurse
- a judge

Is the woman doing the job in each example completely in control of the situation? Has she entered into it freely? If not, what factors have forced her to behave in that way? If she is in control, then will there be any negative consequences for her? Would your answers be different if you lived in another country such as Iran?

Feminists and feminism have been instrumental in helping the *new sociology of politics* to shift its emphasis away from looking at:

- large-scale power
- formal power
- public institutions
- economic power

to understanding the role of power and power struggles that centre upon:

- small-scale power
- private institutions
- power within interactional encounters
- issues of power based upon the oppression or control of the body
- power based upon the limiting or defining of sexuality
- power based through the limitation of lifestyle choice

Varieties of feminist thought

We can make a distinction between the following types of feminist thought and how power is viewed within these varieties of feminisms:

- *Traditional feminism* – analyzed male power in terms of tradition. Women were seen to be excluded from employment opportunities open to men and, as a result, captive in the family home. Domestic labour was seen as a source of inequality, and traditional expectations of childcare stopped women from seeking change. The political solution to these power inequalities was claimed to lie in anti-discriminatory laws that would free women from oppression and inequality (look at Exercise 5.8 to establish your understanding of the role of law in oppressing women).

▓ *Marxist-feminism* – essentially Marxist-feminists placed more importance on class power and on capitalism than on patriarchy. However, there is the recognition that like men in the factory women are oppressed workers in the private family home, performing domestic labour that keeps the wheels of capitalism going by caring for workers and ensuring they can continue to work and be exploited in the public world of work. The solution to power inequality from this viewpoint is to revolt against capitalist power, and the problems of patriarchy will also be solved.

▓ *Radical feminism* – often this position was associated in sociological literature with a form of lesbian politics – in particular with 'separatism' – the idea that women will only be free from male power and domination by being free of men altogether, although there are different types of radical feminist thought. This radical view suggests that all men wish to dominate all women – it is due to their biology and physiological power that men are violent towards women and physical domination and the threat of physical domination allow inequality to continue. Shulamith Firestone (1979) has argued that male power is based upon biological strength and such power inevitably structures the nature of all social relationships – in both the private and public areas of life. It is therefore inescapable.

▓ *Dual-systems feminism* (also called *socialist feminism*) – this theory took as its starting point a criticism of how Marxist-feminism deals with the relationship between capitalism and patriarchy. Whereas for Marxist-feminists capitalism is the more powerful form of inequality and patriarchy serves capitalism, for dual-systems thinkers class and gender, capitalism and patriarchy are as important as each other and they are interconnected. At some times one form of power might dominate over another form of power, but usually they exist in combination. Heidi Hartmann (1981) has described Marxism-feminism as an 'unhappy marriage' since the problems of male domination over women are seen to be imposed upon the theory – Marxism (the male) taking control and dominating feminism (the female). Feminism and the problems of patriarchy are seen as simply 'added on' rather then forming a detailed analysis of how the two forms of power (class and gender) operate in society together. The earlier work of Sylvia Walby (1986; 1988) also reflects the concern to unite an analysis of these two forms of power together. Walby notes that in all of its history, capitalism has always existed with other forms of power and inequality.

▓ *Black feminism* – like dual-systems theory, this type of feminism seeks to look at how patriarchy might link to other forms of power and inequality in society, rather than somehow being separate. Thinkers such as Amos and Parmar (1984) argue that the psychological experience of gender inequality and patriarchal power might feel very different for some women because of their ethnicity. Not all women experience patriarchal power in the same way. For some, racism might further their inequality, but for others their ethnic identity might be a source of comfort and resistance to wider inequality and potential powerlessness.

- *Materialist feminism* – French thinker Christine Delphy (1984) is sometimes described not as a 'radical feminist' but as a materialist feminist. This means that sexual oppression is seen as fundamental to male power in society, but that, irrespective of other forms of inequality, women share common experiences, interests and political goals by virtue of their sex. As such, all women, irrespective of class, are a sex-class and as such are involved in a struggle against the power of the male sex-class. Biological difference is therefore the key to inequality, but men do not rule because they are stronger or biologically superior, they rule due to tradition and violence, but share more in common politically with others of the same sex. Biological sex differences do not cause inequality, but they are the differences around which the two classes struggling for power in society are organized.

- *Triple-systems feminism* – this view tends to be associated with the later work of Sylvia Walby – in particular in her books *Theorizing Patriarchy* (1990) and *Gender Transformations* (1997), where she suggests that ethnicity, class and gender are as important as each other as forms of power inequality in society.

ⓀⓊ

Exercise 5.8

Find out about how male power might be said to be expressed in the law. Using the following questions as a starting point, look at the ways in which the law treats women differently. Find the answers to these questions, and also look for some of your own examples. You can do this on your own or in groups. You could compare your findings with other groups in your class or by looking at the situation in another country:

- What rights do women have with regards to their partner's property if they are married, unmarried, with or without children?
- How do the laws defining male and female rape differ?

- What is the criminal charge for soliciting? Compare this to the criminal charge for picking up a female prostitute.

Sylvia Walby – forms of power in society

In *Theorising Patriarchy*, Walby (1990) suggests that we can identify six areas of social life in which male power dominates:

1. *Employment* – women still suffer from poor pay, lower employment expectations by society in general and a lack of full-time work. This is furthered by expectations of maternity leave that might make some employers think before employing a women to a top position and the fact that traditional women's jobs are still undervalued in society (see Exercise 5.9);
2. *Family relationships and domestic labour* – marriage is for most women still a form of domestic enslavement and captivity, although some women do find family life a safe haven from patriarchy – but this is unusual, and depends upon the individual nature of the relationship;
3. *Culture* – in particular the representation of women's bodies and the so-called 'sexual revolution' has not treated female sexuality the same as male sexuality – especially in terms of the widespread distribution of sexualized images of women that define women as sex objects for the use of the man;
4. *Sexuality* – the definition and limiting of women's sexuality and the labelling of heterosexuality as the normal type of sexuality;
5. *Violence* – is seen to be used to dissuade women from challenging powerlessness;
6. *The state* – while the state has passed a great number of laws protecting the rights of women and does take domestic violence seriously, it still treats single mothers as a problem to be solved.

For Walby, all six are separate yet interlocking structures of patriarchy, and when we talk about male domination and power it is located within these six areas of society. Sometimes these structures might be independent from each other and, at other times, they might combine to oppress women. Walby also acknowledges that inequality does not necessarily bond all women together into a common experience of powerlessness, since other forms of power (class and racism) also intersect gender and patriarchy, making a whole range of combinations of inequality and powerlessness possible. For example, the state has passed anti-discriminatory laws that might limit patriarchy expressed as violence by men against women. Yet at the same time, pornography is more commonplace than before – including highly sexualized images of women in the mainstream media – which might encourage male violence further. Heterosexuality is still seen by the medical profession as the norm and this might influence how the state treats some family relationships.

Ⓐ Ⓐn

Exercise 5.9

Using the following extract, describe the inequalities expressed within it:

The results of the 2007 Annual Survey of Hours and Earnings (ASHE) show that median weekly pay for full-time employees in the UK grew by 2.9 per cent in the year to April 2007 to reach £457. Median earnings of full-time male employees were £498 per week in April 2007; for women the median was £394.

The top 10 per cent of the earnings distribution earned more than £906 per week, while the bottom 10 per cent earned less than £252. Between April 2006 and 2007 the distribution of gross weekly pay narrowed, with a 3.5 per cent increase at the bottom decile, and a 2.8 per cent increase at the top decile.

Median gross weekly earnings for full-time employees were highest for 40 to 49-year-olds at £516 for this age group. Male employees reached their highest earnings in this age group at £575, whereas women reached their highest earnings for 30 to 39-year-olds at £460. Earnings increased until employees reached these age groups and steadily decreased thereafter.

Median full-time weekly earnings in London were £581, significantly higher than in other regions, where they ranged from £402 in Northern Ireland to £481 in the South East.

The occupations with the highest earnings in 2007 were 'Health professionals' (median pay of full-time employees of £1,019 a week), followed by 'Corporate managers' (£702) and 'Science and technology professionals' (£670). The lowest paid of all full-time employees were 'Sales occupations', at £264 a week.

The monetary difference between the median level of full-time earnings in the public sector (£498 per week in April 2007) and the private sector (£439 per week) has widened over the year to April 2007, following annual increases of 3.0 per cent and 2.9 per cent respectively.

(Office for National Statistics (2007) Annual Survey of Hours and Earnings (ASHE) Online: http://www.statistics.gov.uk/StatBase/Product.asp?vlnk=15050)

In *Gender Transformations* Walby (1997) outlines four types of sociological approaches that look at how power and patriarchy operate in society:

1. Ignoring gender as not being as important as other forms of power such as class;
2. Identifying problems of ignoring gender without really looking at gender in any great detail;
3. Adding on the study of gender as part of a wider study of a supposedly more important form of inequality such as class;
4. Providing a full theoretical analysis of how the structures of patriarchy intersect with other forms of power in society.

A full theoretical analysis is certainly what Walby attempts. Walby's analysis presents us with a complex picture of how patriarchal power might operate in society; a picture made up of a web of power relationships between many sources of male power that themselves might support or contradict each other. And, along with this patriarchy, inequalities in power such as class and racism also intersect with these structures of patriarchy to present an even more complex picture of power.

Post-feminism – has power inequality changed?

For post-feminism, traditional patriarchal power inequalities are now a thing of the past. This type of thinking is also sometimes referred to as a 'rational choice theory' since it sees women as able to make a free and reflexive choice about what they wish to have from society. It seems to suggest that if women feel powerless, then they have themselves to blame for 'choosing' to live a life that makes them unhappy. For example, Catherine Hakim (1995) says that since times have now changed, women can choose from all options available – if they are housewives then they must surely desire this option since they have the choice to change this if they wish.

Exercise 5.10

Write down a list of constraints that may be used to challenge Hakim's view that being a housewife is a 'choice'. Think internationally as well as nationally.

Can you think of other examples where women may feel powerless through no fault of their own?

Feminism and the future?

In order to move on from post-feminism, with its suggestion that there is no longer a need for a feminist analysis, Walby identifies ten key points of feminist analysis for the future. These ten points are designed to allow feminist sociology (and its contribution to studying the political nature of everyday life) to continue:

1. Gender politics should be fully included in any discussion of politics in general.
2. Gender politics have an effect upon other types of political struggles such as class or environmental politics.
3. Party politics also have a gendered dimension that should not be ignored.
4. Gender politics includes the study of men as well as women.
5. We cannot understand politics based upon gender without also looking at anti-feminist positions – some women may also be anti-feminist.
6. Although there is a relationship between sex and political affiliation we cannot automatically assume that all men are anti-feminist and all women are feminists.
7. 'There is more than one way of being a feminist'.
8. The different types of patriarchy in society might contain significant differences between each other.
9. We must seek to understand a third important position in gender politics – not just feminist and anti-feminist – but also pro-women non-feminists who might wish to reduce/remove patriarchy in society.
10. 'Feminist politics are not unusual' – and we need to understand why some forms of feminist thought might disappear, as well as why others might rise.
    (Adapted from Walby, 1997, pp. 153–4)

POSTMODERNISM AND THE NEW SOCIOLOGY OF POLITICS

One way of understanding postmodern ideas is to see them as an attempt to discuss the usefulness of the more classical ideas within sociology. With the rise of, and interest in, postmodern ideas from the late 1980s/early 1990s onwards, a radical rethink has taken place within the social sciences in general. This rethink has attempted to understand how the contemporary world may have developed and changed and to understand how sociology should change alongside it.

Simply put, postmodernism is the belief that society has significantly changed since its historical roots in the modernity of the industrial revolution. As the name suggests – we have moved after the modern.

In discussing issues of postmodernity, it is important to be clear about some important terms:

- *Modernity* – this is seen as the time period created by the industrial revolution in Europe. This is described as being modern, not in the sense of now or contemporary, but because this time period was concerned with stripping away tradition and becoming (what they thought at the time was) modern. It represents an emphasis on the importance of science in society and the rise of rationality. This is the very sort of thinking that was responsible for the rise of sociology itself – the belief that humans could master nature and that social change could be directed towards progression, towards a better universal future for all humanity (see Chapter 3).
- *Postmodernity* – this is what is thought to be after the modern. In a sense, the modern itself has now become traditional as time passes. Postmodernity is the time period itself – the actual historical events and the actual society where postmodernism (the theory) helps us to understand how society itself has changed.

Although there is no unified definition and theory of postmodernism, it is possible to identify two broad trends within this way of thinking:

1. *Postmodern optimism* – this suggests that changes to the world and the decline of modernism are liberating and represent a progression for the individual and for society;
2. *Postmodern pessimism* – this suggests that the rise of a postmodern world has brought about radical change that has caused problems in society – which has led to uncertainty, chaos, meaninglessness.

Features of a postmodern society

Within sociology there are those thinkers who have embraced postmodern ideas, and those who think they are an intellectual cul-de-sac, a dead-end. Likewise, a great many thinkers feel that profound change has taken place in society to make us rethink our reliance upon classical sociology, but this change is not necessarily completely post (after) what was before. Many different thinkers have used a wide range of terms to describe what they think these changes after the modern might be; so much so, that contemporary sociology seems littered with 'post' this and 'post' that. Broadly speaking, all these images of the new society are rooted in the observation that great change has taken place so that our present society is fundamentally different from before. Some of the trends are:

- *Post-industrial* – based on the idea that the nature of economics has greatly changed from production to consumption, and the rise of a service economy.
- *Post-scarcity* – the end of want – society produces enough wealth and consumer products for everyone.
- *Late/advanced industrial* – the idea that present day capitalism is a different or more advanced sort of industrial capitalism than before – now based upon consumption.
- *Post-Fordism* – the idea that in terms of production processes, we have moved on from the mass production of a single standardized product ('Fordism') to a situation where we have a wide and diverse range of niche markets making a slightly different product for slightly different audiences who see the purchasing of such products as part of their lifestyle choices. People then identify with what they think having these products might say about them.
- *Post-materialism* – the belief that people in society today engage in political action for reasons other than financial ones, such as sexual freedom, environmental concerns and for the ability to have the sort of lifestyle they wish, and to remove the state's involvement in this lifestyle.
- *Reflexive modernism* – this idea is not so much a type of postmodern thinking or a feature of a postmodern world, but rather an alternative sociological image of what is happening in the present day world. This view suggests that present day society encourages individual reflection unlike ever before and the rise of opportunities to take control and move away from the constraints of previous structures such as class, the traditional family or sexuality.

In general all these ideas are postmodern in a sense, since they all claim that something comes after the sort of society identified by the classical sociologists as modern.

The periods of modernity and postmodernity are often presented as a series of opposites – as if postmodernism does not build upon what went before, but has stripped it away, replacing all the key features of society with their

Table 5.1 Modernity vs Postmodernity

Modernity	Postmodernity
1. Belief that science can understand every aspect of human activity;	1. Science becomes seen as just another story no more true than any other;
2. Belief that there are clear rules of development along which all societies should progress;	2. Rise of chaos and uncertainty – no more guiding rules, no more certain belief in the correct path for society to follow;
3. The importance of class as a source of identity;	3. Rise of a wide range of identities – decline in the importance of class;
4. The belief that politics can discover the right way to live and political struggle can create the perfect society;	4. Apathy with all things political, the rise of identity politics based upon self-identity and lifestyle rather than creating the best society for all;
5. The replacement of tradition with the modern supposedly more rational way to organize life and society.	5. The ironic invention of fake tradition as part of a general playing around with past cultural products.

opposites. This is a broad generalization, but maybe a useful starting point to consider how these ideas might relate to a study of power and politics and to the creation of what we have called the new sociology of politics.

Postmodernity can thus be characterized by the following essential features:

- *fragmentation* – of identity, knowledge and previous dominant structures;
- *rise of relativism* – the belief that no truths can be said – there are no absolutes that can guide society as the correct ways to live any more;
- *uncertainty* – with no guiding truths social life becomes a potential source of anxiety and confusion;
- *diversity* – of beliefs, lifestyles, truths and identities: no single guiding way to live life.

Exercise 5.11

Fill in the gaps from the choice of words at the bottom of the exercise. Then compare your own paragraph with your neighbour's to check your understanding.

In a — — — society, the rise of a service economy overshadowed — — — — in favour of — — —. Modernity was associated with the — — — — — — — — — in Europe, and — — — — and — — — — — were thought to be very important. — — — — — has moved on from modernity. In a — — — — — society, ways of understanding social and political life are changing. — — — — — — — — — — — see the decline of modernism as liberating. In postmodern society there is a rise of — — — and — — with fewer guiding rules. Identity has moved away from — — — — — — to other identities often related to — — — —. Politics may have followed suit in a post-modern society with the rise of — — — — — — — — based on — — — — — — — — — and — — — — — choices.

chaos		
lifestyle	postmodern	production
consumption	postmodernity	postmodern optimists
Industrial Revolution	social class	science
rationality	consumption	uncertainty
postindustrial	identity politics	self-identity

Postmodern politics

John R. Gibbins (1989) offers a collection of terms and images frequently associated with postmodernism and the impact that these changes in the very fabric of society might have had on politics itself:

1. Dealignment of class and political action (separation, so that they are out of line with each other).
2. Discontinuity – how the shape of politics is forever changing and sometimes seems to jump from past periods of political certainty to confusion and chaos.
3. Fragmentation

   a. of interest in voting;
   b. of previous powerful political ideas and parties;
   c. of 'the people' from once solid class groupings to much smaller and looser collections based upon common lifestyles and identities that

might quickly change and change with it the nature of politics in the future – the creation of even more political uncertainty;

4. Overload – of the state and its spending – the belief that welfare cannot continue in the way it has before.

Gibbins poses the question that all postmodernists ask when looking at the present nature of power and politics:

> What changes, if any, have occurred in the political cultures of modern industrial states in the last thirty years? Is there any uniform direction or pattern in the changes that are occurring? Are the changes identified explicable within established cultures and paradigms, or do they signify a break with the past and a new beginning? Does a 'new politics' accompany the new political cultures? (Gibbins, 1989, p. 1)

Gibbins suggests that we live in a period of postmodern politics simply because the decades since the Second World War have resulted in massive and fast-paced social change, which, in turn, has had an effect upon how people see themselves, how they see society and what they want out of life. Gibbins notes that we have witnessed:

- alterations in party policies and party support
- the decline of trust
- the rise of pluralism
- the marginalization of pressure groups
- the emergence of new political movements such as feminism, environmentalism and sexual politics
- the re-emergence of some political ideologies from the past
- the rise of terrorism
- increased exposure to political messages from the media – yet the increased apathy in voting
- the rise of importance of the communication industries to modern day politics

Gibbins and others have concluded that, 'the terrain of contemporary politics seems unfamiliar and very definitely new' (Gibbins, 1989, p. 1) and,

A postmodernist politics and political culture would highlight a dissatisfaction with modern politics, its sameness, customary alliances, its predictability, bureaucracy, discipline, authority and mechanical operation, and would stress the emergence of a politics featuring difference, dealignment and realignment, unpredictability, freedom, delegitimisation and distrust, power and spontaneity. (Gibbins, 1989, pp. 15–16)

The politics of the new

In *Intimations of Postmodernity*, Zygmunt Bauman (1992) seems to suggest that postmodern politics are about rethinking old views and ways of 'being political' itself. Being political – actually 'doing politics' – means something different than it once did. Politics and struggling for power can now involve lifestyle choice and how you might choose to live, rather than simply the activities of elected elites that you might vote for every four years. Although, as Bauman notes, not all types of politics that occur in postmodernity are actually themselves postmodern: the old style of politics and the old sources of power still exist, and sit alongside the new forms of power and the new ways to struggle for power. What we now have is a great mixture of ways to be political – society-wide and localized – and this further adds to the postmodern character of political life since it results in even more mix, even more choice, even more diversity.

Bauman says, however, that the newer, postmodern politics will come to dominate how politics occurs and as a result, the older forms of politics will take second place. He also suggests that postmodern forms of politics might gain more power and support precisely because they are new; thus, they might have more of an impact and more of an appeal to people already disillusioned with previous political issues. Old struggles – such as class and wealth redistribution – come to be seen as legacies from the old days, left over and out of place somehow with the more fresh and vibrant postmodern issues of sexuality, lifestyle and identity. In this sense, Bauman claims, postmodern politics are not more superior, they have just managed to seem more attractive and therefore perhaps seem more trustworthy to those already disillusioned. However, the issues that older political struggles were based on – class, wealth and racism, for example – have not disappeared; they have not been solved as such, it is more the case that other issues have come to attract people's attention: 'Postmodern politics is mostly about the reallocation of attention. Public attention is the most important – coveted and struggled for – among the scare commodities in the focus of political struggle' (Bauman, 1992, p. 247).

Bauman identifies four key types of postmodern political expressions – he notes that they are not the only type of postmodern politics on offer, but are, at present those that have been most readily adopted by people in this changed society:

1. *Tribal politics* – new associations and groups (tribes) are loosely created over new issues to do with identity and these groups establish themselves as a community of similar people.
2. *The politics of desire* – in order to establish identity, people might consume ideas, objects or images in order to show others they are the right sort of person.
3. *The politics of fear* – some people are concerned with the risks and harms that society has to offer and as such will adopt lifestyles that help them to avoid these ills of modern living.
4. *The politics of certainty* – we loose faith in once trustworthy leaders and experts; there is the rise of anxiety in postmodernity and then attempts to replace anxiety with certainty once more, based upon new claims and new sources of trust.

Postmodern politics and freedom

Bauman has suggested that in postmodern politics we have an enhanced autonomy. In other words, more freedom, since there are many more choices to be made in a postmodern political age.

Anthony Giddens (1991), although not a postmodernist as such, has also suggested that, in present society, there is much greater scope for individuals to make choices and to remove some of the constraints of tradition. He refers to this as living in a post-traditional social order. This is both *enabling* and also itself *constraining* since the more structure and tradition is removed, the less certain life becomes and the potential for anxiety rises. Thus, we have increased opportunity and choice, but only if we choose to take up these opportunities. The dramatic change in politics for Giddens is the rise of life-politics whereby individuals are able to be reflexive about their lives and their positions in society more than ever before. As a result of this they can choose between more options, as the range of choices on offer has dramatically increased. These choices concern issues of lifestyle and of identity: we have a much greater say over who we wish to become and this is itself a political struggle since it involves taking responsibility for, and control over, who we end up becoming.

The idea that postmodernity might offer more political freedom is echoed by Ronald Inglehart (1990), who has argued that postmodernism has emerged from a change in society towards post-materialism. In other words, present-day political struggles and issues are concerned with issues involving the quality of life: environmental awareness and protection, increased choice over one's sexuality and freedom to explore individual lifestyle choices. For Heller and Feher (1988) the postmodernization of politics, and the rise of freedom and choice over a diverse range of lifestyle options, is itself a *democratic* process; it is about personal choice, not enslavement to the desires of others or to some abstract notions of tradition. Of course, personal choice is always limited by the options that are available within society and by the individual's ability to make choices. Middle-class people, for example, have always found more lifestyle options open to them then the poor and dispossessed. The majority of people living on our planet at the current time have their personal choices severely curtailed by poverty and want. The freedom to explore lifestyle choices could be seen as exclusive to those of us lucky enough to have enough food, water and shelter.

New technologies and political campaigns

Another aspect of the postmodern condition that has attracted the attention of sociologists of politics is the rise of virtual technologies and the way that they have impacted upon political parties and election campaigns. This is not just the case of the political parties developing websites that would attract new members. Indeed, it has been argued that the people who are most likely to visit mainstream party websites are already politically active and are likely to be sympathetic to the party that they access (see Gibson *et al.*, 2005). In the USA, a personal website has become one of the main ways in which potential candidates 'test the water', heighten their political profiles between elections, establish their policy intentions and rebuff hostile rumours that opponents may have placed in the public domain (Cornfield, 2004).

As new technologies develop, political parties and candidates move to exploit their potential to support their election chances. In particular, the parties in the USA have used the Internet as a means of fund-raising and gathering small donations. The Democratic Party has been quicker than the Republicans to use the internet for this purpose, but it is actually candidates who grab the electorate's interest who benefit most from this source of revenue (Graf *et al.*, 2006). In the 2004 election, supporters of different presidential candidates began to use YouTube to post up videos of their favoured candidate, and the mistakes made by their opponents. Many of these videos gained the status of virals, that is, they seemed to take on a life of their own as the word of their existence spread through the virtual world (Jalonick, 2006). Barack Obama had over 64,000 contacts on MySpace at the beginning of the 2008 campaign and used these contacts as a supporters' base even though he did not create or control it (Williams, 2007). However, it is important not to over-estimate the impact of the internet and new technologies on political campaigns. The television remains the main conduit for political information during an election campaign, mainly because it is a 'lean-back' technology rather than the proactivity needed to utilize their Internet as a source of political knowledge.

CONCLUSION

The new sociology of politics, with its use of ideas drawn from postmodern theory makes some very profound comments about the nature of society and the nature of the human condition within such societies. This is, however, one theoretical voice among many, and within postmodern thinking we see a wide variety of ideas and views. The new sociology of politics is just as plural and diverse as the old ever was. And, in fact, both the older and newer ideas still sit side by side in most sociological discussion, as will be demonstrated in the remainder of this book where these ideas, themes and theories will be applied to key issues within political sociology.

Exercise 5.12

Revision exercise. Now that you have read through this chapter, there are some key terms and definitions that you need to be sure of. Answer the following questions:

1. How can Becker's ideas about labelling (p. 80) be applied to our understanding of power?
2. What do feminists Abbott and Wallace mean when they say that 'the personal is political' (p. 85)?
3. Explain briefly the difference between traditional and contemporary feminist views on the nature of power in society (p. 82).
4. Define what is meant by post-feminism (p. 94).
5. What does Giddens (p. 101) argue is the main impact of postmodernist thought on postmodern politics?

Exam focus

Feminists have altered the way that we think about politics and power. The invisibility of women in the past meant that they were not included by sociologists of politics when they considered the exercise of power. Power was seen as a male domain, while women were confined to the private sphere of the home. Feminism has changed that position, so that women are more likely to engage in politics than they were previously. However, by focusing on male power and the ways that women are subordinated to it, feminists have ignored the differences between women in their relationships to power. Issues of class and ethnicity are equally important to women as they experience the exercise of power.

Using material from the Item and elsewhere, assess the view that feminists have altered the way we think about politics and power.

In your answer make sure that you include the following concepts: patriarchy, the personal is political, public/private spheres, domestic power, separatism, sexuality.

Important concepts

- interpretive sociologies (interactionism) • impression management
- framing • labelling • moral panics • patriarchy • 'malestream'
criticism • 'the personal is political' • socialization • the ideology of
the family • types of feminism • Traditional • Marxist • Radical
- Dual-systems (socialist) • Black • Materialist • Triple-systems
- post-feminism • post-industrial • post-scarcity • late/advanced
industrial • post-Fordism • post-materialism • reflexive modernism
- tribal politics • the politics of desire • the politics of fear • the
politics of certainty • postmodernism • The politics of the 'new'
- enhanced autonomy • post-traditional social order • 'life politics'

Summary points

- Debates within political sociology are concerned with two key questions:

  ○ what is the significance of class in the contemporary world?
  ○ do social structures still constrain human action?

- Interpretative sociological theories suggest that society does not exist as a thing in its own right but is the active creation of humans themselves.

  ○ Goffman sees humans as social actors, acting out parts, following scripts and taking on roles.

- o Becker suggests that powerful groups might seek to label as deviant those whose behaviour might cause them problems.
- o Cohen suggests that working-class attempts to struggle against the inequalities of power they experience in a capitalist society often become the target of moral panics.

- Unlike other theories, feminism is both an intellectual exercise, looking at the existence of patriarchy in society as a whole, and a practical activity, seeking real change in society. 'Malestream criticism' is the idea that sociology has been 'By men, for men and about men'.

    - o *Traditional feminists* focused on inequality in domestic labour, male violence, representation of male and female bodies, socialization of children into gender roles and unequal access to employment.
    - o *Contemporary feminists* have contributed to the new sociology of politics by looking at how female sexuality is defined by male-dominated media, how female bodies are limited and controlled bodies by the medical profession; how an ideology of the family makes it seem natural for women to wish to care for children; and how an ideology of pro-natalism makes it seem a biological fact that women who do not have children are not whole or full women.
    - o Feminism has been instrumental in helping the new sociology of politics to shift its emphasis away from looking at large-scale or formal power to understanding small-scale power.

- There exists a range of feminist ideologies:

    - o Traditional feminism
    - o Marxist-feminism
    - o Radical feminism
    - o Dual-systems feminism
    - o Black feminism
    - o Materialist feminism
    - o Triple-systems feminism

- *Post-feminists* believe that traditional patriarchal power inequalities are now a thing of the past; if women feel powerless, then they have themselves to blame for choosing to live a life that makes them unhappy.
- *Postmodernists* suggest that we live in a period of postmodern politics because the decades since the Second World War have resulted in massive and fast-paced social change. Politics and struggling for power can now involve lifestyle choice rather than simply the activities of elected elites.

    - o Bauman has suggested that in postmodern politics we have an enhanced autonomy.
    - o Giddens describes the rise of life-politics whereby individuals are able to be reflexive about their lives and their positions in society more than ever before.

Critical thinking

1. Do you think that interpretive or interactionist sociologists are over-optimistic about the individual's ability to affect the world around them?
2. 'All the world's a stage, And all the men and women merely players' (William Shakespeare, *As You Like It*). Discuss.
3. Describe examples in which moral panics have been used as a form of social control.
4. Is the personal political?
5. What divides traditional, Marxist- and radical feminists?
6. Is feminism an ideology of the past?
7. Define postmodernism and describe its implications for politics.

Chapter 6

Changing Ideologies and the Transformation of Political Parties in the UK

By the end of this chapter you should:

- understand the views of the major UK political parties
- be able to compare and contrast the views of the major UK political parties
- have an understanding of how political ideologies have changed in the UK in recent years
- be able to apply sociological interpretations to the changing nature of UK political ideologies – in particular the ideas of postmodernity

INTRODUCTION

Harold Wilson, Prime Minister of the UK from 1964 to 1970 and from 1974 to 1976, famously once said that 'a week is a long time in politics'. He meant by this that events change rapidly and such is the nature of governing a society that it is impossible to predict what will happen and what issues will develop. Things can change dramatically even in the space of a few days. The observation that 'things have dramatically changed' is one shared by most contemporary commentators when looking at the current political landscape in the UK. Things seem very different than they did 15 or 20 years ago, and some these changes are indicators of the processes of postmodernization in society in general. For many sociologists and political scientists – and in media discussion and public opinion as represented in the media – there is a general awareness that the political parties in the UK have changed. The business of politics seems different. It is no longer based upon class alliances but instead focused upon lifestyle choices and what we will discuss later as identity-politics. For example:

- The views of the parties seemed to have changed.
- New issues in society, often involving risk have risen to prominence in contemporary political debate.
- The traditional assumption that some parties represented certain sorts of people rather than others seems no longer true.
- The association of class with voting behaviour seems to have declined.
- The political parties seem to have moved on the political spectrum – they no longer offer what they once did.
- Political parties have tried to reinvent themselves, to publicly redefine who and what they think they are.
- The role of the mass media and the advertizing industry in political campaigning has risen to a position of massive importance – especially the role given to spin doctors.

This chapter will start by considering the type of political system the UK has and will discuss the ideas of the main political parties within the UK. It will then, drawing on the list above, offer some contemporary sociological interpretations of these changing political times – looking at what has changed and why it might have done so.

VARIETIES OF POLITICAL SYSTEMS

A political system refers to the way in which the governance of society is structured as a whole. In other words, it refers to how running society is organized. Every political system involves consideration of the following key questions – the particular answers to which would shape the type of political system the particular society ends up with.

Questions that define a political system:

1. How many people should have ultimate power in a society?
2. What type of person or people should run society?
3. Should they be elected or born into the position or can they display their leadership qualities through military service?
4. Can anyone run for election?

5. How much say can the people have over who should run their society?
6. If elections are to be held, how will they be organized?
7. What role will a royal family have in the process of power – if any?
8. Will the government organize business and the media itself, or allow free-market competition – or even a combination of the two?
9. What rights will the people have?
10. What responsibilities will the people have?
11. How will the government be funded and how will it in turn fund military, education and welfare services?
12. How will the legal system be organized – and who will run it?
13. Who would be regarded as having privilege in society – and should privilege be redistributed among everyone, or should inequalities be allowed to exist?

Exercise 6.1

Imagine yourself as part of a committee set up to decide on the governance of a new state. In an ideal world, how would this state be run? Answer as many of the questions that define a political system as you can in deciding how your state should be organized.

Work in groups to do this exercise, and then present your ideas to the other groups in your class.

How different is your ideal from your own political system? Can you think of any places that have the type of government you suggest, or is it unrealistic and if so why?

It is important to point out that the society-wide consideration of these issues does not necessarily occur at a public level – although on some occasions in some societies the people are asked to vote to change some aspects of the political system. Equally, systems develop over long periods of time and, as such, do not always make logical sense. Some aspects of a political system may seem at odds or in contradiction to others, but this is usually due to the fact that traditions change slowly, and not always at the same rate or in the same direction as other traditions. For example, in the UK we have both a prime minister and a monarch. These are two very different traditions. How do they relate to each other? Who has the real power and how do they get it? In France, there is both a prime minister and a president: How do these interact in day-to-day politics?

When looking at governance, we can identify three key types of systems:

- totalitarianism
- oligarchy
- democracy

Totalitarianism

According to Friedrich (1954), a totalitarian society is characterized by the following features:

1. a single political view that allows no alternatives to be elected (if elections are run at all);
2. a single political party;
3. usually a dictator;
4. the use of violence by the state to limit and control opposition;
5. the use of a secret police force and/or military rule;
6. state control of business;
7. state control of the media;
8. the absence of free speech.

Like Weber's use of the ideal-type (see Chapter 3), these features can be applied to different societies at different times to get the 'best fit' possible – not all totalitarian societies will have all of these features, but they will have most of them.

Oligarchy

An oligarchy is a dictatorship that is based on a small elite group of privileged people, rather than just one – it means rule by the few. These few may represent different groups of people, depending on the society in question. For example, the elite group might be:

- religious leaders
- a royal family
- a warrior class or caste/military leaders
- business rulers

Democracy

The word democracy means rule by the people. As commentators such as David Held (1993) note, claims to being democratic are among some of the most powerful sources of legitimacy for a ruling group in the contemporary world. What this means is that if ruling groups can make others see their political system as being democratic, it also tends to be seen as a just or legitimate source of power and rule. There is an authority (to use Weber's term) (see Chapter 3) behind this claim of 'democracy' that gives power and leadership a certain credibility.

The key features of a democracy are:

- regular elections
- the right to free speech
- rights and responsibilities enshrined in law
- rulers and leaders are held responsible for their actions by those they represent
- a degree of choice over who rules

We can identify two key types of democratic political systems:

- *Participatory democracy* – the birthplace of democracy is usually considered to be Athens and the actual word democracy comes from the Greek *demos* (people) and *kratos* (rule). In Athens, people who were defined as citizens participated in mass public elections where decisions were made through debate, argument and agreement. However, not everyone could vote – women and slaves were not considered to have the status of a citizen and were therefore not allowed at these events. Equally, everyone present was made to vote. Famously, officials tied a dyed red rope around the assembled crowd; if voting and debating were slow, the officials would walk forward, slowly closing the rope circle. Any citizen slow to have their say and who stood around at the back was touched by the rope and coloured red: this was a mark of shame – it meant that the citizen in question was slow to take advantage of the democratic process!
- *Representative democracy* – Mass participation in the political process is impossible for modern large-scale industrial societies and, because of this, the particular form of democracy usually found today is representative. This type of democracy is where leaders are elected to represent the wishes of those who voted for them. Unlike participatory democracy, this representative form is open to criticism, as those who are voted to represent may

form themselves into an elite who may look after their own wishes, rather than what their electors would like.

Exercise 6.2 will help to develop your understanding of these distinctions.

Exercise 6.2

Think of examples of governments that are totalitarian, those that operate as an oligarchy and those that have demonstrated both participatory and representative democracy.

Do some research by reading the foreign sections of broadsheet newspapers, using the internet to find out about your examples.

* Where are they located?
* Who is in government? Is it an individual or a group?
* What do they stand for?
* When and how did they get into government?
* Note down anything else of interest.

You could extend this activity by looking at neighbouring countries, the history of the state and the economic conditions.

Problems with democracy

A number of sociologists, philosophers and political scientists have identified some problems with democracy (which is interesting since in our society there is often a common-sense assumption that democracy is the best or even perfect form of political system). These problems are as follows:

 Max Weber (1968) warns that as societies become increasingly large, massive bureaucracies will be needed to help to run and organize society in a smooth fashion. When this happens the unelected invisible bureaucrats themselves may develop more power than those elected since they understand more and are in day-to-day control of the system.

 Max Weber also points out that democracies only work if there is enough choice between parties for people to feel they will have their views represented. If parties become too similar, then how much choice do people really have?

▨ Schumpeter, an economist, argues that the key problem with democracy is that those elected to stand for the people are themselves a ruling elite and as such may rule for themselves, not for the good of the whole. He also notes that due to the large size of modern societies, trying to identify exactly what the common wishes of the people, are is a problem, and it is highly unlikely that people will agree, given how many there are!

▨ Birch makes a similar point to Schumpeter – it is impossible to identify popular will and thus, as a result, impossible to really know exactly what the people may wish.

▨ Marxist sociologists point to the existence of a ruling class who are able to influence the process of political decision-making due to their manipulation of vast amounts of wealth. This is surely a very undemocratic situation since these people are not elected, yet may be able to influence the decisions of those who are.

▨ Finally, with the rise of global interconnections of an environmental, economic and military nature between societies, the right to self-rule of some societies is shaped and influenced by others from outside – especially through international laws and economic regulations. Therefore, those voted to represent the people might only be able to do so, if outside powers agree they can do what they wish to!

The 'victory' of democracy?

As Held (1993) suggests, despite the many actual and possible problems of democratic political systems, the need to be seen as being democratic is a key feature of the contemporary world. Almost every revolution, demonstration and military action is a consequence of people feeling that the existing rulers are not as democratic as they should be. Almost every dictator in the modern era claims to be democratic, as a way of making their rule seem more legitimate and increasing its length.

As Held notes:

> Democracy seems to have scored an historic victory over alternative forms of government. Nearly everyone today professes to be a democrat...yet what these regimes say and do is often substantially different from one another...democracy is a remarkably difficult form of government to create and sustain. (Held, 1993, p. 14)

The idea that democracy may have won some sort of victory of legitimation over other types of political systems is reinforced by Claus Offe (1996). He follows the ideas of Weber and Schumpeter in warning that, although we may have come to expect democracy in the Western world, this does not mean that it is an easy and automatic state for politics to achieve – especially given the problems in trying to identify the will of the people. In fact, Offe goes further still and suggests that it is not very clear at all exactly who the people are, let alone what their will might be, given that not everyone who is eligible to vote at an election actually does.

For Offe:

> In quite a specific sense, there is no alternative to liberal democracy today: there are no theoretical alternatives worthy of attention...I do not mean this in the sense that there are still in existence but which have been rejected as less worthy of being considered valid when compared with liberal democracy, as based on universal, free, and equal adult suffrage. Instead, the opposite is the case: such an alternative no longer exists in modern societies. Democracy, therefore, does not resemble an elected constitutional form...but rather an ineluctable fact...modern societies are condemned to rely solely on the 'will of the people'...democracy has changed from being a virtue we should adhere to and has become a fact that we have to get by with. (Offe,1996, p. 89)

What is interesting is that Offe describes democracy as a situation we are condemned to rely on. What he means by this is that once a society claims it is based upon representing and carrying out the will of the people it would be virtually impossible to gather popular public support for anything else. However, since this will is impossible to measure, such societies that claim to be based on the will of the people have no real way of proving that this is the case. More worrying still, with the absence of a detailed and meaningful measurement of the public will, whose will is really being represented?

Offe highlights three main problems with the so-called victory of democracy:

1. When politicians speak of the will of the people, such a will is *fictitious* since it cannot be seen as a clearly identified entity. In fact, given the vast differences between groups in society, it almost makes more sense to assume no universal will exists at any time;

2. When politicians speak of the will of the people this will must therefore also be fallible (possibly incorrect, making mistakes) – meaning that there are no real guarantees that the will identified is truly what people think and that, even if it is, there are no guarantees that the people are right: they may have got it wrong, they are, by definition, not political experts;

3. Finally, since there is no way to measure the will of the people, claims to know what it really is probably led to its creation in the first place – it is a self-fulfilling prophecy. Once politicians and the media start to talk about public will they are raising ideas that the public might start to think about it, in a way they have not done before. Thus, the will of the people is a *social construction*. It is not real or true, and may actually seduce the people into agreeing with it – because 'everyone else thinks that way'.

Anthony Arblaster (1994) suggests that since the idea and the practice of democracy has existed for a long period of time, definitions of democracy become even more of a problem if we recognize that, over time, such definitions and practices may change. For example, what we think of as highly democratic in one age, may be seen as very undemocratic in another. Thus, the UK was still considered to be a democracy by many before women were able to vote, but today, if a politician argued to withdraw this vote it would be seen as a thoroughly undemocratic. Equally, some societies seem to have the support of the will of the people but still do very undemocratic things, with some degree of public support, such as the persecution of minority groups, or the invasion of other weaker societies.

Arblaster notes that much media and political party-led thinking about democracy is commonsensical in nature: it is based upon an assumption that we all know who really is democratic and who simply claims to be. However, this is a difficult and at times a dangerous way to think about society – who is this 'we' that political parties and the media stand for when they talk about 'our' true democracy?

Exercise 6.3

Look up definitions of democracy and democratic process in various dictionaries – do they differ or are they all the same? If they differ, how do they differ?

ARE WE INTERESTED IN POLITICS ANY MORE?

Despite this apparent victory of all things democratic, there may still be a high degree of scepticism among the people in the UK (some of whom remain unconvinced) that their wishes are as fully represented in the political process as the concept of democracy would suggest. For example, Pattie *et al.* (2004) found that 55 per cent of respondents felt that they had no say in the UK government, despite the right to vote.

Anthony Giddens (1999) in his 1999 Reith Lecture on democracy states that:

> The paradox of democracy is that democracy is spreading over the world...yet in the mature democracies, which the rest of the world is supposed to be copying, there is widespread disillusionment with democratic processes. In most Western countries, levels of trust in politicians have dropped over past years. Fewer people turn out to vote than used to ... more and more people say that they are uninterested in parliamentary politics, especially among the younger generation. Why are citizens in democratic countries apparently becoming disillusioned with democratic government, at the same time as it is spreading round the rest of the world? (Giddens, 1999, pp. 71–2)

Giddens' own answer to his question is interesting since he says that non-attendance at elections does not necessarily indicate a population uninterested in politics – in fact, quite the opposite. For Giddens, although many people in the West have lost faith in politicians, this does not mean they have also lost faith in the whole democratic processes itself. Instead, the act of not voting does not mean apathy, but could itself be a political act: a way of showing discontent in a critical fashion at those making policy decisions. Giddens suggests that we need to look at environmental protests and the widening of protests about rights – in particular those associated with gender and sexuality – to see that young people in the West are still political.

Problems measuring political apathy

Andy Furlong and Fred Cartmel (1997) have suggested that, in the same way that it is difficult to tell what voting actually means for the individuals concerned, it is just as difficult to try and measure what non-attendance at elections means for the individuals involved (see Exercise 6.4). For the media, the non-attendance of the young at elections means apathy or disinterestedness and some sociologists have also taken up this theme, seeing the apathy of the young with politics as a part of a general trend towards the end of politics (see Chapter 2) as part of the postmodernization of social life (see Chapter 5). It could be the case, as Giddens suggests, that non-attendance at elections is part of a wider concern with identity-politics among the young. Alternatively, young people's apathy could be explained sociologically as a media *moral panic* – yet another exaggeration concerning a group in society that those who make the media find difficult to understand – the young.

Exercise 6.4

Denver (2006) uses The British Election Study carried out at the University of Essex in 2001 to suggest that:

- married and widowed people are more likely to vote than single people or those who are living with a partner
- professional and managerial people are more likely to vote than manual workers
- people are more likely to vote as they get older
- owner-occupiers are more likely to vote than people who rent their homes
- the higher the level of education, the more likely people are to vote
- people with higher incomes are more likely to vote
- people with strong party identification are more likely to vote

1. What might the explanation be for these discrepancies in turnout?
2. What difference do you think it may make to the outcome of a vote?
3. What could be done to improve turnout among groups that tend to be less likely to vote?

Furlong and Cartmel note that interest in politics among the young can take many forms, much of which is difficult to measure and directly identify (try it yourself in Exercise 6.5). They specify the following situations:

1. It is possible to express an interest in politics without being actively involved in a formal political organization.
2. It is possible to take part in direct action (demonstrations etc.) without voting or having an affiliation to a particular party.
3. It is possible to be knowledgeable about political issues yet still be cynical about elections actually altering the shape of political events.
4. It is possible to be actively involved in very political actions in the broadest definition of the political possible – such as environmentalism

or gender/sexuality politics, or through lifestyle statements such as body piercing or vegetarianism – while at the same time expressing no interest in politics as defined in its narrowest sense as the activities of elected governments.

Exercise 6.5

Working in groups, or on your own, survey your friends or a sample of fellow students about what politics means to them.

Design a short questionnaire asking questions about political affiliation and issues they consider to be important.

What do your results suggest to you about the nature of political activity among young people?

Park (1996) has suggested that it should come as no surprise that younger people are less interested in politics than older generations – that, in fact, politics has always been like this! Using data from the 1994 *British Social Attitudes Survey* (BSAS) Park notes that people tend to become more interested in politics – defined as the activities of government – after the age of 25. This may be due to increased dependence experienced by those under the age of 25 due to higher education or unemployment, with political awareness only developing as financial independence is achieved.

An alternative view is provided by MacDonald and Coffield (1991) who have suggested that political apathy among the young is the direct consequence of knowing little alternative. Between 1979 and 1997, there had only been successive Conservative governments in power, with little chance for the Labour opposition to gain power, until the transformation of the Labour Party for the 1997 election. Why should the young be interested in politics if all they have experienced are successive periods of similarity? Equally, with the media predicting the second election victory in 2001 of Tony Blair's New Labour party as a foregone conclusion, who can blame the young for being disinterested? The media and some leading politicians appear to share the view that voting changes nothing, so great were the New Labour victories in both 1997 and 2001. The motivations for voting in general and the issue of the voting behaviour of the young in particular are further discussed in Chapter 7.

CONTEMPORARY UK POLITICAL IDEOLOGIES

As part of the democratic process in the UK, every four to five years, general elections are held where the people get to choose their representatives. These elections usually start with massive campaigning where the political parties make election promises and identify their key aims, concerns and policies for the next five years. Although we deal with voting and voting behaviour in Chapter 7 of this book, summarized below are the results of the past few General Elections.

Table 6.1 Election results since 1979

- 1979 – Conservative victory and Margaret Thatcher becomes the first female Prime Minister
- 1983 – Conservative victory – Margaret Thatcher continues as Prime Minister
- 1987 – Third successive Conservative victory – Margaret Thatcher re-elected but replaced as leader of the Conservative Party and Prime Minister by John Major in 1990
- 1992 – Fourth successive Conservative victory (and John Major is narrowly elected as PM in his own right)
- 1997 – 'New Labour' landslide victory under the leadership of Tony Blair
- 2001 – 'New Labour' second victory under Blair
- 2005 – Blair wins again, but stands down in 2007 and Gordon Brown becomes Prime Minister

The 1997 General Election

Labour	= 43% share of the vote (majority 179 seats)
Conservative	= 31% share of the vote
Liberal Democrat	= 17% share of the vote
Others	= 9% share of the vote

Source: House of Commons (2001a).

The 2001 General Election

Labour	= 42% share of the vote (majority of 167 seats)
Conservative	= 33% share of the vote
Liberal Democrat	= 19% share of the vote
Others	= 6% share of the vote

Source: House of Commons (2001b).

The 2005 General Election

Labour	= 35% share of the vote (majority of 65 seats)
Conservative	= 32% share of the vote
Liberal Democrat	= 22% share of the vote
Others	= 11% share of the vote

Source: House of Commons (2005).

The choice on offer to voters in the UK is usually described as a two-party system. This is because there are only really two political parties that can round up enough support in the form of votes to stand any real chance of being elected as a majority government – these are the Conservative Party and Labour. The third key party in the UK is the Liberal Democrats (an amalgamation of the Liberal Party and the Social Democratic Party). As Kirby (1999) notes, there have only been three general elections since 1900 (1918, 1922 and 1931) where the total percentage votes for these three parties together have been lower than 94 per cent! The supporters of the Liberal Democrats feel that their party might be able to achieve a degree of power if we have the situation of a hung parliament. What this means is that if neither of the two leading parties have a large enough majority, the Liberals would hold power in the sense that who they agreed with, and voted with, would beat the other side. Thus, in a hung parliament, the smaller party has a degree of power since it can ask for its demands to be met in return for siding with a party.

Perhaps the two most significant developments in modern UK political ideologies have been:

- the rise of the New Right in the UK and the USA since the late 1970s;
- the modernization of the UK Labour Party in the light of four successive election defeats since 1979.

So there has been the rise of a New Right, the decline of an Old Left (the traditional ideas of the Labour Party) and the rise of a New Left – developed through processes of modernization, each offering its own political ideology.

What are political ideologies?

Political thinker David McLellan (1995) has noted that, 'Ideology is the most elusive concept in the whole of the social sciences.' Ideology means different things to different thinkers and political sociologists often use the term very differently to general sociological theory – especially in comparison with theories of Marxism and various feminisms.

Roger Eatwell (Eatwell and Wright, 1993) identifies that the origins of the word 'ideology' can be traced back to French philosopher Antoine Destutt de Tracy who coined the term 'ideologie' in 1796. This term was originally used to describe the science of studying the human mind – a sort of cross between psychology and early pedagogy (understanding how humans learn). However, this use of the term was soon replaced by the use of the word in a negative sense to refer to incorrect views. The use of the term was seen to be a criticism, since you only had an ideology if you were:

- mistaken,
- false,
- protecting your own self-interests, or
- trying to deceive.

As Eatwell notes, ideologies were what 'they' had. 'We' on the other hand had the truth! The word ideology became used as a criticism to stand for sets of ideas that tried to deceive and tried to justify the rule of groups of people that did not deserve to be in positions of power. This is how modern day Marxist sociologists use the term – to refer to the powerful ideas used by the ruling class in order to trick the masses into going along with an unequal class-based society. This control using deceptive ideas – ideological control – is seen as a major weapon of power used to impose the ruling group's 'will' onto the people, in order to continue their rule over them. To paraphrase a well-known saying, if something is ideological, 'it is not powerful because it is true, but it is true because it is powerful'!

Roger Eatwell identifies three modern sociological questions about ideologies:

1. What functions do they perform in society?
2. How are ideologies created? Are they contradictory? Are they based on morality, based upon myths etc.?
3. Has the existence of such ideologies changed society and shaped history in some way?

In terms of political sociology the term ideology has another usage, related to the remainder of this chapter. The word ideology can also stand for sets of political worldviews held by political parties. The two key political ideologies that have risen to prominence in the UK in recent years can be associated with changes within UK political parties and in turn, changes in society itself.

The Conservative Party and the ideology of the New Right

The term New Right encompasses neo-liberalism, which is most associated with the Thatcher governments in the UK since 1979 and in the USA with the Reagan administration, and neo-conservatism, which is associated with the Bush administration and with the ideas of Christian fundamentalism, due to its desire to reinject morality into society.

The central idea behind all New Right thinking is the view that other political ideologies have damaged society, and what is needed is a return to basics and to traditional morality before social chaos ensues. Interestingly enough, New Right thinking is not in fact traditional (despite its claim to wish to return to traditional values), but it is very radical, arguing for massive transformations in welfare systems and in the introduction of free-market economics as seen in the UK, the USA and in many other societies, such as Australia and New Zealand, since the 1980s.

Key ingredients of the New Right ideology that these countries have introduced include:

- privatization of business away from centralized state control;
- the introduction of economic competition through the free market;
- a desire to return to traditional family values – and a criticism of homosexual and single-parent families;
- a wish to roll back the state – to reduce state welfare to avoid scroungers;
- the removal of state spending on welfare was seen to compensate for the nanny-state of welfare provision that was too costly, and as a result has caused a situation of state overload;
- the removal of the welfare state to avoid a dependency culture where people do not seek employment;
- the view that poverty and unemployment are the fault of the lazy individual;
- zero-tolerance policing.

In the New Right view, the social problems of rising juvenile crime, massive unemployment and crisis-point state spending are the result of liberalism and socialism and the introduction of the welfare state that has allowed immorality and laziness to continue. You can explore your own views on these issues in Exercise 6.6.

(U)(E)
(An)

Exercise 6.6

1. How do supporters of the New Right resolve the apparent contradiction between freeing up the markets and minimizing state interference in business on the one hand, and the promotion of specific moral values relating to social behaviour on the other?

2. To what extent do you think an individual should be blamed for being unemployed?
3. In what ways do supporters of the New Right believe that the welfare state creates dependency? Do you think they are correct in their beliefs?

Authoritarian populism

Marxist-influenced sociologist Stuart Hall (1984) described the movement of popular public electoral support towards Thatcherism during the 1980s as the great moving right show. Many of the traditional working class whose usual voting loyalties fell to Labour had moved to vote for the New Right policies of a Conservative government, who enjoyed four successive terms in government. Hall argues that this shift in voting support is due to the authoritarian populism basis of Thatcherism. In other words, Thatcherism offered a strong sense of leadership and thus had a strong sense of identity. This happened at a time when the Labour Party was generally discredited due to internal fighting. However, it was this same internal fighting that led the way to the modernization of the party that may have been the reason for its success in 1997.

State overload

Jürgen Habermas (1988) has suggested that the success of the New Right is due to the failure of the legitimation of the welfare state. During the 1980s the welfare state cost more than the government wanted to afford, or felt that the electorate would support. As a result the media presented a picture of a state overload – a crisis that needed to be managed by reducing state spending at all costs before the crisis became unmanageable. Habermas says that this policy of reduced state spending and non-interference by the state in the economy was a way for New Right governments to restore their own legitimacy at a time of rising unemployment and economic recession.

The ideology of the New Right has had a massive impact in society and within sociology. Many claim that the ideologies of the New Right paved the way for the transformation of the Labour Party into New Labour. There are some similarities in the welfare policies of the New Right and the New Left, even though they are supposed to be at opposite ends of the ideological spectrum. This can also be seen in American politics, where the convergence of Republican and Democratic parties around the ideas of the New Right was broken only with the election of President Barack Obama in 2009.

The reform of the Labour Party and the ideology of the Third Way

The single most important factor in the transformation from the Labour Party into New Labour (under the leadership of Tony Blair) was considered by many to be the rejection of 'clause four' in the party's constitution. This clause committed the Labour Party to the equitable redistribution of the means of production. This clause was a statement of Marxist-influenced ideals that saw the class system as a major challenge to inequality. In this clause the dismantling of class inequality was the key goal of Labour. It was these policies that traditionally were thought to align Labour with the working class and in particular with the Trade Union movement in the UK.

With the change from old Labour to New Labour a number of left-of-centre thinkers and politicians started to speak of a new way, or rather of a Third Way in politics – a political ideology that moves beyond traditional left versus right political debates. Most notable among these advocates of a Third Way are Tony Blair and sociologist Anthony Giddens (1998; 2000). Others see this Third Way as simple liberalism, and others still have tried to suggest that the political views of New Labour are moving towards some of the ideas of the New Right!

Like the ideology of the New Right in the 1980s, the ideology of the Third Way in the late 1990s and early 2000s has its political counterpart in the USA. Originally, in 1996, the idea of a Third Way was described by the American Democrats as a new progressivism. However, Alan Ryan (1999) has argued that Third Way politics is not really a new idea. Instead, it is an updated form of what once was called New Liberalism and which was last spoken about in UK politics at the turn of the twentieth century. He suggests, 'The truth is that the third way is neither New Labour, as its admirers say, nor warmed over Thatcherism, as its detractors say, but a reversion to a very old idea' (Ryan, 1999, cited in Giddens, 2000, p.13).

Key features of the Third Way

According to Giddens, Third Way policies tend to emphasize the following:

1. an awareness of the importance of the process of globalization in modern society and modern politics
2. a commitment to environmental concerns in the light of the increased forces of globalization
3. a belief in the moral responsibility of the individual and the responsibility of the community

4. a use of free-market economics
5. the stabilization of family life while encouraging sexual equality (see Steele and Kidd, 2000)
6. community renewal policies as a way to tackle crime
7. a desire to be realistic about crime (see Lawson and Heaton, 2009) – to tackle it rather than romanticizing it or blaming it all on poverty
8. to encourage people to see themselves as citizens – having rights but also responsibilities
9. to maximize equality of opportunity
10. to reduce differences in wealth (see Kirby, 1999).

Exercise 6.7

Take three or four of the statements from the list about the key features of the Third Way, and find evidence that illustrates New Labour's commitment to these principles.

You may already know some examples, or you may need to look in current newspapers or their archives.

The Third Way and its critics

Giddens, himself a Third Way theorist, summarizes the main criticisms of the idea of a Third Way as follows:

1. The concept lacks genuine political direction – it is little more than a new slogan or catchphrase.
2. The idea of a Third Way lacks true substance – it is simply a liberal position somewhere in between the old left and right.
3. Since it seems to embrace free-market economies, it is not really a left-of-centre theory at all – and as such it fails to attack class inequality.
4. It accepts the global marketplace as inevitable in today's society and as such will never attempt to redistribute the vast inequalities of wealth that exist in the UK, and between the West and the non-industrialized worlds.
5. It has no distinctive clear economic policy except to let the market rule.
6. It has no effective way to cope with environmental concerns – especially since it values globalization which has been responsible for many environmental problems and risks.

In response to these criticisms, Giddens states:

> What is at issue is making left of centre values count in a world undergoing profound change... Third way politics, as I conceive of it, is not an attempt to occupy a middle ground between top-down socialism and free-market philosophy. It is concerned with restructuring social democratic doctrines to respond to the twin revolutions of globalisation and the knowledge economy. (Giddens, 2000, p. 163)

The New Left and communitarianism

A key feature of the new political ideology of New Labour in the UK that is in keeping with this new Third Way is a commitment to the principle of what is known as communitarianism. This idea is often associated with sociologist Amitai Etzioni (1995) who, in his book *The Spirit of Community* outlines the following three important features of a communitarian approach to politics. This approach is based upon a focus on the rights and responsibilities of the relationship of the individual to his or her community:

1. Families need to ensure they develop the correct moral values in their children, and provide a stable arena for socialization.
2. Schools should develop good citizens – young people should have both discipline and a sense of responsibility towards others.
3. The government should try and get the local community involved in the decision-making process. The community should be given a political voice over local decisions that affect it.

Some have suggested that these policies are little more than New Right ideology in disguise – especially the fact that both seem to wish to reduce state welfare in some areas and to make families responsible for the discipline of young people. This implies that the New Left (like the New Right) sees a crisis facing society regarding problem families and problem socialization. In their defence, New Left advocates, such as Giddens, point out that the key difference is that the New Right do not seem to care if inequality persists and that those who suffer disadvantage are seen to deserve it, whereas for the New Left inequality must be tackled and reduced, but the community still has a major responsibility in ensuring a healthy and safe social environment for all by instilling a sense of community into young people. As Giddens says, 'a stable sense of self has to be anchored in a community – such as one's family of origin, or ethnic, religious or national communities. Communities are the source of the ethical values that make a wholesome civic life possible' (Giddens, 2000, p. 63).

The key ideological difference between this and New Right thinking is that while the New Right places a similar emphasis upon the family, it sees families as a source of individuality, and argues that it is the moral responsibility of individuals to sort their own lives out. For the communitarianists it is the family's place in the wider community that is important.

Giddens, however, warns of some of the dangers of too much emphasis upon the community:

> if they become too strong, communities breed identity politics, and with it the potential for social division, or even disintegration. Even in its milder forms, identity politics tends to be exclusivist, and difficult to reconcile with the principles of tolerance and diversity upon which an effective civil society depends. (Giddens, 2000, pp. 63–4)

HOW HAS THE POLITICAL IDEOLOGICAL LANDSCAPE CHANGED?

There is a sense within the media and within the sociological literature that we are living through new political times. This sense of political change is further increased because the political parties themselves are engaging in a very public reinvention of themselves.

Before the 1970s, politics was seen to be a rather set and stable process – the parties could be clearly identified with either the middle class (Conservative) or the working class (Labour) and voting was assumed to be relatively stable. Any voter not voting in line with their class interest was seen to be deviant (see Chapter 7 for a more detailed discussion).

At that time politics was associated with:

- *partisanship* – the electorate were loyal, often passing down this party loyalty through the family and across the generations;
- *stability* – people tended to vote in line with their class background;
- *alignment* – class and politics were intimately linked and entwined with each other.

The rise of the New Right and the swing of the working class towards Thatcherism seemed to challenge the traditional view that politics was class-based, although it is unclear if the New Right contributed to this process of *dealignment* or benefited from it. Perhaps it was a combination of the two. We now have the situation where to encourage mass appeal and make itself more electable, or perhaps through a genuine ideological commitment, the Labour Party has moved itself towards the middle ground.

Ⓚ

Exercise 6.8

See if you can identify some sociological terms in the word search from the clues below:

```
T W U Z I I T U Z K B Q X O R
B F Z P N I D E N T I T Y N M
M S I N A I R A T I L A T O T
P H E H W K D L M O K W L L A
S Q P A R T I S A N K V T I Q
L S X P O I B P A G N H E G N
G I V P O L U S E P G B E A C
I J R B C M A R X I S M H R M
J Y G P Z J G B R Q V V U C X
P M Q F T F E L L L T V W H S
N W O R B N O D R O G E M Y I
A R S D R T A F Q X Q J X I I
W M V O Q D Q W T C A M X J F
D J R Z K D I U R G H X H K O
J Y G O L O E D I Z D D D F R
```

- Loyalty to a party across generations
- Leader of the Labour Party at the end of 2008
- The beliefs or 'worldview' of a political party
- Parties can be - - - - - or - - - - - of centre
- Politics based on lifestyle choices is called - - - - - - - - - politics
- A system in which society is defined by a single political view and state control of the media
- Socialism stems from this
- A system led by a small elite group

Beyond left and right?

Sociologists such as Giddens suggest that we need to stop thinking about politics in terms of the basic distinction between left and right and go beyond this outdated and rather limited conceptualization of politics. We now have a new form of politics based upon:

- the movement of political parties away from traditional loyalties;
- the movement of voters away from traditional class-based patterns of voting;
- increased apathy regarding politics – especially among the young;
- the creation of new social movements (see Chapter 7) and the development of lifestyle politics based upon a search for individual identify;
- the increased significance of the forces of globalization – and the resulting implications for national and individual identities.

Giddens (1994) has argued that the rise of this new form of modern day politics has come about through three related currents that underpin the modern Western world:

1. The increase of *globalization* - and an increased awareness of this process by ordinary people in society;
2. The rise of a post-traditional social order – where old values are constantly reassessed and rejected for being old and out-dated;
3. The rise of *reflexivity* – where people reflect upon the world in which they live more than ever before.

Giddens argues that these three processes have developed due to the rise of *manufactured uncertainty* to the modern world. What this means is that ordinary people in modern society are able to calculate the various risks and problems that modern living brings – risks that have been created or manufactured by humans themselves. These are not natural risks but problems caused by humans, in their attempts to take control and to master nature. For example, nuclear war, increased dependence of the poorer nations on the richer, skin cancer due to ozone depletion, rising crime in urban areas due to civil unrest are all human-created risks. All of these have been manufactured by advanced industrial society. The awareness of this uncertainty – and the awareness that humans are responsible for its existence – leads to an apathy towards traditional politics and a search for something new. For Giddens, the Third Way offered by the Labour Party in the UK is one such political solution to the problems of *manufactured uncertainty*.

How left was New Labour after coming to power?

Anthony Giddens (2001) has suggested that the reason why New Labour won both the 1997 and the 2001 elections was that it promised something new for the electorate. Its solutions to key issues and political problems in society were realistic and suitable for the contemporary world. Giddens notes that all so-called left parties in Europe have also had to undertake a radical transformation to make themselves electable. Giddens sees such change as a much-needed response to an ever-changing world. He suggests that New Labour has managed to take authority away from the Conservatives over political issues such as:

- the use of a market economy;
- taxation;
- the centrality of work and the problem of mass unemployment draining resources from society;
- being tough on law and order.

For Giddens this appropriation of traditional Conservative areas of political debate is part of a positive move to the centre-ground of politics. For others, the adoption by New Labour of some policies and areas once associated with the Conservatives and the right of politics suggests that New Labour is nothing more than an old right party in disguise.

For Marxist-influenced sociologists such as Alex Callinicos (2001) New Labour's so-called Third Way represents little more than the adoption of global capitalism, and therefore the adoption of political policies that will lead to increased inequality and the furthering of the class system. While at the same time we see what we could interpret as a mass rejection of the UK political system (due to low turnout at elections) we also see the rise of global protests that are anti-capitalist in nature – most notably in Madrid (1984), Seattle (1999), Montreal (2000), Genoa (2001), Florence (2002), Paris (2003) and London (2004). These protests claim to be against globalization or, at least, against the way in which trans-national corporations create inequality across the globe (see Chapter 9 and Exercise 6.9).

Exercise 6.9

Find the names of some transnational companies and look at their activities in the countries in which they operate. Do you think that you have found evidence to support the claim that these trans-national corporations create inequality? Are there any benefits for the people with whom they are working?

For critics such as Callinicos, New Labour's Third Way represents a rejection of the true or authentic left-of-centre Labour politics. In the UK, Callinicos suggests that anti-capitalist and anti-globalization movements are drawing membership from many people who were once traditional Labour supporters before the party transformed itself for the 1997 election.

Taking a closer look at the values that guide New Labour, Callinicos notes that Tony Blair did make use of traditionally left-of-centre socialist concepts – he talked of morality, of community and of equality. However, the meaning of these words is very different from the way in which old Labour used to use them.

For example, in a lecture given in 2000, Blair defines the 'traditional values' at the heart of New Labour as:

> For me, they are best expressed in a modern idea of community. At the heart of it is the belief in the equal worth of all – the central belief that drives my politics – and in our mutual responsibility in creating a society that advances such equal worth. Note: it is equal worth, not equality of income or outcome; or simply, equality of opportunity. Rather, it affirms our equal right to dignity, liberty, freedom from discrimination as well as economic opportunity. (Blair, 2000, cited in Callinicos, 2001, pp. 45–6)

As Callinicos notes, this speech sounds left-of-centre and indeed, the aim to re-address inequality in society has always been the key difference between left-wing and right-wing politics. This need to address inequality is ever more pressing, with global differences in wealth more dramatic than ever before. However, for Callinicos and other critics, what is interesting about this desire to make the individual have mutual responsibility is that it centres around traditional values – very similar to New Right claims in the past. Equally, Callinicos accepts that community is better than individuality, but asks the question – 'Whose community is it?' He feels that the community that ties us together in the New Labour vision of the world is imposed through harsh and authoritarian means – just like New Right governments between 1979 and 1997. Callinicos suggests that this so-called community is one imposed by the elite New Labour thinkers – guardians of everyone else's morality. Part of this imposition includes zero-tolerance policing, the withdrawal of state benefit for some and a moral criticism of single parents – not that different from the previous Conservative Party.

Exercise 6.10

It is important that you can evaluate the ideas of the writers whose work you read. Take Blair's speech, and Callinicos's comments on it, and write a paragraph summarizing the views of each.

However, the economic woes that began in the USA in 2009 with the banking crisis and that were quickly followed by a strong economic downturn in the United Kingdom and the rest of the world have further transformed the political landscape. The sight of President Bush, the most New Right of all New Right leaders, effectively nationalizing large swathes of the banking sector suggested that all political ideologies would have to step back and re-examine their principles in the light of the economic downturn. The deregulation of markets that has been a prime aim of many government's policies since the 1980s has led to a situation where banks all over the world are so heavily indebted that they came close to breakdown. Regulation was reintroduced to the political agendas of all political parties whether they hailed from the traditional left or traditional right.

The death of class?

Mackintosh and Mooney (2000) suggest that although class might have eroded as a source of voting, this does not mean that it is dead as a source of identity. People still might feel a sense of who they are through class, and surveys such as the 2005 *British Social Attitudes Survey* (BSAS) still asks questions about class and people still respond that this is a meaningful concept for them. In the 2005 survey a small majority of respondents to the BSAS said that it was difficult to move between classes in the modern UK.

Exercise 6.11

How important is social class in contemporary voting behaviour? List the other forms of identity that might affect voting behaviour. Why are these important?

The postmodernization of politics?

The changes outlined above have led some sociologists to adopt the theory of postmodernism (see Chapter 3) to try and explain the nature of the contemporary political landscape.

The key features of a postmodern world are:

- the rise of relativism – the truth is no longer certain, clear or absolute;
- concern with identity and personal lifestyle creation;
- the decline in tradition;
- a loss of faith in science and religion;
- a loss of faith in meta-narratives – the big stories or grand ideas used to previously explain the world;
- a loss of a sense of progression in social change;
- the decline of dominant and shared meaning.

Agnes Heller and Ferenc Feher (1988) describe the rise of postmodern politics as based on the fact that we have many different claims to political truth. It is no longer the case that politics is about government or class struggle. It is now about issues of lifestyle, sexuality and identity.

Politics is now what postmodernists describe as de-centred – it has been taken out of the hands of governments, and placed in the hands of the individual. Politics and political struggles for power have become individualized and localized.

Anthony Giddens agrees with postmodernists that we live in a changing and volatile world. However, he disagrees with postmodernists on the nature of this change and the future direction it might take. For Giddens we are postmodern in the sense that society has moved on, but he describes this as a post-traditional social order. By this Giddens means that postmodernization has given individuals the freedom and ability to be reflexive. This means that, as individuals, people can reflect upon their beliefs and their futures and can take individualist and localized action to create the sort of lifestyle and identity they wish. Politics is changing to accommodate this increased individualization, but for Giddens there are still certain truths for politicians to search for. For example, he believes that those on the left should try and find a Third Way through the political ideological traditions of the past.

Understanding the 2001 and 2005 elections

The results of the 2001 and 2005 General Elections in the UK are interesting since only 59 per cent and 61 per cent respectively of those eligible to vote did so. This in itself might be seen to be problematic in terms of democracy, since if not everyone votes how much can we really say that the party elected reflects the will of the people? The turnout for the 2001 election was the lowest in the UK since 1918 (and dramatically different from the 71.4 per cent turnout from the previous election in 1997). In the 2001 election New Labour received 42 per cent of the votes, and the low turnout means that they were voted in by only 25 per cent of the actual electorate. In the 2005, these figures were even lower; New Labour received 37 per cent of the vote and was voted in by 23 per cent of the electorate. There are a number of reasons that might help to account for these low turnouts:

1. For some sociologists, low turnout might be evidence of the rise of apathy among the voters and a sense that the democratic process does not really change anything.
2. Alternatively, low turnout may reflect a disappointment with the increased similarity of the political choices on offer. Some sociologists, such as Anthony Giddens, have described this as the parties moving beyond left and right into what is called the 'middle ground'.
3. Low turnout may be evidence of the increased postmodernization of politics in contemporary Britain (see Chapter 7). People become less involved in the mass political process which might be interpreted as a rejection of mass politics, and support the idea that political parties offer little to ordinary voters.
4. Finally, we might note how, prior to the election, the media seemed to suggest that the outcome would be another landslide victory for New Labour – it seemed almost inevitable. Given this, many people may have felt it was pointless to vote since it was seen as a foregone conclusion. This is different from the 1997 election where people may have had more of an incentive to vote – to change the four successive election victories of the Conservative Party.

Cohen (2001) puts the 2001 election result in context when he points out that since the turnout was the lowest since 1918, effectively this means it was the lowest turnout in the *whole* of the *democratic history* of UK voting, since working-class men did not get the vote until 1918 and women did not have the vote until 1929. Clearly, until all adults were able to vote, it is very difficult to see the UK as a true democracy.

CONCLUSION

There is general agreement among many commentators that politics in the UK has changed dramatically; the decline of so-called traditional party alliances and the rise of new revised political ideologies means that politics in the UK in the early twenty-first century is very different to the postwar era since the 1940s. There is both a sense of volatility about the outcome of voting and decisions made by political leaders and yet also a sense of new beginnings. Old class-based politics might be declining (although the evidence is not conclusive that this is no longer a source of identity) and new political solutions are being sought in a very public way to new political problems, globalization (see Chapter 9) being a key feature in these debates. The next chapter takes up the concerns of the death of traditional voting behaviour in more detail.

Exam focus

Identify and briefly explain *three* political values associated with either the Conservative Party or the Labour Party.

This is what is termed a shorter-mark question as there are clear limits to what you have to do and therefore the marks allocated to the answer will not be very many. You would therefore not spend too much time in an examination answering this question, but you must be thorough in meeting all of the requirement s of the question. There will be marks given for identification of a political value and further marks for explain what is meant by the political value. However, note that you only have to *briefly* explain, so this is not an essay-type response.

Values for the Labour Party might be:	Values for the Conservative Party might be:
State provision of services	Private provision of services
Equality	Free markets
Fairness	Meritocracy

In briefly explaining state provision of services, you might write something like:

The Labour Party believes that the state has an important role in providing the basic necessities of life such as the health service, education and support for the elderly. They believe that private provision would not meet the needs of poorest in society.

For meritocracy in the Conservative Party list, you might write:

The Conservative Party believes that everyone should have the opportunity to use their talents to better themselves and achieve what their abilities allow them to do. People should not be held back on account of their social origins.

Now try to do the same activity with the other four values that have been identified.

Important concepts

- political systems • Totalitarianism • Oligarchy • Democracy
- types of democracy • Participatory • Representative • the victory of democracy • Political apathy • identity politics • the New Right
- neo-liberalism • authoritarian populism • state overload • the modernization of the UK Labour Party • the Third Way • the New Left and communitarianism • globalization • post-traditional social order
- the death of class

Summary points

- A *political system* refers to the way in which the governance of society is structured as a whole:

  ○ *totalitarianism* is when the ruling regime adopts a single political view that allows no alternatives;
  ○ an *oligarchy* is a dictatorship based on an elite group;
  ○ *democracy* means rule by the people and can either be *direct* or *representative.*

- A number of thinkers have identified some problems with democracy but it is now very widely accepted as the only legitimate system of governance.
- The UK is a *representative democracy*, but recent years have seen a rise in *political apathy*. However, it is difficult to measure political apathy, and it may be that younger people are getting involved in politics in new ways.
- The two most significant developments to modern UK political ideologies have been the rise of the New Right in the UK and the USA since the late 1970s and the modernization of the UK Labour Party in the light of four successive election defeats.
- Key features of *New Right* Conservative ideology include: privatization and the free market; traditional family values; a reduction in state welfare; the view that poverty and unemployment are the fault of lazy individuals and zero-tolerance policing.
- Key features of *Third Way* policies include: a acceptance of globalization tempered by a commitment to environmental concerns; a belief in the moral responsibility of the individual and the community; an acceptance of the free market; the stabilization of family life while encouraging sexual equality; community renewal policies as a way to tackle crime and stressing the rights and responsibilities of citizens:

  ○ The Third Way has been criticized on the grounds that the concept lacks genuine political direction.

- *Communitarianism* argues that families need to ensure they develop the correct moral values in their children, and schools should develop good 'citizens' with a sense of responsibility towards others. Before the 1970s, politics was associated with *partisanship stability* (and *class alignment*). The rise of the New Right seemed to challenge the traditional view that *politics* was class-based.
- Giddens suggests that we need to stop thinking about politics in terms of the basic distinction between left and right; the rise of a new form of politics has come about through three related currents:
  - the increase of *globalization*;
  - the rise of a post-traditional social order;
  - the rise of *reflexivity*.

These three processes have developed due to the rise of *manufactured uncertainty* in the modern world,

- However, for Marxist-influenced sociologists such as Callinicos the Third Way represents little more than the adoption of global capitalism.

Critical thinking

1. What are the disadvantages of democracy?
2. Is democracy now the dominant political system in the world?
3. Why is it so hard to measure political apathy?
4. 'New Labour and the modern Conservative Party agree with each other more than they disagree.' Discuss.
5. Describe what some see as internal contradictions within the New Right and the Third Way ideologies.

Chapter 7

Understanding Individual Political Participation

By the end of this chapter you should:

- understand the changes that have taken place in voting behaviour since the Second World War
- understand the changes that have taken place in sociological discussions of voting behaviour since the Second World War
- understand sociological interpretations of voting patterns
- be able to evaluate sociological interpretations of voting patterns
- understand why some sociologists claim we are living through a time of political apathy
- be able to evaluate sociological reasons for the growth of pressure groups
- be able to evaluate sociological reasons for the rise of new social movements

INTRODUCTION

For many people in society, politics is seen to involve the workings of and decisions made by governments. Ordinary people's involvement in politics only occurs every four to five years with a general election, or perhaps with local elections between these times. For many, politics is seen as something detached from everyday life and concerning things over which they have little or no control.

Recently, some sociologists and some commentators in the media, have started to see voting behaviour itself as a problem:

▦ Voters are not turning out as much as they did in the past.
▦ There is seen to be considerable apathy among the young.

■ Some people do not believe that voting has a significant influence on society. This view is often supported by the idea that the parties are too similar or perhaps that politicians are corrupt and do not listen to those who they represent.

In Britain, at the 2001 General Election only 59.1 per cent of voters turned out to vote, compared to 71.4 per cent the election before in 1997. In France in 2007, voter turnout in contrast stood at 85 per cent and in the US presidential election of 2009, it was 64 per cent. Turnout for local elections is also significantly lower than in general elections, since some voters see local elections as less important. It is even noted among some political commentators that voter turnout is also dependent upon the weather – the more rain, the fewer people leave the house to vote!

Himmelweit *et al.* (1985) noted that the very phenomenon of an election in a large-scale mass representative democracy such as the UK raises some interesting problems for sociology and for the public alike:

■ The sociological problem posed by voting is how we are to understand what each vote means. How and why do some parties receive more support than others? Is it due to what people think, or due to what parties do to influence what people think?
■ Another sociological problem surrounds the issue of voter apathy; what does this mean, and what do people themselves actually think about the process of voting?
■ The problems that voting poses for the voters themselves is also an issue. How significant is the act of voting for the individual in relation to wider society? Do voters think that voting changes anything?
■ How do voters come to decide whom and what to vote for? What factors might influence them, and what experiences and knowledge do they draw upon? Explore this in your locality in Exercise 7.1.

(A)(E)

Exercise 7.1

Design a questionnaire to look at voting behaviour. Choose who your sample population might be – you might consider people of different ages or different sexes, or you could use some other criteria, such as occupational background or education.

Design a simple set of questions to ask about voting behaviour and reasons why your sample members vote the ways they do. You might like to carry this out in groups and build up a picture of voting behaviour in your area.

Perhaps different groups could choose two different variables. Be aware of ethical issues, as you are likely to ask questions that are usually considered quite personal.

Himmelweit *et al.* have suggested that, although voting is a mass activity, many individuals who make up the masses choose to opt out or perhaps vote ritualistically – they might vote out of habit, duty or a feeling that it is their right, yet at the same time feel that their individual involvement in the political process is insignificant.

As Himmelweit says:

> Despite the importance of the aggregate decision, the majority of the electorate are little involved. They believe that their individual decision, being one of millions, makes little difference to the outcome, and the public as a collection of individuals does not see itself as having much influence on political events or even on the conduct of the party of their choice. This is not surprising. After all, it is only at election time that the public's views are seriously canvassed and any interest taken in their lives, their fears, their babies … to be taken off the shelf, dusted down and asked to perform once every four or five years neither generates much enthusiasm for the act of voting, nor convinces the public that it is worth their while to invest in the study of political issues. (Himmelweit *et al.*, 1985, p. 2)

These observations by Himmelweit and colleagues made in 1985 are still echoed in the sociological literature and within the media today, and perhaps raise interesting questions for our present model of democracy (see Chapter 4). For example:

1. Are voters well informed about political issues?
2. Are all voters equally well informed?
3. Do voters feel valued and represented by the parties they vote for?
4. Do people need more information about political ideas?
5. Is voting taken seriously?

If many people do not believe that our present form of voting represents their interests, can we then say that we have true democracy? Clearly, the problem of representation (if it exists as a problem at all) is a key feature of any large-scale democracy, since not everyone can be involved all of the time.

This chapter will explore the various models that sociologists have used to explain voting behaviour.

SOCIOLOGY AND PSEPHOLOGY

The study of voting and voting behaviour is referred to as psephology. Traditionally this sub-branch of political science and political sociology has tried to explain voting with reference to the background of the individuals and groups involved – and in particular with the key variable of class. In recent years, the literature has moved away from class as a key variable in voting, and has considered a much wider range of factors. Such factors that might influence an individual's vote could include:

- class background
- educational experiences
- parental views
- occupation
- trade union membership
- views of friends and families
- media opinion and bias
- political campaigns run in the media by the parties themselves
- party literature and canvassing
- the image of the party leaders
- financial considerations

Himmelweit *et al.* have suggested that voting is a prime source for good sociological debate and investigation since, unlike some other forms of decision-making, it is very regular. For example, the event reoccurs within a standardized time period (give or take a few months); the event reoccurs with the same political parties – and gives a standardized choice each time; and, finally, the event occurs with the same people voting each time (give or take those who have died and those who have become first-time voters between each election). Given the regular and routine nature of voting, it is surprising that sociology still knows little about what voting really means.

CHANGES IN VOTING SINCE THE SECOND WORLD WAR

Much sociological literature on voting today argues that voting has changed significantly in recent years – and often relates this observation to the possible decline of class as a key variable.

Before the 1970s voting in the UK was seen to be characterized by:

- Stability
- Alignment
- Partisanship
- Loyalty

Stability – it was generally considered that voting and class background went hand-in-hand with each other: if you were working class you voted Labour – the traditional party of the worker – and if you were middle class you voted Conservative – the party that wished to keep society as it was – to conserve existing privilege. Thus, voting patterns were stable over time.

Alignment – since class and voting were seen to be so closely related, they were said to be 'in alignment' with each other – if you were working class it could be predicted that you would vote Labour and not to do so was seen to be unusual and in some sense deviant – going against the interests of your class background.

Partisanship – given the alignment of class and voting, family socialization was seen to play a strong role in continuing these voting patterns over time and, as such, voters became partisan – they unquestioningly supported the party of their class background and stayed loyal to this party over a long period of time.

Loyalty – today, we have seen the rise of what are called floating voters – voters who are not partisan, not loyal to the tradition of one particular party, but who may change their vote from election to election on the basis of what they think each party might offer them (see Exercise 7.2).

The patterns of alignment are summarized in the classic voting studies of Butler and Stokes (1969) who suggested that throughout the 1950s and 1960s social class and socialization from parents were the most important factors in explaining why people voted as they did. In fact, they felt that class was more significant in British voting than in any other English-speaking country.

Ⓤ

Exercise 7.2

What do you think are the main concerns of floating voters in contemporary society?

Deviant voting

The key problem for the observations made by Butler and Stokes is that if voting is characterized by class loyalty, then why was it possible for the Conservatives to win any elections – in particular three elections running after the Second World War in 1951, 1955 and 1959. If we assume that the working classes have more people than the middle classes, then according to the ideas of alignment, Labour victories should have been assured for years. This must mean that either the importance of class was beginning to disappear, or that a considerable proportion of working-class people were what we call deviant voters and were voting for the Conservatives instead – against their traditional class loyalties.

We can identify a number of reasons for this so-called deviant voting:

1. Some working-class people could be defined as deferential voters, because they tend to defer to their 'betters' – Conservative MPs might be associated with upper-class backgrounds and seen to be more worthy to make important decisions than trade-union-backed Labour MPs.
2. Some working-class members might feel themselves to be middle class due to increased income or because they have bought their own home. This is called subjective class: how you feel your class to be, rather than how it might be measured by a sociologist.
3. Some elderly working-class people might remember how some Conservative governments before the Second World War claimed to speak for the common man and might still be loyal for this reason.
4. Some middle-class people might have been upwardly mobile and still remember their working-class roots and they might still vote Labour out of previous loyalties.
5. Middle-class people in the caring and service professions such as teachers, doctors, nurses and social workers might vote Labour since they felt this party would support the welfare state more than the Conservative Party would.

The death of class?

An alternative model to that of Butler and Stokes' idea of alignment and deviant voting is to suggest that since the 1960s and certainly into the 1970s the UK has experienced a process through which class has lost significance as the key to explaining voting behaviour. For example, Heath *et al.* (1985) have argued that the nature of the working classes has dramatically changed since the 1960s to the extent that they are no longer the traditional working classes that Butler and Stokes associated with aligned voting. For Heath, class has dramatically declined as the most influential factor in voting. This means that we have moved from a period of alignment to one of *dealignment*; and from stability to *volatility*. Volatility refers to the unpredictable nature of voting patterns – the inability to assume voting loyalty from people because of their class or other backgrounds.

There seem to be a few key sociological explanations that help us to interpret what has happened to traditional class-based politics in general, and voting in particular:

1. The idea that class has lost significance in the lives of people in society, although the significance played by class inequality in wider society might still exist.
2. The idea that class has declined in significance in society and therefore also in people's minds, possibility replaced by other newer forms of identity and lifestyle-based forms of inequality.
3. The idea that class has not declined but has changed: in particular that the *traditional working class* found in the work by Butler and Stokes has transformed into a *new working class*, or even *new working classes*.

Exercise 7.3

In the light of the points above about traditional class-based voting, and using the articles reproduced below, answer the following questions about voting behaviour in the 2005 General Election.

1. Describe the 2005 voting patterns for each of the three parties with respect to class.
2. Can you explain the differences between the parties?
3. How has the class pattern of voting changed since the 1997 election?
4. Why do you think this was?
5. What has happened to voting behaviour in relation to gender, and why?

    Source: 'Who deserted Labour? – Analysis by David Cowling' (Editor, BBC Political Research) http://news.bbc.co.uk, accessed 7 May 2005

Labour has won power – but suffered a 6 per cent drop in the share of its vote. The Liberal Democrats were the main gainers. But just as Labour has been ejected from some of the Tory-leaning suburban seats it won in 1997, its support among key middle-class social groups also shows signs of haemorrhaging. However, it has done better than expected among women, where it eliminated the gender gap, which in the past meant women were more likely than men to vote Conservative.

But Labour is no longer ahead of the Conservatives among lower-middle-class voters (C1), which they cultivated in 1997. And its support among working-class voters and council tenants has dropped sharply. However, it has hung onto much of its support among owner-occupiers with a mortgage, who used to be the bedrock of Conservative support.

Labour's appeal in 1997 was across all social classes (and all tenures). Tony Blair managed to win a greatly increased share of the middle-class vote, including a plurality over the Conservatives among lower-middle-class (C2) voters and home owners, while holding on to Labour's working-class vote.

Based on our polling data in the 2005 General Election, Labour's support is eroding at both ends. Two out of three of the opinion polls (NOP and ICM) suggest that the Conservatives narrowly beat Labour among the C2 group this time. And Labour's share of the unskilled working-class vote has declined sharply. According to ICM, Labour was supported by 58 per cent of these voters in 1997, and just 45 per cent in 2005. However, Labour has retained support among owner-occupiers with a mortgage – who perhaps are giving Labour credit for low interest rates.

They still have a 39 per cent to 30 per cent lead compared to the Conservatives (in 1992, the Conservatives led in this group by 48 per cent to 30 per cent). Finally, the Liberal Democrats have increased their share of the upper-middle-class vote – mainly at the expense of the Conservatives.

Table 7.1   Who voted for the parties? Percentage of support in 2005 (percentage in 1997)

	Tory	Labour	Liberal Democrat
Men	33 (28)	38 (47)	21 (17)
Women	32 (35)	38 (43)	23 (17)
AB (middle class)	37 (43)	32 (30)	24 (21)
C1 (lower middle class)	34 (35)	35 (37)	24 (21)
C2 (skilled workers)	32 (28)	43 (52)	18 (13)
DE (unskilled workers)	28 (21)	45 (58)	19 (15)
Age 18–24	24 (25)	42 (50)	26 (17)
Age 25–34	24 (27)	42 (50)	26 (17)
Age 35–64	33 (31)	38 (43)	22 (18)
Age 65+	42 (38)	35 (42)	18 (15)
Home owners with mortgage	30 (32)	39 (41)	23 (19)
Home owners owning outright	43 (42)	30 (36)	20 (16)
Council tenants	16 (15)	56 (65)	19 (13)
All voters	*33 (31)*	*36 (43)*	*23 (17)*

Source: ICM. All campaign polls (sample 13,730 in 2005, 10,000 in 1997 weighted for outcome): GB only.

We can identify a number of sociological views on the rise of dealignment

Embourgeoisement

For sociologists such as Zweig (1961) the shift away from class – from align-ment to dealignment – has resulted from changes to the wider class structure in Western societies in general. In particular, there has been a movement of upward social mobility from the upper working classes into the lower and middle middle classes, resulting in the expansion of the middle of the class structure. One way to imagine this is to think of the traditional class struc-ture as a triangle, and the new expanded class structure after the process of *embourgeoisement* (becoming middle class) looking more like a diamond: the class structure has grown in the middle. As a result, argues Zweig, traditional working-class support for Labour changes, as people are upwardly mobile out of the traditional working class.

Class dealignment

Ivor Crewe (1986) has also suggested that we have seen the rise of a new mid-dle class and that, along with this, the traditional basis of class – occupation and money – has been replaced by other more important forms of economic divisions and inequalities between and within the different classes. These are called new forms of sectoral division: divisions now based upon home owner-ship, union membership and region that make traditional class identity more complex than it was before.

The rise of the new working class

For Goldthorpe *et al.* (1968), we have not witnessed the rise of a new middle class, but rather, a change within the old working class. They argue that there has been the creation of a *new working class* – still working class, but very dif-ferent from the traditional working class that still exists in Northern regions in the UK, for example. This new working class has what is described as an instrumental orientation to voting and to trade union membership. This means that they are not unquestioningly loyal to their traditional working-class par-tisan patterns of voting (the Labour Party), but instead float their vote. They vote for the party that appears to benefit them the most in the short term, especially in regard to how much money they will take home each month.

The continuation of class?

Despite the modern day sociological literature that has built on the legacy of ideas from Crewe, Heath and others, there are still many other sociologists who have argued that the death of class has been greatly exaggerated, and that class continues to be significant in voting behaviour. We can identify this argument within the work of Marshall *et al.* (1988) and in Callinicos and Harman (1987).

Looking at class struggle

Callinicos and Harman (1987) have suggested that it is wrong to assume automatically that it was natural for all working-class people to have supported the Labour Party and therefore the shift of the working classes away from Labour is somehow a rejection of tradition. Instead, for Callinicos and Harman, we need to reinterpret these claims to show that there has always been a much more complex relationship between class, identity, trade union membership, beliefs in socialism and voting. They argue that there never was a 'golden age' of class alignment. Therefore, it is not surprising that we have dealignment now.

Sectoral division

Marshall *et al.* (1988) have suggested that the observations made by sociologists such as Crewe – that traditional class has been replaced by newer forms of sectoral division – is not a new feature of class. They argue that sectoral division has always been a feature of how class has worked in the UK. Thus, class has not changed but has been replaced by more complex forms of division.

This view has been criticized by some thinkers associated with the New Right in sociology – in particular Francis Fukuyama (1992) and Peter Saunders (1990) who have both claimed that class is dead in modern society. For Fukuyama this represents the end of class struggle and an acceptance among the populations of Western societies that capitalist forms of social organization are the most acceptable for the modern age. For Saunders, like Crewe, the death of class has been replaced by newer forms of division that, in turn, take the place of class in shaping opinions, interests, desires and self-identity. The most notable of these is home ownership as a form of identity and status.

Exercise 7.4

American writer Fukuyama argues that class is dead in contemporary society. Do you agree?

In *British Democracy at the Crossroads*, Dunleavy and Husbands (1985) suggest that although social class is withering as an influence upon voting and newer forms of division have risen to importance, these very new forms have attached to them new political ideas that themselves suggest that class is dead. For example, the Conservative Party – and in particular those on the New Right (see Chapter 6) – have suggested for a long time that class was dead. Of course, it is Conservative politicians who have most to gain from persuading people that class is dead. First, they themselves are much more likely to come from the sort of class backgrounds that are privileged; others are less likely to oppose this privilege if they can be persuaded that it does not really exist. Second, if working-class people believe that society is now classless, they might be more likely to vote Conservative since they will no longer identify themselves so strongly with Labour as a working-class party.

Exercise 7.5

Write a paragraph that could explain the results of the 2005 General Election using the previous section of this chapter.

You may want to use some of the following terms in your paragraph:

- floating voters • deviant voters • embourgeoisement • class dealignment
- sectoral division • the rise of the new working class

Is dealignment evidence of the postmodernization of society?

Postmodern voting?

The idea that class has been replaced with newer forms of identification is echoed in postmodernist ideas on society (see Chapter 5). For example, Jean-François Lyotard (1984), in his book *The Postmodern Condition*, has argued that the rise of postmodernism results in the decline and fragmentation of previous structures. What this means is that previously stable truths in society have become increasingly exposed as simply one version of the truth among many other truths. With this plurality of things to believe in and ways to live life, people begin to increasingly experience what has been described as ontological insecurity: anxiety about what society is like, and even who we feel we might be as people – anxiety over our very sense of self-identity. For Lyotard, when people experience these feelings of anxiety, they often seek out new forms of personal expression and identity in order to feel that they can regain control over who they are. Thus, postmodernization liberates people from structures like class that tell them what to do – and lets them decide for themselves who they wish to be. In keeping with this, they can choose aspects of their life now separated from traditional class identity – such as voting for any party they choose.

Although not postmodernists, both Anthony Giddens (1990) and Jurgen Habermas (1987) have suggested that a new politics has replaced the old. A major part of this replacement is the rise of volatility and de-alignment and the freeing of political expression from tradition and in particular the creation of more political choices. Habermas' claims of increased voter apathy are also explained by this change from old to new politics, since to be political today means something different than before. In contemporary society a person does not have to vote to be political. Instead, adopting a particular lifestyle can be seen as a reflexive political act. Some writers refer to this as micro politics – a way of asserting who a person is, and making a statement about their identity, even if this is at odds with previous forms of self-expression for that individual.

Some commentators such as Bauman (2000) have used the famous phrase from Marx and Engels, 'all that is solid melts into the air', to describe the postmodern condition: all that we once held to be true is over, and individuals need to pick up the pieces of tradition that are left and make new meaning out of them. For example, French postmodernist Jean Baudrillard (1983) argues that we have witnessed the 'end of the political', by which he means that the masses have become disillusioned with party politics. They have become what he calls a 'silent majority' – disillusioned and disinterested. These people are only connected with politics when party politicians try to convince them to vote for their particular brand of politics. However, the masses have given up on seeing politics as anything that can lead to liberation, truth or freedom from inequality. This disillusionment with the political, however, is seen as a 'fatal strategy' by Baudrillard, since it leads to increasing hopelessness and the inability to be represented by those political leaders claiming to doing so. If the masses are silent, then their views cannot be heard by those claiming to carry out their wishes! This is a very pessimistic view indeed.

Exercise 7.6

Do you think the masses can be said to be a 'silent majority', as Baudrillard suggests?

Carry out a straw poll in your class, asking the following questions:

- How many of you have ever been to a political rally?
- How many of you have ever been on a protest march?
- How many of you have ever signed a petition?
- How many of you have ever supported a campaign to change something?
- How many of you know how your parents vote?
- How many of your parents campaign for a political party or pressure group, or some similar organization?
- What does your poll tell you about your attitude to politics and representation in general?

Political apathy might be a modern day media concern and, for some, indicative of the onset of postmodernization, but there is a substantial amount of evidence that suggests that the so-called recent trend towards apathy and disillusionment towards party politics has existed for a while. For example, in 1974 Alan Marsh carried out a study on people's political involvement in the UK. He says,

> Twenty-three percent [of respondents] will not even read the political section of newspapers and a cumulative 69 percent will do no more than talk about it; the remanding third do get involved to some degree, but only 8 percent have ever had anything to do with an election campaign. (Marsh, cited in Topf, 1989, p. 55)

Although the majority of Marsh's sample did not get involved – did not try and join or help political movements and parties – the majority also felt that politics was pointless and that the parties themselves did not work for those who voted for them. For example, looking at Marsh's data further:

> In answer to the question: 'How much do you trust the government in Westminster to do what is right?', some 61 percent of respondents replied 'only some of the time', or 'almost never'. Sixty percent said that 'almost never' or 'only some of the time' did they believe that people in politics speak the truth, and the same percentages said they believed that British governments of either party placed party interests above the needs of the country and its people. (Topf, 1989, p. 56)

It would seem that if political disillusionment is the reason for the low turnout at the 2001 and 2005 General Elections in the UK – and whether this is an indicator of postmodernization or not (explore this further in Exercise 7.7) – these feelings might not be new to the political climate of the UK.

Exercise 7.7

The graph below shows the turnout in all general elections since 1945. Write a paragraph to explain how postmodernists might interpret the evidence in this graph.

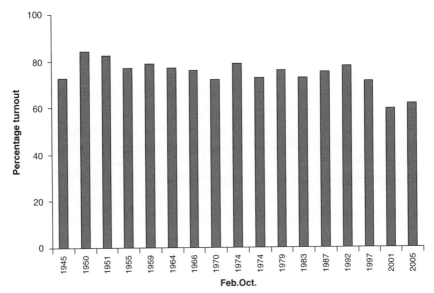

Source: House of Commons (2001b and 2005).

The UK general election of February 1974 was the only election since the Second World War to produce a hung parliament. The Conservatives, led by Edward Heath, polled the most votes by a small margin, but lost their overall majority when the Ulster Unionist MPs decided to align themselves with Labour, led by Harold Wilson. Heath attempted to make a deal with the Liberal leader Jeremy Thorpe and when this failed, he resigned and Wilson took over as Prime Minister, calling another general election in October of the same year.

Problems with the idea of deviant voting

The idea that we have changed from alignment to a situation of dealignment poses problems with the notion of deviant voting. If an increasing proportion of voters have voted deviantly (against traditional class lines) then the more it occurs the less, strictly speaking, we can call it deviant. The new norm for voting appears to be the old deviant: to vote in ways other than according to old class loyalty! With this observation, many sociologists now seek alternative voting models to those used in the past.

CONTEMPORARY MODELS OF VOTING BEHAVIOUR

We can begin looking at modernday models of voting by making a distinction between two types of models generally used by sociologists:

- *Expressive models of voting* – look at how voters are influenced by social characteristics from their background – such as class, trade union affiliation, occupation, home ownership, etc.
- *Instrumental models of voting* – are much more common in the contemporary literature and treat voters as individuals making rational and calculated decisions. In these models we see an image of voters as consumers of party politics.

We can identify a number of *instrumental models* of voting that do *not* look at class allegiances as the basis for voting decisions:

1. *The consumer model* – this suggests that voting is like any act of consumption – such as shopping. The individual considers all the goods on offer in the competitive marketplace and chooses the product that offers best value – each individual chooses to measure value. This view is held by Himmelweit *et al.* (1985).
2. *The tactical voter model* – this model has been suggested by the Liberal Democrat Party and the Labour Party at different times. The fact that it is often discussed in the media might serve as evidence that voters are more calculating today and less loyal than they once were. This model suggests that individuals might not necessarily vote for the party they wish to obtain power, but might vote to remove a party from power. For example, if a Labour Party supporter in a strong Conservative area wanted to reduce the amount of MPs that the Conservatives have, they might vote

Liberal Democrat instead. The voter might not want to see them win over-all, but believe they have the best chance of removing those they like the least! This is clearly a very tactical way to go about voting.

3. *The pocket-book voter* – suggested by Heath *et al.* (1985). This model suggests that many people make voting decisions on the basis of what party they think will cost them the least – in other words, they vote for the party who will give them the best deal financially. This is often associated with issues of taxation and, today, issues of minimum wage payments and state benefits.

4. *Lifetime learning model* – suggested by Rose and McAllister (1990), this model argues that voting decisions are the result of a whole lifetime of experiences – parental socialization, morality, values, economic conditions of the time, media campaigns etc. All these factors – and many more – combine to make voting decisions highly complex.

5. *The rational choice model* – like the consumer model above, this model, developed by David Downs (1957), suggests that voters are rational: they weigh up decisions and think about the sum total of benefits that parties might bring them over others. This decision is therefore highly calculated.

6. *The subjective class model* – this view is associated again with the work of Heath. He points out that by looking at class, sociologists might not be able to predict voting patterns, but that this is not the same as arguing that class is dead. Individuals might have a subjective definition of their own class position that they may use to help them to think about voting. This would make it seem as though dealignment has occurred, but in fact class is still important, just not the impersonal so-called objective measurements used by sociologists.

What is interesting to note about these various *instrumental models* is that they might be seen to combine together. For example, it might be rational to vote tactically and this choice might be the result of an individual's own subjective sense of class that they have developed across a whole lifetime of experiences.

VOTING: WILL WE EVER HAVE A CLEAR PICTURE?

As we have discussed, voting behaviour is complex and varied. Perhaps the reason why so many models exist to explain voting behaviour is in part explained by the fact that so many individuals are involved. With so many different choices and decisions being made, it would be a mistake to assume that because all these decisions might look the same (they are all crosses on a ballot paper) they might be the same. They are clearly not. A vote for the same party might be made for very different reasons depending on the individual voting.

In recent years sociological views on psephology have moved away from models that look at group behaviour and towards models that look at individual behaviour. These seek to understand the act of voting, like many other forms of decision-making, as being influenced by a wide range of factors that include social class, but also ethnicity, gender, regional factors and other factors linked to class, such as home ownership and trade union membership. The importance of each factor will vary from election to election, depending on the issues of the day and the changing policy positions of the different parties.

The complexity of voting behaviour means that it is very difficult to predict how an individual will vote, but what is clear is that turnout in elections and membership of political parties is declining. This may be a sign of political apathy resulting from a disillusionment with party politics and the Westminster process, or it may be that people are choosing to become involved in politics in different ways, such as pressure groups and new social movements.

PRESSURE GROUPS AND NEW SOCIAL MOVEMENTS

Pressure groups and New Social Movements (NSMs) are seen by pluralists as a vital part of the political decision-making process; they consist of groups of like-minded people who seek to influence policy-making on a narrow range of issues, either by lobbying policy-makers directly, or by attempting to convince members of the public of their point of view, so that politicians are put under pressure. Unlike political parties, they do not normally put up candidates in elections and are not interested in becoming policy-makers.

These groups are considered to play a key role in ensuring democracy because they allow issues that may otherwise be ignored by the main political parties to be publicized and discussed. Minority groups and their interests may not be important to parties on the grounds that they may not lead to many votes; pressure groups and NSMs are a means by which the tyranny of the majority can be challenged. They allow ordinary people to become directly involved in political change and, particularly in the case of NSMs, are genuinely 'bottom up' initiatives. On the other hand, it can be argued that pressure groups and NSMs are damaging to democracy: they are unaccountable and can act irresponsibly, or can present information to the public that is inaccurate or misleading. They can mean that a small group of activists can have a disproportionately large influence, especially if they have good financial backing. Finally, they often operate by whipping up public emotion and outrage, and this can lead to poor policy decisions.

Pressure groups

Pressure groups vary in their aims, the methods they use and their organization and membership. For example, some pressure groups are created in order to protect the interests of their members. Examples of these so-called sectional pressure groups are trade unions (defending the pay and conditions of their members), Surfers against Sewage (protecting their members' leisure activity) or Fathers for Justice (defending their members' rights to have access to their own children). Other groups exist in order to promote a cause that they perceive to be neglected by government. Examples of these promotional or cause groups are Greenpeace, Amnesty International, the Animal Liberation Front etc. Some groups are both sectional and promotional; the Countryside Alliance defends its members' rights to take part in certain leisure activities, such as fox-hunting, and also defends the livelihoods of those involved in this activity. However, they also claim to be defending freedom and a traditional way of life as a cause.

Pressure groups can also be classified as either insider or outsider. Insider groups are consulted by government as part of the decision-making process. They are more likely to consist of sectional groups, such as the Confederation of British Industry (CBI) or the British Medical Association (BMA), as these groups have expertise in a particular field and the government may well want to take their members' interests into account. However, some promotional groups are also insiders. Shelter, for example, campaigns to reduce homelessness but its membership does not consist of homeless people acting in their own interest. The government is willing to consult formally with groups like this because it approves of their aims and their methods.

The primary aim of *insider* groups is to convince the policy-makers directly to change their policies. They lobby MPs and Lords and are consulted by them. The may even have seats on government policy committees and agencies. The National Farmers Union (NFU), for example, is a central part of government decision-making when it comes to dealing with outbreaks of disease in farmed animals. Some pressure groups are actually set up and funded by the government. Examples of these co-called 'ultra-insider' groups are the Equality and Human Rights Commission and Consumer Focus. Promotional groups are more likely to be *outsiders* and, with less direct access to government, these groups tend to focus on persuading members of the public of their cause, in the hope that this will in turn influence government. Outsider groups have more freedom in the methods they use to get public opinion on their side. They can organize public demonstrations and rallies (e.g., the Stop the War coalition), publicity stunts (e.g., Fathers for Justice) or take part in civil disobedience or peaceful direct action (e.g., Greenpeace). Some pressure groups engage in violent protest and there is a narrow line between this and terrorism. Some animal rights organizations, for example, have targeted individuals involved in using animals for medical research, attacking them or their property.

It is not clear whether groups are more effective as insiders or outsiders (see Exercise 7.8); as insiders they have access to decision-makers, but they have to act responsibly and may lose their independence. However, it is probably the case that most outsider groups would like to become more insider in their status. The Countryside Alliance, for example, would very much like to be consulted by government, but this is unlikely to happen as long as its members continue to attempt to evade the law on hunting with dogs, or to invade the House of Commons as happened in September 2004.

(An) (E)

Exercise 7.8

The Labour Party was initially set up by the trade unions, and unions were closely consulted by the 1974–9 Labour Government. Since 1979, trade unions have seen their status change largely from insider to outsider. A recent example of this process took place among the five teacher unions in England and Wales. In January 2004, they were all invited to sit on a consultative body on teachers' pay and conditions (the Rewards and Incentives Group (RIG)). One of the conditions of membership of RIG was that unions had to sign up to an agreement that classes in primary and secondary schools could be taught by non-qualified assistants. This was to enable the government to stick to its promise to provide more marking and preparation time for teachers without having to train and recruit more teachers. The National Union of Teachers (NUT) felt that this was unprofessional and would not agree to this condition. As a consequence the NUT was excluded from RIG; by sticking to this principle, it transformed itself from an insider group to an outsider one, with potentially less influence.

Do you think the NUT was right to lose some of its influence in order to stand by a principle which it had no hope of winning anyway, or do you think that the other unions were right to provide the government with credibility for a policy that they probably did not agree with simply in order to remain on the inside of the consultation process?

New social movements

New social movements (NSMs) arose in the 1960s and 1970s in liberal democratic societies and they apply to movements such as feminism, environmentalism, the peace movement, anti-racism etc. Like pressure groups, they consist of groups of people with broadly similar ideas on particular issues. One set of issues that NSMs tend to campaign on are concerned with defending the natural and social environment from the perceived threat of the modern industrial world. Anti-nuclear groups (e.g., CND, Greenpeace), environmentalist groups (e.g., Friends of the Earth) and animal rights groups (e.g., Respect for Animals) come under this heading. Other NSMs focus more on groups of historically marginalized people; for example, women, ethnic groups, lesbian, gay, bisexual and transgender people (LGBT) people or people with disabilities.

NSMs are different from pressure groups in a number of ways:

- They tend to have much more informal structures with a very limited bureaucracy. The anti-globalization movement, for example, does not have official leaders or offices or even a membership base. Rather than being run by a representative elite (which is often the case in pressure groups – all trade unions have an elected National Executive committee, for example) they seek participatory democracy. This leads to them being more diverse and fragmented, with a number of different spokepersons and no leadership structure.
- They use the same kinds of tactics as many pressure groups (public demonstrations, stunts, civil disobedience, illegal direct action, media campaigns, etc.) but as outsiders they are not consulted by government and unlike trade unions they do not use threats to withdraw labour (although they do organize boycotts).
- According to Hallsworth (1994), members of NSMs tend to be young and more concerned with quality of life rather than material comfort. They are mostly middle class, with public sector workers (teachers, nurses, social workers, etc.) or the children of public sector workers over-represented among their numbers. They also contain a higher proportion of students and unemployed people than society in general.

NSMs are mass movements that tend to appear very rapidly in response to a narrow issue (e.g., the Anti Poll Tax Federation in the 1980s); they are often quite short-lived (e.g., the anti-veal protests in Dover in 2006) and followers tend to be very passionate about the issue concerned.

Technology and new social movements

One of the key elements in the proliferation of NSMs has been changes in communications technology; the internet and email in particular, but also mobile phones, fax machines and satellite broadcasting, have enabled large groups of people to combine in a common cause very quickly and to get their message spread around the world.

Perhaps the first major development in communications technology to have a global effect occurred in the 1960s when images of the earth from space were transmitted to television sets around the world. This created a widespread appreciation of the importance of maintaining 'spaceship earth' in good ecological health, and this was followed up in the 1980s by images from space showing the depletion of the ozone layer. Technological advances in the field of communications have advanced extremely quickly; in 1965, for example, 85 per cent of the world's telephone lines were in Europe and the USA, with a single transatlantic cable handling fewer than 100 calls at a time. Thirty years later, there were 1.2 billion telephones in 190 countries, and a transatlantic call was one-thirtieth of the cost. By 2005, there were 76 million mobile phone users and 49 million land-line users in India. By 2006, 10 per cent of Japanese telephone users had adopted VoIP (voice over Internet protocol) technology (Cohen and Kennedy, 2007).

The percentage of the world's population with access to the internet has increased ten-fold in the last 20 years and this has facilitated all sorts of political activity. Websites, email and discussion groups have allowed individuals and organizations to produce and circulate literature very cheaply, to build up data banks of information, to communicate instantly and cheaply with large numbers of people separated by vast distances, to gain support worldwide for particular causes. The internet has allowed new social movements to by-pass the expensive and time-consuming processes that were previously necessary to mount simultaneous protests by millions of people across the world.

The development of the internet has mirrored the rise in international social movements, and has, according to some commentators, contributed to the movement of power away from nations states to non-governmental alliances and coalitions. Arquilla and Ronfeldt (2001) use the term 'netwar' to describe a new spectrum of conflict that is emerging in the wake of the information revolution. They argue that the Internet has allowed informal, leaderless groups to organize very rapidly against established governments and that it is crucial for governments, the military and law enforcement to begin networking themselves. Giddens (2006) quotes a US army report as warning that, 'A new generation of revolutionaries, radicals and activists are beginning to create information age ideologies in which identities and loyalties may shift from the nation state to the transnational level of global civic society.'

The use of the information highway by radical anti-government forces is exemplified by the Zapatistas in Mexico. The Zapatistas used the Internet as part of their guerrilla tactics against the Mexican state to mobilize global support for their struggle (see Castells, 2004). Establishing internet sites both within Mexico and outside with the help of sympathizers, the Zapatistas conducted a campaign to publicize their aims and the activities of the Mexican army, while encouraging supporters to lobby their own governments to support the indigenous people's land rights that were at the heart of the struggle. The success of the information strategy led to the establishment of a dense network of non-government organizations throughout the world, linked through the Zapatistas, that includes women's groups and human rights organizations in many arenas. Following on from their campaign, other protest groups have used digital technologies to organize effective and 'spontaneous' actions against specific targets. The use of mobile phones in 2001 to gather a million people together to protest at the collapse of the impeachment trail of President Estrada of the Phillipines is a well-documented example (see Cabras, 2002)

However, it is also the case that many of the old social movements and pressure groups have turned to digital technologies and are finding new ways of seeking to influence governments and policy-makers. Bimber (2003) has documented cases where traditional lobbying groups in the USA have been transformed organizationally by the use of the Internet. For example, the internet allows an organization to have a much broader recruitment appeal, especially in areas where they may be organizationally weak. For example, the Countryside Alliance was able to recruit among the young and urban through the use of the Internet (Lusoli and Ward, 2006). In addition, many of these groups have used the internet as a way of mobilizing supporters to bring pressure to bear on legislators. For example, 150,000 emails were sent to members of Congress at the behest of the National Coalition against Domestic Violence when Congress was deliberating on a pertinent measure. Though this is an example of the potential for mobilization of grassroots opinion, it is possible that legislators and other powerful groups may see this tactic as one of 'cheap talk', that is, a way of lobbying at little cost and inconvenience to the lobbyists.

Some commentators are sceptical of the long-term impact of virtual technologies on political decision-making. They argue that it is difficult to organize sustained political action only through virtual media and that the core activities of pressure groups will continue to be carried out through traditional methods (see Diani, 2000). Therefore the main effect of new technologies is a reinforcement of the professional activities of lobbying groups. Others argue that there are new elements emerging in the deployment of the new technologies. They allow the rapid mobilization of 'flash mobs' or 'smart mobs' to protest a particular cause and do not depend on leaders to organize, but on connectedness (see Rheingold, 2002). What digitalization also allows is the cross-national mobilization of groups who may have little in common nationally or ideologically, but which might form strategic alliances at particular moments in history (see Bennett, 2003). Bimber *et al.* (2009) argued that the main impact of the internet on the activities of pressure groups is due to its flexibility. That is, the internet permits organizations to operate in a number of ways effectively. It facilitates large-scale hierarchal structures to mobilize and recruit members, but is also capable of supporting small-scale intensive and interactive relationships that lead to entrepreneurial pressure group activity and new ways of carving out influence.

New social movements and postmodernisation

According to Stephen Crook *et al.* (1992), NSMs represent a shift from the old politics of modern societies to a new, postmodern, politics. Features of this new politics include:

- a much weaker class basis for party politics;
- a move from politics based on sectional interests (e.g., working-class people supporting Labour because it is in their economic interests to do so) to politics based on causes that affect everyone (e.g., campaigning against activities that may lead to climate change);
- a move away from the reliance on representative elites and towards a greater degree of participatory democracy;
- a shift of focus away from the activities of the state and towards those of the mass of people within civil society;
- a recognition that the personal is political; politics is no longer simply a set of ideals but is also linked to lifestyle choices. People who campaign against climate change, for example, are expected to live their own lives in a certain way, cutting down on energy use, recycling, etc.

Crook *et al.* (1992) attribute this change from old to new politics mainly to the breakdown of class distinctions, which they argue have been largely replaced by lifestyle and consumption patterns. People are more likely to define themselves as green than working or middle class. They also stress the importance of the mass media in broadening people's outlook and making it harder for them to focus on narrow sectional interests.

According to Crook *et al.* these factors have led to a permanent shift in the nature of politics. However, it is questionable whether there really has been the decomposition of class that Crook *et al.* claim, and it may be that NSMs and the new politics is a response to modern capitalism rather than to a postmodern, post-class society. Anthony Giddens (1990) argues that globalization and increases in ecological and conflict-related threats have led directly to NSMs, but that party politics remains very influential in modern societies, alongside nation states, international organizations and the power of big business. Giddens recognizes that NSMs have increased in importance, but he stresses that they have existed for some time and we are not witnessing a new postmodern politics with NSMs at the centre.

Alex Callinicos (2003) argues that NSMs are part of an anti-capitalist movement that has arisen specifically in opposition to the growth of global capitalism in the late 1990s. Naomi Klein (2000, p.3) similarly attributes the rise of new politics to 'the astronomical growth in the wealth and cultural influence of multinational corporations over the last fifteen years', which she argues can be traced back to 'a single, seemingly innocuous, idea developed by management theorists in the mid-1980s: that successful corporations must primarily produce brands as opposed to products'. Callinicos and Klein are both political activists, actively promoting the anti-capitalist movement they describe. As such, it is possible that they are guilty of over-exaggerating the impact and extent of the international anti-capitalist movement, but the G8 protests and the European Social Forum, for example, are clear evidence of the existence of a new and significant political phenomenon.

Whether NSMs represent postmodernist politics, or a product of late modern society, they do comprise a new type of politics that has arisen out of new risks facing human society, the rise of globalized capitalism and changes in media and communications technology.

Exercise 7.9

Discuss the following questions in small groups:

1. Do you tend to buy certain brands of clothes, shoes and drinks?
2. Do you think this is because the products are superior to those of other brands?
3. If so, why?
4. If not, why do you prefer these particular brands?

5. Do you agree with Klein that companies now tend to promote their brand logo rather than their products?
6. Why do you think they do this?
7. Do you agree that people should refuse to buy products linked to global brands?
8. If not, why not?

CONCLUSION

Since 1945, turnout in general and local elections has fallen, and voting patterns have changed. They are no longer so clearly based on class and now seem to be much less predictable than they used to be. In response to this increase in dealignment and volatility, contemporary sociologists have developed a range of different models of voting behaviour, but none seems to provide a complete explanation of this complex form of behaviour. Some argue that the current disillusionment with the party political process is a postmodern phenomenon, while others argue that changes in the nature of capitalism towards globalization, innovations in media technology and the perception that the world is now at greater risk of war and environmental disaster has led people to abandon party politics in favour of the new politics of social movements.

Exam focus
Question
Examine the view that social groups such as classes are no longer important in influencing how people vote.
When attempting to answer this question in an examination, the biggest difficulty you are likely to face is the enormous amount of information that you have about voting behaviour and the limited amount of time you have to get it down, This means that you have to be *selective* about what you choose to include – indeed, this is an important skill in itself and demonstrates your ability to interpret questions and apply material to the question set. Another thing worth noting is the mention of social classes. This is the setter of the question trying to be helpful by giving you one social group to go at. This means that you have an immediate focus for your answer. However, it does not mean that you necessarily have to restrict yourself to looking only at social classes. You might want consider gender or ethnicity as having or not having continuing influence on the way people vote. It is also worth thinking about what is meant by 'examine the view'. Although there is no explicit evaluation word in the question (such as 'assess') evaluation is implied by the phrase

'examine the view'. It would be unlikely that a high mark answer could be written that did not have some evaluation in it.

Therefore, write an answer to the question, selecting only relevant material and making decisions about how many social groups you are going to include. Time yourself for an hour (this is a common enough time given for an essay question of this type) and see whether you have completed a good answer by asking yourself the following questions:

- Does my introduction set out what it is I am going to write about?
- Does the main body of the answer flow logically from one paragraph to another?
- Have I presented both sides of the argument?
- Are there more than two sides to this argument?
- Have I included sufficient evidence about all the sides of the argument I have explored?
- Have I come to a conclusion that flows from the main body of my answer?
- Have I been evaluative enough?

To check this last point, go through your answer with a highlighter and highlight any evaluative words, sentences or paragraphs that you have included? What proportion of your answer is highlighted? You should be aiming for about a third.

Important concepts

- psephology • stability • alignment • partisanship • loyalty
- deviant voting • dealignment • embourgeoisement • sectoral division • the 'new working class' • postmodern voting
- expressive and instrumental models of voting • pressure groups
- new social movements

Summary points

- The study of voting and voting behaviour is referred to as 'psephology'; voting has changed significantly in recent years with decline of class as a key factor.
- Before the 1970s voting in the UK was seen to be characterized by *stability*, *alignment*, *partisanship* and *loyalty*.
- People who voted against their traditional class loyalties were labelled as *deviant voters*.
- Heath argued that the nature of the working classes has dramatically changed since the 1960s; we have moved from a period of alignment to one of *dealignment* and from stability to *volatility*.

- There are a number of sociological views on the rise of dealignment:

  - *Embourgoisement*: the upward social mobility from the upper working classes into the lower and middle middle classes;
  - *Class dealignment*: the traditional basis of class has been replaced by other forms of economic divisions and inequalities between and within the different classes;
  - *The rise of the new working class*: voting for the party that appears to benefit them the most in the short term.

- Callinicos and Harman argue that the death of class has been greatly exaggerated and that there never was a golden age of class alignment.
- Marshall argues that class has not changed but has been replaced by more complex forms of division.
- Baudrillard suggests that class dealignment is evidence of a postmodern society and that we have witnessed the 'end of the political'.
- There are two types of modern day models of voting: *expressive models of voting* and *instrumental models of voting*.
- Instrumental models of voting include:

  - The consumer
  - The tactical voter
  - The pocket-book voter
  - Lifetime learning model
  - The rational choice
  - The subjective class model

- The complexity of voting behaviour means that it is very difficult to predict how an individual will vote, but turnout in elections and membership of political parties is declining; people are choosing to become involved in politics in different ways, such as *pressure groups* and *new social movements* (NSMs).
- Pressure groups and NSMs consist of groups of like-minded people who seek to influence policy-making on a narrow range of issues; they are not interested in becoming policy-makers themselves
- Pressure groups can be classified as *sectional* or *promotional*. They can further be classified as *insider* or *outsider*.
- NSMs have informal structures and they tend to be young and middle class. They are outsiders and tend to use tactics such as public demonstrations, stunts etc., and are more concerned with quality of life rather than material comfort. They appear very rapidly in response to a narrow issue and are often quite short-lived.

  - One of the key elements in the proliferation of NSMs has been changes in communication technology
  - Some argue that NSMs represent a shift from the old politics of modern societies to a new, postmodern, politics.

Critical thinking

1. Do you think that individuals make a free choice when they decide whom to vote for?
2. What is meant by the term 'deviant voting'?
3. Is class dead?
4. 'Conventional party politics is in decline and new social movements will become the dominant form of politics in Western democracies.' Discuss.

Chapter 8

Theories on the Role of the State in Society

By the end of this chapter you should:

- understand sociological definitions of the term 'the state'
- understand sociological theories on the role of the state in society
- be able to compare and contrast different sociological ideas on the state
- be able to evaluate different sociological ideas on the state
- be able to identify how sociological ideas on the state have changed over time

INTRODUCTION

When looking at how power operates in society, a great deal of sociological analysis considers the rise of the state in modern society and the ways in which it uses power over the citizens within its territory. Although a relatively recent social phenomenon in terms of the history of humanity as a whole, the growth of the nation state has been a key feature of all societies over the past 200–300 years. From the early city states such as Athens in ancient Greece to the modern day nation states, we have seen the growth in large-scale organization and bureaucracy and the employment of a large group of people whose job it is to exercise legal power in society. As Birch (1993) comments:

> The entire surface of this planet, with the single exception of Antarctica, is now divided for purposes of government into territories known as nation-states... Only 200 years ago, there were fewer than twenty states with the shape and character that we should now recognise as deserving describing as nation-states. (Birch, 1993, p. 13)

Anthony Giddens (1986) suggests that a sociological analysis of the state is vital – especially given its growth and increasing involvement in social life. In fact, he is rather surprised that, given its importance, the systematic sociological study of the state has been rather ignored by sociologists until recently. Giddens points out that:

- The state plays an increasingly direct role in supervising the economy in capitalist societies.
- The state in capitalist societies tends to employ roughly 40 per cent of the workforce – whether in its administrative institutions or in state-owned or regulated economic areas.
- States increasingly influence the import and export of goods to and from other nation-states across the globe.
- The state increasingly intervenes in social life through organizations such as the police, the law and the prison agencies.
- The state regulates welfare provision, heath and educational services.
- States increasingly involve themselves in ordinary family life – the so-called private realm of social activity – through its policies and laws.

Given the growth of the state, an analysis of its power is a key question for political sociology.

DEFINITIONS OF THE STATE

In the words of Anthony Giddens (1981), we can define the state as follows:

> The nation-state, which exists in a complex of other nation-states, is a set of institutional forms of governance maintaining an administrative monopoly over a territory with demarcated boundaries (borders), its rule being sanctioned by law and direct control of the means of internal and external violence. (Giddens, 1981, p. 190)

The state is one of the ways in which a society is organized. It is the mechanism through which the decisions made by leaders are legitimized and carried out. Nation states operate within specific boundaries (even if these are contested between different nation-states through political or armed conflict) and they have legal control over the population within these boundaries.

Giddens, following Max Weber (see Chapter 3), notes that a key feature of the state is its ability to use legitimate violence against those within its political and geographical boundaries. It is also worth noting that the boundaries of the state might extend beyond one geographical area – many nation states might have territories in other parts of the world. Also foreign embassies within other nation states are treated as the sovereign soil of the nation state which is represented by the embassy in question.

Weber offers his own detailed definition of the state as follows:

> The primary formal characteristics of the modern state are as follows: it possesses an administrative and legal order subject to change by legislation, to which the organised activities of the administrative staff, which are also controlled by regulations, are oriented. This system of order claims binding authority, not only over the members of the state, the citizens, most of whom have obtained membership by birth, but also to a very large extent over all action taking place in the area of its jurisdiction. (Weber, 1978, p. 56)

See how this applies across the world by doing Exercise 8.1.

Exercise 8.1

Think about the role of Britain as a state. See if you can list the places outside the immediate geographical location of the United Kingdom which are officially British.

Is there a difference in our involvement with different states outside the UK – for example, between the Falkland Islands and Australia? Discuss or find out about any recent news coverage of the control of these places.

You could also find out how many places across the world were once considered to be British (by the British state).

- Are all states geographically compact? Look up Kaliningrad.
- Do all regions of a state accept the central authority of that state? Look up South Ossetia.
- What is the relationship between the USA and Puerto Rico?
- What implications do these examples have for the definition of the state?

Essential characteristics of the modern state

For Giddens (1993), although he recognizes the rather ambiguous nature of the state – it is quite difficult to identify its exact features – the following three elements are essential to all states and their organization:

(a) centralized organs of government,
(b) claims by centralized government to legitimate territorial control,
(c) a distinct dominant or elite class, having definite modes of training, recruitment and status attributes. (Giddens, 1993, p. 193)

Ⓘ Ⓐ

Exercise 8.2

Read the following extracts from an article about how the nation-state of Saudi Arabia was created, and identify evidence of the three elements identified above by Giddens as essential to all states, that is:

- centralized organs of government,
- claims by centralized government to legitimate territorial control,
- a distinct dominant or elite class, having definite modes of training, recruitment and status attributes.

Fiefdoms and Bureaucrats: Building the Saudi State 1953–1980s, *Lecture given by Mr Steffen Hertog to the Saudi-British Society, 13 October 2005*

... the modern Saudi nation state started its evolution only in the early 1950s, when the first functionally differentiated, formal ministries and agencies were created and the Council of Ministers was set up in 1953.

The fact that much of the early state-building was already based on oil income led to several idiosyncrasies in the creation of modern institutions: as the income came from abroad and hit Saudi society unprepared, there was much leeway for the leadership to determine the shape of new ministries. This meant that institutional design was largely a product of elite politics, i.e. negotiations between senior princes, influenced by a limited number of commoner advisors. Ministerial design hence reflected specific balances of power, and ministries were 'granted' to specific factions, i.e. the Ministry of Defense to Prince Mansour and his full brothers and the governorship of Riyadh to Sultan and then Naif. More strikingly, institutions were structured so as to reflect the seniority of their heads, as when the Ministry of Air Force was allocated to Defense so as to avoid too much authority to accrue to Communication under Talal.

Trusted commoners would also be allowed to design institutions according to their interests, as in the case of the Ministry of Finance under Abdallah Sulaiman, who used his sprawling bureaucratic empire to further his own business interests and rear a whole stratum of business partners (including the Sharbatli family, who reportedly first endeared themselves to his brother and deputy Hamad Sulaiman through a gift of fruit). However, the minister also used his discretion to help with the setting up of the Saudi Arabian Monetary Agency, which was designed by American advisors and subsequently proved to be one of the best central banks in the Middle East.

Changing institutions also reflected elite politics during the years when the distribution of authority between King Saud and Crown Prince Faisal was unclear. Each of them promoted different institutions: Faisal used the formal bureaucracy and the Council of Ministers to solidify his rule, whereas Saud relied on the traditional royal court to bolster his following. Strikingly, Saud would also try to promote modern institutions – like a 120-member Majlis Ash-Shura which never came into being – to further his own interests. Conversely, Faisal would be reluctant to give up the traditional post of Hijazi viceregent. It was, however, in the area of defense administration that a constant fluctuation of status and institutional attachment of Royal Guard and National Guard most vividly reflected the balance of forces of the day.

Elite politics fluctuated much less once Faisal had emerged as the main figure in Saudi politics. The set-up represented by the October 1962 cabinet under him was one which should define Saudi politics thenceforth: 'sovereignty ministries' under senior princes – from maternal branches which should keep these institutions until today, and most technocratic posts for commoners.

While much was accomplished, the concentration of authority in a few senior players made for the 'island' character of specific ministries, whether controlled by commoners or royals – an enduring feature which has come to complicate the Saudi business environment today.

What does this article suggest is the role of bureaucrats in the state? Does this support or contradict the ideas about essential elements of the modern state put forward by Giddens?

Taking the work of both Giddens and Weber together, the nation state includes:

- the geographical territory within which it can act;
- the mechanisms through which leaders become leaders (elected or not);
- the legal system;
- the welfare system;
- the government body and its decision-making process – whether through a parliament or not;
- the armed services;
- the legal system;
- law enforcement bodies.

For Dunleavy and O'Leary (1987) it is possible to identify five essential features of the modern state:

1. The state is a separate institution from others in society – it encourages a separation of the private from the public.
2. The state is the supreme power within its territory – it creates the laws and has control over all legitimate uses of force;
3. The state has control over territory, but also the population within its territory. This control is enshrined in the law, and this law applies to everyone – including those people who themselves work within the institutions that make up the state;
4. Those who work within the institutions of the state are recruited in a fair and bureaucratic fashion: there are written rules governing what qualifications individuals need to gain employment in these institutions, and what their duties are once they are appointed;
5. The state has the right to demand money from those in its territory in the form of taxation to help fund what the state does within its territory.

(K)(U)

Exercise 8.3

Write a list of examples of Dunleavy and O'Leary's five elements of the modern state. Think of at least one example for each.

Dunleavy and O'Leary's five elements of the modern state:	Examples
The state is a separate institution from others in society	
The state is the supreme power within its territory	
The state has control over territory and the population within its territory	
Those who work within the institutions of the state are recruited in a fair and bureaucratic fashion	
The state has the right to demand money from those in its territory in the form of taxation	

The dark side of the state

Looking at the five elements of the state offered by Dunleavy and O'Leary, we can make the criticism that it is a very liberal list. In other words, it seems to suggest that the state is a fair and democratic institution and that, since its power is based in written law, this ensures continuity and promotes fairness – the state is regulated for the good of all.

However, some commentators are critical of this image of the state. For example, both Weber and the economist Schumpeter (see Chapter 3) criticize the rise of the bureaucracy that surrounds the development of the state in a large-scale society. They suggest that those who work for the state become an elite group and that even if their position has legal controls associated with it, they are the very people who have the elite power to write this law in the first place. This – in their view – is a highly undemocratic situation since those who control the bureaucracy may become very powerful, yet they are largely unelected.

This observation is very similar to the idea of the 'iron law of oligarchy' developed by Robert Michels (1911) – an associate of Weber's. Michel claims that all mass democracies – due to their large scale and the degree of bureaucratic organization that this involves – have a tendency towards a form of oligarchy rather than democracy – the rule of a few in the interests of the few. This is because mass democracies are so large, it is impossible for everyone to have a say, except through the representatives they elect. However, those who are involved in the day-to-day running of the state have a separate existence from those elected to lead, and are able to develop a very significant power base of their own.

Ⓘ Ⓐ

| Exercise 8.4 |

What evidence is there in the following extract of the form of oligarchy that Weber and colleagues suggest might emerge in a large-scale state?

Police probe exile's claims about Russian 'revolution'

Police in Britain and Russia launched separate inquiries into the multimillionaire Boris Berezovsky yesterday after he disclosed to the *Guardian* that he was plotting a 'revolution' to overthrow President Vladimir Putin. In Moscow, where investigators said they were opening a criminal investigation into the tycoon's calls for the use of force to secure regime change, infuriated government ministers demanded that he be stripped of his refugee status and extradited to stand trial.

In comments which appeared to be calculated to enrage the Kremlin, Mr Berezovsky told the *Guardian*: 'We need to use force to change this regime. It isn't possible to change this regime through democratic means. There can be no change without force, pressure.'

He added that he was in contact with like-minded people within Russia's ruling inner circle, offering advice, finance, and 'my understanding of how it could be done'. Asked if he was effectively fomenting a revolution, he replied: 'You are absolutely correct, absolutely correct.'

In his *Guardian* interview the tycoon claimed he was already bankrolling people close to the president who were conspiring against him. His remarks set off a storm in Russia, where the state-controlled TV stations led reports on the *Guardian* interview and a host of pro-Kremlin MPs queued up to denounce him.

Mr Berezovsky, 61, made his fortune, currently estimated at around £850m, during the Boris Yeltsin years, when he bought state assets at knockdown prices during Russia's rush towards privatisation.

Although he played a key role in ensuring Mr Putin's victory in the 2000 presidential elections, the two men fell out as the newly elected leader successfully wrested control of Russia back from the so-called oligarchy, the small group of tycoons who had come to dominate the country's economy. A few months after the election Mr Berezovsky fled Russia, and applied successfully for asylum in the UK.

Source: Ian Cobain, Ian Black and Luke Harding,
The Guardian 14 April 2007

The state and bureaucracy

The state can be seen to be highly bureaucratic: it is run by elected leaders yet it is administered by a whole series of civil servants – officials, clerical workers, minister's advisers, etc. For Weber, the growth of bureaucratic organizations was a key feature in the development of modernity across Western Europe – and the state can be seen as one of the most heavily bureaucratic institutions in the history of the modern world.

In defining bureaucracy, Weber himself places importance on the growth of a hierarchical form of organization within the specific bureaucratic institution and the coordination of the work of individuals. Bureaucrats work in line with collective goals and within written formal procedures that dictate what tasks are done, how they are done and in what order they should be done.

Weber suggests that the growth of bureaucratic forms of organization – the state being a prime example of this – is a feature of the spread of the process of rationalization across society after the industrial revolution. This is a key feature of what we have called modernity (see Chapter 5). For Weber, the modern world is characterized by the processes of:

- *secularization* – the decline of religion;
- *disenchantment* – the loss of a belief in the spiritual and supernatural;
- *desacrilization* – the loss of the sacred in society.

And along with the decline in religious thinking, there is a rise in scientific and technological thinking. This is what Weber calls the process of rationalization. Rational thinking for Weber is characterized by the breaking down of tasks into a universal order of smaller tasks. This type of organization can be seen, for example, in the growth of assembly-line production in factories. Weber argues that bureaucratic forms of organized government are more efficient: they turn institutions that are based upon bureaucracy into machines – where people and their individual jobs within them are like cogs in the machine.

> The fully developed bureaucratic apparatus compares with other organisations exactly as does the machine with the non-mechanical modes of production. Precision, speed, unambiguity, knowledge of the files, continuity, discretion, unity, strict subordination, reduction of friction and of material and personal costs – these are raised to the optimum point in the strictly bureaucratic organisation. (Weber, cited in Giddens, 1971, p. 159)

The 'iron cage of bureaucracy'

Weber was very aware that with the growth of bureaucracy, this rational and efficient form of organization would also lead to a dark side of modern life: what Weber called the 'iron cage of bureaucracy' (see also Chapter 3). Weber suggests that the growth of large-scale bureaucratic states results in a kind of organizational trap, where individuals become concerned with the means (the procedures) and not with the ends (the goals) of their small part in the whole task. This results in the sort of society where people lose sight of the goals and eventually the rationality and efficiency of bureaucracy becomes part of the cage: stopping development, holding back change. Thus rationality ends up highly irrational: the goals become the means to keep the machine running. The ultimate goal of the state becomes to keep itself existing and unelected officials end up running the state in the interests of the state. Weber describes a very dark future for industrial societies when he writes:

> Together with the machine, the bureaucratic organisation is engaged in building the houses of bondage of the future, in which perhaps men will one day be like peasants in the ancient Egyptian State, acquiescent and power-less, while a purely technically good, that is rational, official administration and provision becomes the sole, final value, which sovereignty decides the direction of their affairs... This passion for bureaucracy is enough to drive one to despair. It is as if in politics... we were deliberately to become men

who need 'order' and nothing but order, become nervous and cowardly if for one moment this order waves, and helpless if they are torn away from their total incorporation in it...and the great question is, therefore, not how we can promote and hasten it, but what can we oppose to this machinery in order to keep a portion of mankind free from this parceling-out of the soul, from this supreme mastery of the bureaucratic way of life. (Weber, cited in Kumar, 1978, p. 107)

Ⓤ

Exercise 8.5

Rewrite the quote from Weber above, using more contemporary language, without losing Weber's meaning.

THE STATE, CITIZENSHIP AND SOVEREIGNTY

The growth of nation states across the globe raises two other features of the modern world:

1. The issue of sovereignty;
2. The issue of citizenship.

- *Sovereignty* – each nation state is seen to have sole control over its territory. The land (and the people) within its political boundaries are there to be controlled in a way that the particular nation state wishes;
- *Citizenship* – (see Chapter 9) the population born within the territory of a nation-state and living there, are the citizens of that particular nation-state. This means that within the laws of that political territory there are both rights and duties that affect the lives of the population. For example, in the UK we have the right to vote in general elections and the right to free education under the age of 18, but we also have the duty to pay taxes and to follow the law. If we reject our duties, this might result in the use of force against us – force that would be legitimate since it would be based in the law.

Zygmunt Bauman (1990) suggests that the duties citizens have within a nation state makes them belong to the nation state in question. This belonging works in two ways: we belong in the sense that nation state *identity* is created for us – we are given a *nationality* by being the subject of the rulers and the laws of a specific nation. This in turn creates a community that we imagine we are a member of (see Chapter 9); we develop a notion of 'us' and 'them' that tells us who we are. Secondly, we belong to the nation state in the sense that those who run the nation state are able to tell us what duties we are obliged to perform, in return for what rights we have. We are the subject of those who lead, run and administer the laws of the nation state; we are subjected to their rule – and punished if we do not adhere. This means that nation states operate a considerable amount of *social control* upon those within their territories.

Exercise 8.6

Using the definition of a *citizen* cited in the text, write a list of ways in which you perceive yourself to be a citizen of Great Britain. What are the defining characteristics that make you a citizen of Britain and not the USA, for example?

Bauman notes that, for the individual, belonging to a nation state is both a situation of protection and of subordination at the same time:

> *The fact that being a subject of the state is a combination of rights and duties makes us feel simultaneously protected and oppressed. We enjoy the relative peacefulness of life which we know we owe to the awesome force always waiting somewhere in the wings to be deployed against the breakers of peace.* (Bauman, 1990, p. 163)

Or, as Weber famously observed: 'Within the velvet glove, there is a fist of steel.' What he means by this is that behind the relative security that life within the protection of a state might offer, there is the constant threat of legally sanctioned violence. This makes those who decide the laws – and those who administer them – very powerful; they have the right to choose whom to define or label as deviants and to control them accordingly.

Our position as subjects is also contradictory, since for many people the state intrudes too much into our private lives:

> We believe that we owe our security and peace of mind to the power of the state, and that there would be no security or peace of mind without it. On

many occasions, however, we resent the obtrusive interference of the state into our private lives. The state-imposed rules often seem too numerous and too pernickety for comfort; we feel that they constrain our freedom...Our experience of the state is therefore inherently ambiguous. It may happen that we like it and dislike it at the same time. (Bauman, 1990, pp. 163–4)

As Bauman also points out, the degree to which we experience belonging to the state as a source of security or as oppression might depend on the social position we have within the hierarchy of society. It may well be the case that those who are higher up the social system – and therefore have more power – find themselves less constrained by the state. This may be because they have the financial resources and status needed to do what they wish, or that their attitudes, beliefs and lifestyles more closely match those who make the decisions within the state in the first place.

Sovereignty and globalization

With the onset of globalization, issues of both sovereignty and citizenship have recently become more complex. For example:

1. Although the state has legitimate power within its territory, leaders and governments of other nation-states might consider that it has used this power in illegitimate ways. This is particularly true of claims of human rights abuses or of the ethnic cleansing that we have seen in some states at the turn of twenty-first century, for example, in Bosnia or Rwanda. On these occasions, global political bodies such as NATO or the UN might seek economic and even military sanctions against these countries – thus calling into question the sovereignty of the nation state. In this way, citizens of one nation state might find themselves being identified at risk by other nation states. It may be the case that in order to protect citizens of a state the UN, may seek to overturn existing laws or impose new laws within that state. For example, in 1994 the UN set up the International Criminal Tribunal for Rwanda (ICTR) and in 1991 the International Criminal Tribunal for the Former Yugoslavia (ICTY) specifically in order to prosecute individuals in those countries, not for breaking their own laws but for violating international humanitarian laws.

2. With the growth of transnational companies, some states might find themselves unable to influence the policies of large corporations if they are not geographically based within their territory of control. Thus, if

governments pass laws that some corporations do not like – especially concerning workers' rights, minimum wages or taxation – these corporations often seek alternative territories in which to base their activities. This can often have the effect of leaving states with problems such as unemployment and higher importation prices (and lead to exploitation in the states to which these corporations have relocated). Situations such as this also question the power of the nation state.

Exercise 8.7

Globalization has had a very significant impact on notions of what a nation is, and what we mean by sovereignty. Read the following material and write a list of the advantages and disadvantages of the process of relocating factories and businesses of large corporations to different parts of the world.

The decision to move production from one country to another is driven by economic considerations. These include the cost of labour, but also issues such as transport infrastructure incentives from the government of the recipient countries and the taxation regime. There are also social dimensions and political considerations in this calculation. Restrictions on trade union activity in the receiving country or a less stringent legal framework as regards human rights or fewer limitations on the employment of child labour might prove attractive to a cost-conscious company.

The cost to the original country of the loss of jobs and production are also not just economic. Of course, the workers who lose their employment suffer economically and the country loses tax revenue. But where a company has dominated the employment opportunities in a region, there are social consequences far beyond individual loses. Whole towns can fall into decline as a consequence of decisions made remotely, by executives who have no connection with the locality and who are making those decisions driven by global forces that often seem out of their control.

The state, nations and national boundaries

Giddens notes that it is not the case that states develop naturally within geographical boundaries. Instead, it is more that states develop quite artificially across different religious, ethnic and cultural boundaries, creating large-scale unified wholes, which are not unified according to any pre-existing cultural ideas:

it is probably not usually the case that state institutions develop within an already constituted 'society' that remains more or less unchanged. On the contrary, the development of states very often fuses previously unarticulated social entities and may at the same time break up others that have existed hitherto.

(Giddens, 1993, p. 194)

For example, the various nation-states that make up the continent of Africa cross many original ethnic boundaries, artificially taking groups of peoples who did not share a common culture and forcing them together within a shared nation state. At the same time these boundaries can split some groups between the artificially created territories of two separate nation-states. If we look at a modern day map of Africa we see that the shape of many countries is based upon a series of straight lines – and does not appear to have taken account of geographical or past settlement. This is because the present day map of nation states in Africa owes a great deal to the legacy left by the colonial empire building of Western Europe in previous centuries. Traditional territories were artificially divided by colonial rulers trying to get their fair share of the land and the wealth it contained, irrespective of the identity of the inhabitants.

Giddens notes that although we might think of nation states as unchanging, they are in fact quite fluid: political change often results in geographical change to nation states and their territories (see Exercise 8.8).

Exercise 8.8

Look at a present day map of Africa. Which states appear to you to have the most arbitrary boundaries? Take two adjacent states, and examine their colonial past. Try to find out which countries colonized them, and for what reasons. What effect has this had on their national identity – e.g., the national language, style of government and the economy? States in west and southern Africa are particularly interesting in this respect.

European Union and its governance

The issue of the sovereignty of the state is also affected by the growth of transnational political units, such as the European Union, which are more than just economic or military alliances and which may have many of the attributes of the nation state. The governance of the European Union has been subject to a great deal of analysis about its impact on the individual member state's powers and independence of action. The key issue here is the degree of federalism (the extent to which power is concentrated in central political institutions, in this case the European Parliament and/or European Commission) that exists or that is desirable in a collectivity of states that agree to pool sovereignty in order to create a larger political unit to act on the global stage. It is fairly clear that the European Union has succeeded in the two main arenas for which it was created; that is, to prevent a recurrence of war between the large European powers (but less successful with the smaller ones such as the former Yugoslav states) and to build up the economic prosperity of its citizens. However, the original theoretical impetus for the EU (usually identified as a neo-functionalist attitude) assumed that there would be steady progress towards the greater integration of the political institutions of Europe through a process of spillover (see Rosamund, 2000).

Spillover describes the situation where the handing over of power to European institutions for specific and limited purposes leads to a further concentration of power at the European centre as the implications of the first transfer are worked through. For example, Jensen (2000) showed how the creation of the single market (which was done with specific functions in mind) led to the further regulation of health and safety legislation across the EU, in order to achieve the free movement of people and goods. Political spillover can also occur where individual member states, in order to protect their own interests, act in concert with another state or states over a different issue, thus tying the two issues together in ways that often lead to a more central control over the member states.

This neo-functionalist approach has been criticized both for its interpretation of the detail of events in the EU, but more importantly, at the theoretical level. Moravcsik (2005), among others, has argued that political spillover indicates that the central players in the European Union are not some supra-national European political or bureaucratic elite, but the nation states themselves. Therefore the EU should be seen, not as some federal state, but as subject to intergovernmental actions, where the individual member states remain as the main political actors. This position is called 'intergovernmentalism' and it also suggests that the policy issues that are controlled by central European institutions are those that do not impinge on the fundamental sovereignty of individual states, such as the right to levy taxes. This right has remained at the national level, even when it is affected by policies created at the centre. Where movement towards more central controls can be identified, it has largely been the result of the negotiated preferences of national leaders pursuing their own national interests, rather than a commitment by political elites to push forward an integrationist agenda. Critics of intergovernmentalism argue that the theory underestimates the roles and influence of both supranational actors in the European Union such as the Commissioners, who are able to exploit national differences to pursue their own agendas, and of transnational interest groups such as the business community who can act powerfully on the European stage when their economic interests are involved.

Others (Sandholtz and Stone Sweet, 1998) argued that the simple distinction between the intergovernmental and the supranational as opposing characteristics of the EU should be abandoned, because some aspects of EU policy are supranational and others are clearly intergovernmental. It is the density of transactions in a particular field of social life that leads to the establishment of trans-national regulations to monitor them and establish a level playing field in the European arena. In addition, theorists have pointed out that the European Project operates at several different levels and that there has not been a one-way process of concentration of power at the centre. Rather power has moved both up and down the system, towards Brussels and towards the regions, while considerable power still resides in the hands of national governments. It is this lack of connection between the day-to-day reality of the European Union and the traditional theories that has led to new approaches to the EU.

The rational choice instrumentalists focus upon the formal rules and processes within the EU and examine how the interests of individuals are mediated through the European institutions. By focusing on the changing nature of the 'game' of Europe, they demonstrate that the interests of individual member states can be served at times by the ceding of power to the central organizations of the EU and that this is a rational outcome, not one drawn from some ideological commitment to federalism (see Pollack, 2002). Moreover, sociologists have developed this approach by looking at the culture of European institutions and how the emergence of common ways of looking at problems can lead to the construction of European identities. In this way, the role of communication and persuasion within European institutions is highlighted, so that the more formal analysis of the rational choice theorists is rounded out by a more sociological emphasis. Moreover, the norms and values at the European level are filtered down into national dialogues and policy discussions, which represents the Europeanization of national politics (Börzell and Risse, 2003).

Another approach to the EU suggests that its governance has been affected by globalization and its associated processes, so that there has been a shift from an interventionist agenda towards a more regulatory body. Rather than actively intervening to achieve its policy aims, the EU has moved towards a role where it seeks to regulate the actions of others (states and interest groups within and beyond those states) through the development of rules of engagement, especially over the operation of the single market (see Majone, 2005). As such, the EU is less interested in integration in many other areas of policy such as welfare, because they distract the European institutions from their dominant regulatory role.

THEORETICAL VIEWS ON THE STATE

Broadly speaking, sociologists have interpreted the state as either:

1. a force for protection, compromise, justice and *fairness*; or
2. a force for oppression and *control* – maybe serving its own interests or those of an elite group.

It may well be the case that all states can be considered in both lights – maybe at different times, or at the same time for different groups within society. Broadly speaking, functionalist and pluralist theories concentrate upon the fair and democratic workings of the state, whereas the more radical theories such as Marxism and neo-Marxism look towards the elitist and oppressive workings of the state. In more recent years, it is possible to identify a third approach to the state:

3. Seeing the state as in crisis or a situation of overload.

This third position is associated with New Right and New Left theories (see Chapter 6).

The democratic state?

Functionalist and pluralist thinkers such as Durkheim (1988) and Dahl (1961) (see Chapter 3) both see the state as a protective body distributing social justice: the state is seen to represent the wishes of all and to negotiate between alternative views and wants.

For Durkheim the state was concerned with the governance of morality in society. In other words it was answerable to the collective wishes of those in society and governed for the benefit of all.

For Dahl (1961), the state avoids conflict by operating as a regulating body between opposing views, groups and wishes. The state's own decision-making is a result of compromise between the interests of groups, pressure groups and social movements within the community of the nation as a whole.

The democratisation of everyday life

In some respects this is the pluralist view – the state as a democratic body open to the interests of the population – and is reflected today in some of the writings of Anthony Giddens. For example, Giddens (1994), in the book *Beyond Left and Right*, suggests that the modern day age is characterized in the West by an increase in the *democratization of everyday life* and, in particular, an increase in what he refers to as an 'emotional democracy'. This refers to the fairness, openness and democratic nature of close personal relationships in the private aspects of our life.

Giddens suggests that modern states are highly pluralistic: they are based upon shared rights and a sense of *trust* between groups within the community as a whole. People enjoy many more rights and freedoms than ever before – freedoms won through a series of protests made by previously marginalized and outside groups over the last century. This means in Giddens' view that modern day states are moving closer towards a more intimate and personal kind of democracy. In this form of democracy the state helps, supports and encourages fairness and freedoms within private life – in particular in the realm of the family, sexuality and personal relationships.

Giddens notes that the dialogue between the general population, and those who lead and administer the state, is becoming more open. He describes this as living in an ever-increasing dialogic democracy – where decision-making by those in power is based upon communication with those subjected to this power in an open fashion. This dialogic democracy is based upon the development of trust between all groups so that all subjects can communicate freely with one another within the territory of the nation state in question.

Life-politics and the pure relationship

For Giddens modern day politics is a form of life-politics: it is about making personal decisions and choosing ones' own actions. Changes in the nature of society have made this freedom and autonomy increasingly possible, but along with this comes an increased sense of anxiety since we are not told how to act, but have to decide for ourselves and in doing so decide who or what our self is to be.

Giddens defines this life-politics:

Life-politics is a politics, not of life-chances, but of life-style. It concerns disputes and struggles about how (as individuals and as collective humanity) we should live in a world where what used to be fixed either by nature or tradition is now subject to human decisions. (Giddens, 1984, pp. 14–5)

Giddens' ideas on the nature of the democratic state have parallels with the ideas of Jürgen Habermas (1991) in his discussion of the 'pure relationship' in society. Habermas suggests that freedom and fairness in society will only develop once we have a 'pure form of communication' not based upon self-ish needs and sectional interests. Before this can take place we need to solve inequality and oppression so that people can experience pure communication and in the end develop trust and eventually harmony in society. For Giddens these pure forms of relationship not only apply to people in day-to-day life (the micro level of society), but to the nature of the ideal relationship between states and their subjects on a more macro level. These pure relationships are based upon compromise, negotiation and honesty – and are in turn only possible if people have autonomy: if individuals are able to shape their lives in the way they wish.

As he notes:

In a world of high reflexivity, an individual must achieve a certain degree of autonomy of action as a condition of being able to survive and forge a life; but autonomy is not the same as egoism and moreover implies reciprocity and interdependence. (Giddens, 1984, p. 13)

Giddens, like Habermas, notes that true dialogic democracy will only be achieved in society once inequalities between groups of a material or economic nature are resolved or drastically reduced: otherwise pure communication based upon trust is impossible if some are able to be more autonomous than others:

Democratisation combats power, seeking to turn it into negotiated relationships, whether these be between equals or are relations of differential authority. Yet democracy, dialogic or otherwise, plainly has its limits. These limits concern especially the intrusive influence of inequality. Dialogue does not depend upon material equality, but it does presume that differential resources aren't used to prevent views being voiced or for a drastic skewing of the conditions of dialogic interchange. (Giddens, 1984, p. 132)

Damaged solidarities

Giddens says that the state, in this new age of dialogue and emotional democracy, has two key goals:

1. it must help to repair previously damaged solidarities and
2. it must help to develop generative politics.

- *Damaged solidarities* – Giddens argues that the state needs to help communities and groups to communicate better and to develop more trust so that they can move away from previously damaged relationships.
- *Generative politics* – the state should encourage, and help to bring about, the autonomy of its subjects: it should help people to generate new ideas and to take control of their own lives. As Giddens says, this is a form of politics that allows people to make things happen for themselves. Giddens says that this autonomy will only happen once we have *active trust* between the state and the subjects of the state.

Exercise 8.9

Summarize the key points of the theories that support the idea that the state is democratic and based on fairness. Use the following names:

Durkheim
Dahl
Giddens
Habermas

One of the ways that postmodern states have attempted to repair damaged solidarities and reconstruct links between citizens and state is by harnassing new technologies. The explosion of digital technologies in the last half of the twentieth century and early part of the twenty-first created opportunities for experiments in what has become known as 'e-democracy'. While these have mainly been located in the technology-rich industrialized nations, there are projects all over the world that seek to use the Internet and related technologies to facilitate communication between the citizenry and the state. The potential for connections was identified through the creation of a number of virtual community groupings, most notably the Minnesota E-Democracy Forum, which is a locally based political discussion forum (see Dahlberg, 2001). Governments have tried to emulate these forums and move beyond the non-interactive information-giving websites that are the main one-way service provided on the internet by governments throughout the world.

Two models of use of the internet have emerged. The first is where governments provide access online to citizens for consultative purposes. In the USA there is a central portal for citizens to comment on proposed changes to rules put forward for consultation by government departments (Coglianese, 2004). Secondly, there have been projects established for a more interactive deliberative use of electronic forums where citizens, officials and politicians can engage in debating policies. The aim of these is to inform the decision-makers in a non-binding way of the arguments surrounding particular proposals. The Hansard Society has been instrumental in these projects in the UK, but they have been copied in other countries such as Canada (see Chadwick, 2006). While projects that have a specific purpose are usually successful, sustaining long-term consultative and deliberative forums is much more problematic. Digital activists tend to burn out after a period of time or move into other areas of online experience, while those who are persuaded to participate through incentives (such as free Internet access or even computers) tend to lose interest once the incentive has been given, as was the experience of the local authorities in Italy (see Berra, 2003).

The oppressive state?

A very different image of the state has its intellectual roots in the ideas of Marx and Engels (see Chapter 3).

Is the state the puppet of capitalism?

The classic or orthodox Marxist interpretation of the nature of the state is to see it as the puppet of the ruling class. Those who own the means of production in society are in turn able to control and shape what governments do – what decisions they make, how they spend their money, what laws they pass about the operation of business and what groups they seek to define as deviant and therefore try and control. Ownership of the means of production, in this view, is ultimate power: those elected to represent the people simply end up following the wishes of those who have economic power. The classic Marxist statement on this issue, in *The Communist Manifesto*, originally published in 1848, is: *'The executive of the modern state is but a committee for managing the common affairs of the whole bourgeoisie'* (Marx and Engels, 1967, p. 82).

These Marxist theories are highly critical of interpretations of the state as a fair and democratic body – ideas contained in the work of Durkheim,

Parsons (see Chapter 4), Dahl and in some of the ideas of Giddens. The Marxist argument from those such as Alex Callinicos (2003) is that the modernday state might seem to take into consideration the interests of pressure groups and might appear to reach compromise between various interests in society. However, in reality, this so-called compromise operates within a framework where business interests are ultimately treated as a top priority and all other interests lack substantial power in the face of those who wield economic power over individual governments – namely, the owners of transnational corporations.

Does the state have relative autonomy?

Many contemporary Marxist-influenced thinkers have sought to reinterpret the ideas of Marx and Engels in the light of changes taking place in the world since their death (see Chapter 4). This has led to the rise of various neo-Marxisms in recent years. In particular, we are now offered two competing interpretations of what Marx really thought about the role of the state in a capitalist society.

- *The Traditional Marxist view* – In his early work – such as *The Communist Manifesto* (1848) – Marx suggests that the state is the 'committee' of the ruling class: in this view those who wield economic power through economic ownership hold ultimate power.
- *The neo-Marxist view* – In his later work – such as in *The Eighteenth Brumaire of Louis Bonaparte* (1852) – Marx can be reinterpreted as suggesting that on some occasions the state might be an independent political force from those who have economic ownership, operating in pursuit of the state's own interests.

  The basis of this second view – later expressed in the ideas of Louis Althusser (1971) and Antonio Gramsci (1971) – is the historical example of the French state of Louis Bonaparte circa 1850, originally discussed by Marx. In this situation the state acts independently of the owners of capital and manages the conflict between the workers and the owners. In managing this conflict, the state takes its own independent action, but action that ultimately helps those with economic power to destabilise protests made by the workers.

Taking this idea further, Louis Althusser (1971) argues that society is what he calls 'over-determined'. In this view, the Marxist notion that the economic base (ownership of the means of production) directly determines the superstructure (culture) of society is too simplistic. Instead, aspects of culture can have a degree of autonomy or independence from the economic rulers, and on occasions are not shaped by them. Thus the state can sometimes have relative autonomy from the ruling class. Ultimately, however, this is only a *degree of independence* – the state will (more often than not) side with and support the interests of the powerful economic owners.

Hegemony

Gramsci (1971) takes this alternative Marxist interpretation of the state further still, and develops the idea of *hegemony*. In Gramsci's view we can think of the state as being divided into two halves:

1. *civil society* – the legal connections of individuals within the territory of the state, based upon law, regulations and duties/responsibilities;
2. *political society* – the use of violence and control by the state as a mechanism of social order.

For Gramsci, civil society is the private world of society, and political society is the public realm of social life. Gramsci argues that these two halves of the state combine and that the continuation of ruling ideas is ensured through 'hegemony protected by the armour of coercion' (Gramsci, 1971, p. 263).

However, ruling class ideas are *not* directly fed to the masses through the existence of a *dominant ideology* that the state itself directly subscribes to and enforces. Instead, the state operates independently: regulating society and managing its own affairs separately from the ruling class. Yet, since the masses only see the fair and legal operations of the state directly, they come to see society as fair and they believe that the state fairly regulates between their interests and the opposite interests of the ruling class. In fact, since the state only has relative autonomy from the ruling class, the workers are 'tricked' into thinking that all is fair with society, yet they actively go along with state policies that ultimately lead to their further oppression and exploitation. This active consent with the state in workers' own eventual oppression is described as hegemony. Further still, if working-class consent eventually breaks down, and hegemony crumbles into organized protest, the state still has the legal right to use violence against the masses – so, even if they do protest, they will still end up being controlled.

Disorganized capitalism

For Scott Lash and John Urry (1987; 1994) the modern age can be best described as a period of globally disorganized capitalism. Individual nation states lack power in the face of the transnational nature of global capitalism:

these global capitalist businesses have shifted production to Third World nations and have created new markets globally to seek ever-increasing profit. They are not answerable to the laws that operate within the territories of individual nation states since, by its nature, global capitalism itself is not confined to one nation-state in particular. It has a transnational existence – it is super-national: over and above individual nations, beyond the scope of individual states to regulate its activities. There is much evidence to support this view, and also evidence that nation states can sometimes overrule trans-national businesses. For example, until fairly recently the Indian government prevented Coca-Cola from manufacturing or selling its products in that country. Now that it is permitted, Coca-Cola has been accused of over-extracting underground water for its bottling plant, causing irrigation problems for local farmers, and has been taken to court by at least one state for pollution offences. However, Lash and Urry would argue that, in the end, the state was not able to prevent the activities of the capitalist business.

The state and surveillance

The ideas of Michel Foucault (1991) – often referred to as poststructuralist – look at the role that the modern state performs in the act of surveillance of the population: both as a collective body and upon the individual body itself. Foucault begins his analysis by making a comparison between the operation of the prison and of the state in both public and private society – arguing, as many feminists have done (see Chapter 5) that the distinction between the private and the public is lessening.

In his book *Discipline and Punish* (1991), Foucault looks at the 'panopticon' – a particular type of prison invented by the Victorian Jeremy Bentham circa 1843.

Bentham designed the panopticon as a prison where the inmates could be under constant surveillance – at all times. The panopticon was designed with the prison cells around the outside of a circular building with their windows and doors facing towards the middle of the circular building which housed the prison guards. Thus, the guards could see everyone, but prisoners could only see the guards. Bentham designed his prison in this way so that the thought of surveillance was ever present in the minds of the prisoners. Even if no guards were actually watching, it was always *possible* that they might be – and as a result it reminded prisoners that there was *always* the possibility of being caught *if* they did anything wrong.

For Foucault the design of this type of building has parallels with the state's organization of its territory: surveillance, discipline and control are the major preoccupations of the state and its associated bodies, and this surveillance happens all the time, even in so-called private institutions. Just like the prisoners in Bentham's prison, in society there is always the chance that someone might be watching; always the chance that those watching the spaces we inhabit – schools, hospitals, work places, city centres – might decide to watch us.

Power and surveillance

As Foucault notes, 'the body is also involved in a political field; power relationships have an immediate hold on it; they invest it, mark it, train it, torture it, force it to carry out tasks, to perform ceremonies' (Foucault, 1991, p. 25). Foucault imagines power as a vast and complex web or net that encompasses the whole of society. It is not a thing to possess, although some groups can manipulate more power than others. Instead power is best thought of by Foucault as a network of relationships of surveillance upon individuals. As Sarup (1993) comments about Foucault's work, power can be seen to spread out across all the spaces and institutions that human bodies are organized into in society – 'its threads extend everywhere' (p. 74).

Foucault notes that this surveillance is exercised upon us by a vast array of specialists who claim expertise over a particular field of society – and these experts thus control how we come to think and speak about the area of social life in question. For example, doctors have power over definitions of heath and illness in society, and they have a legitimate state-sponsored right to perform surveillance over our bodies. Foucault sees the judges who exercise this surveillance as being everywhere at all times – again, just like the guards in the panopticon:

> The judges of normality are present everywhere. We are in the society of the teacher-judge, the doctor-judge, the educator-judge, the 'social worker'-judge; it is on them that the universal reign of the normative is based; and each individual, wherever he may find himself, subjects to it his body, his gestures, his behavior, his aptitudes, his achievements. (Foucault, 1991, p. 304)

Power and knowledge

Those who are able to take control over definitions of knowledge come to have more power than others and are able to perform surveillance upon the others: telling them what to do, how to do it and when to do it, in order to be considered to be normal. This means, for Foucault, that power and knowledge are two sides of the same coin.

> We should admit that power produces knowledge ... that power and knowledge directly imply one another; that there is no power relation without the correlative constitution of a field of knowledge, nor any knowledge that does not presuppose and constitute at the same time power relations. (Foucault, 1991, p. 27)

In other words, things are not powerful because they are true. Instead, they are true because they are powerful. This relationship Foucault terms 'power-knowledge' and he suggests that those who have the ability to define and determine what we think and say about areas of life over which they are expert get to control how we think and speak about ourselves. In other words, these groups (for example – doctors, lawyers and social workers) control the *discourses* (specialist ways of speaking) that we use to think about ourselves:

> power produces; it produces reality; it produces domains of objects and rituals of truth. (Foucault, 1991, p. 194)

> truth isn't outside power, or lacking in power ... truth isn't the reward of free spirits ... truth is a thing of this world: it is produced only by virtue of multiple forms of constraint ... each society has its regime of truth, its 'general politics' of truth: that is, the types of discourse which it accepts and makes function as true. (Foucault, 1984, pp. 72–3)

> 'Truth' is linked in circular relation with systems of power which produce and sustain it, and to effects of power which it induces and which extend it. (Foucault, 1984, p. 74)

Those who get to define this truth are very powerful indeed. The state can be seen as both a regulating mechanism by which these powerful claims of truth are legitimated in society and as the arm of surveillance that seeks out those who are not living their lives according to the normal rules of behaviour. The state then punishes them for not accepting what they should be doing and when.

Refer back to Exercise 8.9 – now summarize the key points of the theories that argue (in contrast) that the state is controlling and based on exploitation. Use the following names if you want to:

Marx and Engels
Callincos
Gramsci
Althusser
Lash and Urry
Foucault

You can use the notes from these two exercises, 8.9 and 8.10, to write a short explanation of the differences in the theoretical approaches to the role of the state in society.

The overloaded state?

Increasingly, among both New Right and New Left commentators, we are seeing claims of the coming crisis of the state – in particular the welfare state. These claims of crisis or of an overload of state spending have also been echoed in the media and by politicians – creating at times a *moral panic* surrounding the future of welfare provision in the UK. We have seen the increasing popularity in the last quarter of the twentieth century of the view that something will need to be done to stop state spending – especially on those who might not deserve it – before we reach a situation where the state cannot deliver its welfare promises.

Brittan (1975), who predicted the rise of this state crisis over 25 years ago, suggests that the modern state is in a very difficult financial and political position. In order to receive popular public support governments promise more and more, but in doing so they can deliver less and less. Thus their legitimacy might fall even further in the eyes of the public, especially when their welfare needs are not catered for.

The New Right

The New Right has attempted to overcome the problem of legitimacy in the eyes of the public by making popular its ideological view that deviant groups in society are themselves responsible for draining the resources of the state. In particular these groups include the unemployed (the underclass), criminal subcultures, 'social security scroungers', black migrants, the elderly, dependent and single-parent families – especially single *mothers* and their 'absent father'.

New Right thinking on the nature of the state (see Chapter 6) can be summarized as follows:

- A strong state is essential – especially to protect normal society from rising levels of crime and delinquency (caused, in their view, by the lack of authority in society, especially because of the absence of strong father figures in some families).
- The state cannot afford to provide benefits for those not willing to seek work: the unemployed are seen to be lazy and if benefits are stopped they might be encouraged to seek employment.
- The welfare state is described as a nanny state – it encourages dependency and stops people from taking autonomy over their own lives.

The idea that the state is overloaded is still present in much political, public and media debate today and to a certain extent is reflected in the Third Way policies of the New Left and in particular of the 'New' Labour Party in the UK (see Chapter 6).

Legitimacy and the state

Jurgen Habermas (1988) describes the problems facing the modern day state as problems of legitimacy or, as a legitimation crisis. He argues that periodically the state in capitalist societies suffers from a lack of legitimacy. The masses (the subjects of the state) begin to question the ability of the state to deliver the goods needed for a comfortable life and to question those in positions of power. Habermas suggests that the popularity and rise of the New Right's almost anti-state theories in Western Europe and in the USA reflect this legitimation crisis. This ideology is a response to problems of increased illegitimacy of those who rule, who are trying to protect their own positions and who in turn scapegoat minority groups for the perceived problems of overloading.

CONCLUSION

An overwhelming theme of many sociological theories of the state is their focus upon the nation state's use of violence within its own territory and its sovereignty to do so. However, with the increasingly complex and globalized world that we live in, the sovereignty of nation states is increasingly called into question. Chapter 8 has looked at how the state attempts to regulate the interests and conflicts of groups within society and Chapter 9 looks at the implications of the process of globalization for definitions of the sate and of nationality in the modern age.

Exercise 8.11

Explain the meaning of the phrase 'the overloaded state'. Do you agree with this idea – if not why not?

Examination exercise

For this activity, there will be no exam question for you to answer. Your task is to do the opposite and work out your own examination questions for this area of political sociology. You must come up with four questions in total. However, these will be pairs of questions, with each pair coming from the same sub-area of the topic. In effect, then, you will have to devise two different questions on the same area. This will get you thinking about how different questions might be framed about a common topic. In addition, think about the stem or command words (assess, etc.) that you can use when constructing your questions. You can introduce variation through using different command words in your questions.

To assist you in doing this exercise, we offer two questions that look at definitions of the state. Our first is a shorter-mark question. Ask yourself 'What makes it so?'.

'Define what sociologists mean by "the state".'

The second would demand a longer response and is framed in a very different way.

'How sociologists define the state determines the questions that they ask about its activities.' To what extent do you agree with this statement?

Important concepts

- the nation state • the 'iron law of oligarchy' • the 'iron cage of bureaucracy' • sovereignty • citizenship • globalization
- the democratization of everyday life • life-politics and the 'pure relationship' • damaged solidarities • generative politics
- hegemony • power-knowledge • the overloaded state

Summary points

- Giddens suggests that a sociological analysis of the state is vital, as the state is the mechanism through which decisions made by leaders are legitimized and carried out within specific geographic boundaries.
- Dunleavy and O'Leary identify five essential features of the modern state:
  - it is a separate institution from others in society;
  - it is the supreme power within its territory;
  - it has control over the population within its territory;
  - those who work within the institutions of the state are recruited in a fair and bureaucratic fashion;
  - it has the right to demand money from those in its territory in the form of taxation.
- Michels criticizes the state by describing the 'iron law of oligarchy'.
- Weber refers to the 'iron cage of bureaucracy'; the ultimate goal of the state becomes to keep itself existing and unelected officials end up running the state in the interests of the state.
- The growth of nation-states across the globe raises two other features of the modern world: *sovereignty* and *citizenship*.
- Bauman suggests that the duties citizens have within a nation-state makes them belong to the nation-state in question. This means that nation-states operate a considerable amount of *social control*.
- With the onset of *globalization*, issues of both sovereignty and citizenship have become more complex.
- Functionalist and pluralist theories have tended to see the state as a force for protection and fairness, whereas more radical theories such as Marxism and neo-Marxism see it as a force for oppression and control.
- Giddens suggests that the dialogue between the general population, and those who lead and administer the state, is becoming more open ('dialogic democracy').
  - Modern-day politics is a form of 'life-politics'; it is about making personal decisions and choosing one's own actions.
  - Habermas suggests that freedom and fairness in society will only develop once we have a pure form of communication not based upon selfish needs and sectional interests.
  - In this new age of dialogue and emotional democracy, the state must help to repair previously damaged solidarities and to develop generative politics.
  - The classic or orthodox Marxist interpretation of the nature of the state is to see it as the puppet of the ruling class. Althusser argues that the Marxist notion that the ownership of the means of production directly determines the superstructure of *society* is too simplistic; the state can sometimes have relative autonomy from the ruling class.

○   Gramsci argues that we can think of the state as being divided into *civil society* and *political society*. The state only has relative autonomy from the ruling class, the workers are tricked into thinking that all is fair with society, yet they actively go along with state policies that ultimately lead to their further oppression and exploitation. This is described as hegemony.

- Foucault – often referred to as *post-structuralist* – argues that surveillance is exercised upon us by specialists who claim expertise over a particular field of society. Things are not powerful because they are true. Instead, they are true because they are powerful. Increasingly, both *New Right* and *New Left* commentators talk about a coming crisis of the state.

Critical thinking

1. What is meant by a 'nation state'?
2. Is the state a good or a bad thing?
3. How important is state sovereignty in the world today?
4. What is meant by the term 'hegemony'?

Chapter 9

Globalization, Nationalism and Revolution

By the end of this chapter you should:

- be able to define the terms 'nationalism' and 'globalization'
- understand sociological theories of nationalism and globalization
- be able to evaluate sociological theories of nationalism and globalization
- understand why, according to sociological theories, some societies experience revolution and protest
- understand sociological accounts of terrorism and warfare in the modern age

INTRODUCTION

For many sociologists, a key feature of the rise of a modern society is the relatively rapid spread of nation states across the globe – a movement which has developed over the past 200 years. Along with the creation of nation states we see the rise of the ideology of nationalism – the political view that belonging to a particular nation state creates identity. Nation states were seen to have sovereignty over their own particular territories as separate elites able to exercise control and create order.

With the rise of globalization, the position of nation states is becoming less clear. What does nationality mean in a globalized world? What sovereignty is left for individual nations given the interconnectedness of world economy, travel, trade, culture and political decision-making? Yet despite the increased global nature of politics and power, in many nation-states we see a return to nationality (often of a fundamentalist nature) in an attempt to protect the sovereignty and identity of the nation in the face of change. There has also been the rise of anti-capitalist riots across a number of nation states, with protesters claiming to have an anti-globalization agenda.

It is difficult to predict the direction of global politics in a time of such change.

UNDERSTANDING NATIONALISM

In his book *Keywords* – a historical review of the origins of words and concepts important to modern culture – Raymond Williams (1976) suggests that the word 'nation' has been in use in the common English language since the end of the thirteenth century, although the term was originally associated with race rather than its modern day political use. The modern use of 'national' originates from the start of the seventeenth century, and was initially used to refer to the whole of a population of a society or country. Subsequently, from the late seventeenth to the late eighteenth centuries 'national' developed its political sense still used today: it referred to a population within a specific territory who are the *subjects* of those who rule the territory.

The concept 'nationalist' appeared in the late eighteenth century and the most recent addition has been 'nationalism', as late as the middle to end of the nineteenth century.

Max Weber (1948) raises some interesting problems with definitions of 'the nation'. In particular he argues that there are competing and ambiguous definitions of this term, which is interesting, given that in common-sense thought and language most people would probably feel they know this term well.

Weber identifies a number of problems when thinking about what a nation is:

1. 'The nation' is not strictly speaking the same as 'the people of a state' – although that is how it is popularly used. This is because within many modern states we see smaller groups of people who claim that their state is independent of the state they are controlled by (Basque separatists in Northern Spain, for example). This is often the result of political change in the past where one state annexes a smaller country, or a stronger military force swallows smaller countries on its borders through military expansion. In these cases the powerful leaders might declare themselves a nation but a significant proportion of the population would disagree.

2. Nations do not necessarily have a shared common language that produces a shared identity: some language groups think of themselves as belonging to the wider nation while others do not. Equally, some people might speak a language associated with another nation as a first language, yet still feel they belong as a legal citizen to the nation they live within.
3. Often nations are not based upon a unified religious belief or even on similar racial or ethnic groups.

Ultimately, the term nation is used to refer to a solidarity of people within a given territory, although, as Weber himself notes, the people in question might themselves disagree that they do share such a solidarity.

Weber concludes that the term nation is about values more than it is an objective fact that can be easily measured. What you consider a nation to be in general – and in particular what you might consider your own nation to be – depends on what values you have. Thus, although Weber himself did not use the term, we can say that the idea of the nation is highly ideological. The term means a number of things depending on the beliefs and characteristics of those who use it. The only definition that Weber himself feels we can offer is: 'A nation is a community of sentiment which would adequately manifest itself in a state of its own; hence, a nation is a community which normally tends to produce a state of its own' (Weber, 1948, cited in Hutchinson and Smith, 1994, p. 25).

Exercise 9.1

One of the main elements of this chapter is a discussion of what we mean by a 'nation' and the concept of 'nationalism'. What do you think a nation is? What do you think people might have in common if they were to have a 'national identity'? Write a list of factors that could be identified as influencing national identity.

Whereas Weber looks at the role played by shared communal feelings – which in turn lead to the creation of a political body to manage the collective affairs of this community – an alternative definition is offered by Anthony Giddens (1985). Giddens uses the phrase 'bordered power-containers' to describe nations. This can be seen as both a political and geographical term. In particular, it places emphasis upon the territory (the 'place' or 'space' in question) that has borders, and the fact that within this space there is a body that has the legal right to exercise control.

The historical origins of the term 'nationalism'

John Hutchinson and Anthony D. Smith (1994) chart the historical origins of the ideology of 'nationalism'. Nationalism is an idea that has been one of the most powerful in the modern world. It has resulted in many wars, revolutions, independence movements and in acts of terrorism. These occur in the name of liberation from a nation, or in protecting a nation from others who wish to change it in some way.

Hutchinson and Smith (1994) describe key factors that have shaped what we call nationalism:

▪ Nationalism first become popular as a motivation behind political action in North America and Western Europe in the late eighteenth century.
▪ In particular, Hutchinson and Smith single out the following key historical dates:

1. The 1775 partition of Poland;
2. The 1776 American Declaration of Independence;
3. The first and second phases of the French Revolution – 1789 and 1792.

▪ The ideology of nationalism was built in some senses upon millennial Christian movements that sought to achieve freedom and salvation from oppressive rulers.
▪ Nationalism was also perpetuated through the creation of the printing press and newspapers.
▪ Early nationalist ideas drew on some understanding of ancient Greek philosophy – in particular the idea of the city state in Athens.
▪ The growth of free towns as trading centres spread the ideas of self-rule and individualism.

Claims of nationalism as a driving force behind warfare – the defence of the nation and of national identity – became a popular and shared sentiment that motivated solidarity among soldiers in national armies. This can be traced back to the battle of Valmy in 1792, in which the French Armies of the North and Centre stopped the advance towards Paris of a Prussian army. This battle is seen as one of the most significant battles of the French Revolutionary Wars, as it allowed the survival of France's new armies and hence of the Revolution itself.

Nationalism and moderntiy

Ernest Gellner (1983) argues that it is not that nations create feelings of nationalism, but rather, that the ideology of nationalism – of wanting a unified identity within a territory – creates the nations themselves. By this he means that before the values of nationalism, the idea of the nation – in terms of how we think about it today – was impossible. Gellner sees the rise of the ideas of nationalism to be a product of the rise of modernity – the industrial age brought with it the need to manage the process of industrialization through a common cultural outlook – called a national identity.

Gellner goes further and suggests that if taken at first glance nationalism is not what it actually seems: it claims to be a movement towards self-rule and self-identity, but it is actually about the imposition of an elite culture onto the masses in order to create an artificial solidarity that gives all those within this culture a common direction.

> Nationalism is not the awakening of an old, latent, dormant force, though that it how it does indeed present itself. It is in reality the consequence of a new form of social organisation, based upon deeply internalised, education-dependent high cultures, each protected by its own separate state. It uses some of the pre-existing cultures, generally transforming them in the process, but it cannot possibly use them all. (Gellner, 1983, cited in Hutchinson and Smith, 1994, p. 63)

Gellner takes from Durkheim the idea that religion – in Durkheim's terms 'the sacred' – is needed for social solidarity: it is an opportunity for society to 'worship itself' since sacred symbols are often used by societies as sources of identity. Gellner suggests that nationalism is a movement that replaced religion at the time of the transition from an agricultural economy, based upon localized centres of trade and power, to the conditions necessary for industrialization to take place. This is why nationalism first developed in Western Europe and North America. It is a pre-condition for industrialization and it serves to unite a population ready for the great changes that industrialization brings. It creates a homogeneous (shared) culture often through the invention of beliefs and values that simply serve as symbols of an imagined identity.

Using Gellner's ideas about nationalism, think of an example of a state that has used the concept of nationalism to create a sense of identity and unity? Can you identify any core beliefs and values that were used to create a sense of 'belonging'?

Anderson (1991) echoes the ideas of Gellner and of Hutchinson and Smith – that nationalism is based upon the need to create a sense of stability and order in society through the creation of artificial and often imagined traditions. The rise of the mass production of printing is seen as essential to nationalism since it provides an effective way to develop a population able to share values through a mass education system. Gellner (1964) also suggests that nationalism is not really about self-rule but more about self-education since it is through mass participation in education that collectivity can be reinforced. Nationalism might be based upon invented traditions, and might be based upon arbitrary symbols, but for Gellner, it is nonetheless real in its consequences and was really needed – the need for homogeneity was vital and so nationalism responded to this need.

> It is nationalism which engenders nations, and not the other way round. Admittedly, nationalism uses the pre-existing, historically inherited proliferation of cultures or cultural wealth, though it uses them very selectively, and it most often transforms them radically. Dead languages can be revived, traditions invented, quite fictitious pristine purities restored . . . the cultural shreds and patches used by nationalism are often arbitrary historical inventions. Any old shred and patch would have served as well. (Gellner, 1983, cited in Hutchinson and Smith, 1994, p. 64)

Exercise 9.3

For this exercise you will need to work in groups, with a large sheet of paper and pens for each group. Each group should design a poster presentation, outlining the key elements of nation, nationalism, national identity and so on. The form your poster takes is up to you, but it should be clear, concise and convey your understanding of these central concepts. Think of using words, images and symbols to make your poster as clear and meaningful as possible.

'Natural' nationalism

In contrast to the ideas of Gellner, Anderson and Hutchinson and Smith, Edward Shils (1957) argues that nationalism is a feature of all human societies and it is natural for it to be so. He believed that the force or motivation towards nationalism is in every human collective grouping, lying dormant, ready to be stimulated. This sort of claim seems to be part of the imagined traditions that Gellner argues that nationalism is based upon: if the ideology of nationalism can make it seem that the movement towards nationalism is a natural and inevitable one, it makes it seem more legitimate. Thus, it could be argued that Shils has fallen for the very ideology that nationalism uses to make itself seem real.

A position that is between Gellner and Shils has been adopted by Anthony Smith (1986). He suggests (like Gellner) that nations are a recent phenomenon and as such are not natural, since many do not have within them the sort of collective shared identity that we imagine them to have. However, he also suggests (unlike Gellner) that the pre-conditions for nations existed before the idea of nationalism, since many nations today have their origins in ethnic communities that existed long before industrialization. Smith argues that this is particularly true if we look at the symbols and imagery used by nations to establish their identity, as these often refer back to traditional ethnic ties.

Exercise 9.4

Summarize the main points in the interpretations of the origins of nationalism. Note the ideas of Anderson, Gellner and Smith, and then compare these to the ideas of Shils.

Gellner is critical of this view, arguing that nations use previous traditions in an ad hoc, almost cynical fashion. He argues that they use past tradition (and reinvent and change traditions) in an arbitrary fashion; just because some symbols are used to create collectivity, there is not necessarily a logic behind which ones get chosen.

Exercise 9.5

Draw together some examples of ethnic symbols that are elements of a nation's identity. For example, you may consider the flags or national anthems of particular states. Are there other national symbols – can you find out about the origin of these? What do they mean and are they symbolic of the whole nation?

Nationalism and citizenship

Marxist historian Eric Hobsbawm (1992) suggests a different interpretation to Gellner of the source of nationalism. For Hobsbawm, nations are created by feelings of nationalism (and not the other way around) – a point Gellner would agree with – however, in this view nations are the consequence of the setting up of states, rather than the moving force behind the desire to set up a state in the first place. What this means is that nationalism is the legitimation used by those who set up states to make people (and perhaps other outside rulers) see their states as legitimate: as genuine and correct. In this view, it is citizenship – belonging to a state – that is the identity that nationalism is really based upon.

Hobsbawm suggests that the rise of ideas of citizenship came about in modernity. This was, in part, due to the emphasis in the French Revolution of the common rights of all French citizens, and the removal of the French royal family from its position of privilege. The idea was that all French citizens under the new French state had common rights, obligations and duties and that living under the same state created a common identity for all alike – the identity of belonging to the French state – being a citizen.

However, with the rise of mass warfare and the need to encourage a population to fight for the state they belonged to, Hobsbawm argues that ideas of national identity based upon citizenship changed to ideas based upon feelings of patriotism. This is the belief that one identifies with others from the same nation, on the basis of being from the same nation: of having a common heritage. This basis of identity is a more secure and lasting symbol that can be used to encourage a population to fight for the identity of the nation – much more powerful than asking people to go to war to help to continue the state they live under.

The role of communications in nation creation

Anthony Giddens (1993) – like Gellner and Hobsbawm – points to the important role played by printing technology in the original creation of the idea of nationalism. Giddens argues that much is written today about the growth of an 'information society – the fact that:

1. communication over vast distances can take place almost instantly;
2. information itself is a valuable commodity – and one that can be the basis for power;
3. electronic communication such as television can provide the basis for shared cultural symbols.

However, for Giddens, nations have always been, in a sense, information societies since the very creation of the idea of nations and the spirit of nationalism was based upon the widespread ability for state rulers to distribute rules, monitor and classify subjects and effectively manipulate economics. All of these activities essential to a nation state require paper, literacy, and printing.

> It would be difficult to overestimate the generalised impact of printing in the shaping of modernity. Printing is the first major step in the mechanisation of communication and, in making documents and texts widely available...So far as the state is concerned, the most important consequence of the easy and cheap availability of printed materials was an enlargement of the sphere of the 'political'...What printing made possible, and what it was increasingly used for...was a very profound furtherance of the surveillance operations of the state. (Giddens, 1993, p. 264)

National identity

Zygmunt Bauman (1990) suggests that feelings of nationalism (of having a national identity) are very powerful and that nationalism is ultimately rational – living as a citizen with the security and structure that it creates is preferable to the alternatives. For example, it makes sense to seek protection and it makes sense that, if we follow our duties, the state will protect our rights. For Bauman, a sense of national identity is about trust and fate. It is about obeying a greater good, yet the greater good is the very fact that everybody obeys: it is the worship of obedience itself. This is the real unifying symbol that national identity is based upon.

Bauman, and others, refer to nationality as an 'imagined community'.

Imagined communities

An 'imagined community' is actually a real entity – despite the fact that its reality lies in the minds and imaginations of those who share it. It is real in the sense that it comes to be seen as real; its symbols come to mean something to those who subscribe to it. It comes to be used by people in a meaningful way; thus, we can talk of being British or of an English way of life and understand what is meant by this, even though its reality is a perceived and imagined one.

As Bauman says:

A nation is from start to finish an imagined community; it exists as an entity in so far as its members mentally and emotionally 'identify themselves' with a collective body most of whose other members they will never confront face to face. The nation becomes a mental reality as it is imagined as such. (Bauman, 1990, p. 171)

This imagined community provides those who treat its symbols as real with a sense of belonging to a greater, wider whole. It provides identity since it says that we are part of 'us' and that equally, we are not 'them' – they are different from us in some way. Thus, this imagined community comes to tell us who we are and who we are not.

This idea is developed by Anderson, who suggests that the reality of nations – besides their territories and populations – is the fact that they can be imagined as collectives by those who feel they are part of the collective itself. They are based upon the imagination of relationships with others, which itself becomes a true relationship. This is true for all nations purely in the sense that they are so large, feelings of collectivity must be imagined: we cannot have a relationship with everyone.

A key set of symbols used by nationalist ideologies to create this imagined community is what Bauman refers to as a 'myth of origin'. What he means by this is that nations seek to make both the feelings of nationalism and their own bordered territory seem to those in the imagined community as having a natural existence: of being firmly rooted in past traditions and in the nature of humanity itself. In England, for example, the story of King Arthur and the

Knights of the Round Table describes the birth of a new rational age and a united land, based on moral values of decency and tolerance. Another example of an English myth of origin is based on an actual historical character, Sir Francis Drake. He is considered as a national hero who circumnavigated the globe in the interests of his country and destroyed the Spanish Armada, saving the nation from invasion. Drake's loyalty and bravery are portrayed as ushering in a golden Elizabethan age. Both King Arthur and Sir Francis Drake reinforce the concept of England as a nation that has existed for a very long time, and also they represent cultural values which are presented as natural or God-given. Bauman suggests that nations command obedience by making it seem natural that populations would wish to belong to their nation.

[The demands made by nation-states] ... are most persuasive if the nation is conceived of as the fate rather than a choice; as a 'fact' so firmly established in the past that no human power may change it now; a 'reality' which can be tinkered with only at the tinker's peril. Nationalisms try on the whole to achieve just this. The myth of origin is their major instrument. (Bauman, 1990, p. 172)

What this myth suggests is that, even if originally a cultural creation, in the course of its history the nation has become a truly 'natural' phenomenon, something beyond human control. The present members of the nation – so the myth says – are tied together by their common past. The national spirit is their shared and exclusive property. (Bauman, 1990, p. 173)

Exercise 9.6

Look at a myth of origin (for example, from Africa, Australia or India). Does this myth do what Bauman argues? If so, how? What elements of the myth unite the population that tell or retell the myth?

Nationalism and language diversity

Benedict Anderson (1991) suggests that nationalism and national identity – the 'imagined community' – was a response, historically, to the decline of

Catholicism in Western Europe and in particular with the decline of Latin as a common or universal language. Anderson suggests that language is a key element in the establishment of a community. It creates a strong basis for commonality: the sharing of meaning, the common use of symbols and the ability to pass down shared myths and stories. However, with the decline of the use of Latin as a universal language, and the moving away from Catholicism in Europe, a new basis of identity and order needed to be created. However, as pointed out by Giddens and Gellner, the rise of printing technology in modernity, enabled shared languages to be distributed, and as a result a new basis for identity was able to be created around languages and the territories in which common languages and dialects were used. Thus, nationality came to be associated with an imagined community of fellow language speakers that became the basis for collective identity.

New nations and nation states are still being created around the world as the empires of the nineteenth and twentieth centuries are dismantled. The collapse of the Soviet Union, for example, led to a dramatic increase in the number of independent nation states. However, there is an argument that the age of the nation state has been brought to an end by the rise of globalization. Kenichi Ohmae (1995) argues that, as a result of globalization, national borders and national identity are becoming less important. In the face of large, transnational corporations, nations themselves have less economic power and people increasingly identify with local or regional identities. The next section examines the phenomenon of globalization.

UNDERSTANDING GLOBALIZATION

Jan Aart Scholte (2000) suggests that the term globalization – one of the buzz words of contemporary politics, culture and sociological thinking – is little understood, despite its rapid rise to popularity as a description of the contemporary world:

> If asked to specify what they understand by 'globalisation', most people reply with considerable vagueness, inconsistency and confusion. Moreover, much discussion of globalisation is steeped in oversimplification, exaggeration and wishful thinking. In spite of a deluge of publications on the subject, our analysis of globalisation tend to remain conceptually inexact, empirically thin, historically and culturally illiterate, normatively shallow

and politically naive. Although globalisation is widely assumed to be crucially important, we generally have scant idea what, more precisely, it entails. (Aart Scholte, 2000, p. 1)

Aart Scholte (2000) cites a comment made by Renato Ruggiero, first Director General of the World Trade Organization, who describes globalization as a process in the contemporary world that 'overwhelms all others'. Equally, media magnate Ted Turner said, in 1999, that 'globalization is in fast forward, and the world's ability to understand and react to it is in slow motion' (UNDP, 1999).

Aart Scholte offers five possible definitions of the term globalization to be found within the existing sociological literature:

1. Globalization can be understood as a process of *internationalization*: the rapid spread of cross-border relations between nation states; the operation of politics on an international level.
2. A second definition is that of *liberalization*: the process whereby restrictions on movement between countries is reduced and as different societies are opened up to each other, the spread of open and tolerant dialogue between cultures is encouraged.
3. Another definition might be that of a process of *universalization*: in other words, the spread of common objects, values and experiences to peoples separated from each other by space.
4. Fourthly, globalization might be seen as a process of *Westernization* or of *modernization*: many commentators have noted that being global sometimes means the ideas of the West – and in particular of capitalism – being adopted by other parts of the globe.
5. Finally, globalization might be seen as *deterritoriality* or of *supra-territoriality*: in other words, a change in relationships of space and time across the globe – the reducing of time, the increasing nearness and closeness of previously distant spaces.

This fifth point – that globalization is a reduction in global relationships of time and space – is the view held by Aart Scholte. He sees globalization as: 'A process which embodies a transformation in the spatial organisation of social relations and transactions' (Aart Scholte, 2000, p. 16).

Malcolm Waters (1995) says that although the term 'global' dates back over 400 years, the modern usages of words like globalization, globalize and globalizing did not occur until around 1960. At this time there was something new about the word and the process. Clearly international connections have existed since the beginnings of human histories, although strictly speaking these connections cannot actually be 'inter-*national*' until *nations* themselves were established over the past 200 years. However, globalization is seen to be very modern; for some it is postmodern. It is a product of late twentieth century–early twenty-first century living.

Waters defines globalization as: 'A social process in which the constraints of geography on social and cultural arrangements recede and in which people become increasingly aware that they are receding' (Waters, 1995, p. 3).

TYPES OF GLOBALIZING PROCESSES

We can identify a number of types of globalization, or rather, a number of different ways in which time and space – the distance between nations – has been reduced and universalized in recent years:

- *Economic globalization* – where finance and the management of finance and trade becomes the interrelated concern of global governments: money flows electronically through the stock exchanges of the wealthy nations of the globe, the state of the economy of one affecting the economy of another. A second aspect of economic globalization is the rise of a global capitalism whereby trade, markets and workforces become global and transnational companies exist beyond individual nation states.
- *Cultural globalization* – beliefs, values and cultural products are now distributed across the globe. For example, we can watch American cable TV or Indian Bollywood films in the UK. Different religions can also be imported across the globe. These processes are due to widespread migration patterns across the globe and the global expansion in electronic communication.
- *Political globalization* – governments from separate nation states are now connected through trade organizations, political allegiances and through international laws.
- *Environmental globalization* – the awareness of the interconnectedness of the environment between different nations, and the global attempts by collections of some nation states to use international law to protect the environment from damage.

Exercise 9.7

List examples of each of the types of globalization that Aart Scholte outlines. Are any of these forms of globalization more obvious than others, and if so how?

Economic globalization	Cultural globalization	Political globalization	Environmental globalization

In essence, the world seems a smaller place, and we are more aware of this than ever before. Globalization can be seen in the following features of what is now considered to be everyday life:

1. the internet;
2. cable TV;
3. the widespread availability of 'foreign foods' as a 'normal' part of the diet of ordinary people;
4. international travel – for both business and tourism;
5. telecommunications across the globe – in particular the development of a global telephone system;
6. the availability of clothes and dress styles from other parts of the globe;
7. the spread of branded products made by large corporations across the globe, such as Coca-Cola and Sony.

A runaway world?

There is a growing sense that globalization is of great importance to society and to the analysis of society by sociologists. There is also a sense that globalization is a new and dramatic development across the globe. In the sociological literature some theorists imply that globalization has run away from us: changes on a global scale and of global significance are happening all too quickly. For others, however, it is representative of the now and the new, and it is the start of a new future for politics and culture.

Anthony Giddens, in his series of 1999 *Reith Lectures* for the BBC entitled 'A Runaway World', describes globalization as a highly complex set of changes; a number of different movements pushing and pulling often in quite different directions across the global stage where issues of identity, politics, power and security are now played out. For example, he notes that globalization involves the following related and connected processes:

1. The globalization of 'in-here' as well as 'out-there': in other words, globalization involves a sense in the minds of people that things have changed, that identity is now different, that the world is a smaller place.
2. The autonomy of the local (and even national) is being eroded, and the international stage is more important – decision-making and therefore power is now a global act.
3. However, globalization is also about 'pushing downwards' – making the local seek more interdependence in the light of changes to its autonomy that it might perceive globalization to have.
4. The process of globalization is contradictory as it involves both the rejection and removal of traditions – it is post-traditional, but also the revival of local culture and traditions, localization, is often a response to globalization.
5. Giddens also describes the process of globalization as 'squeezing sideways': it creates new zones or areas of culture and power within nations – for example, the rise of global communications has made the area known as Silicon Valley important in America since this is where computer chips are made – this local zone has become very powerful globally because of its importance to global communications.

We can suggest that the process of globalization is experienced across the world in a highly contradictory fashion:

- it creates security and anxiety;
- it protects and it creates risks;
- it creates opportunity and it takes away autonomy;
- it encourages redistribution and it furthers inequality.

For example, as Giddens notes, 'Globalisation, of course, isn't developing in an even-handed way, and is by no means wholly benign in its consequences. To many living outside Europe and North America, it looks uncomfortably like Westernisation – or, perhaps, Americanisation' (Giddens, 1999, p. 15).

Giddens suggests that globalization provides new autonomy – for the local and the individual – since it offers new models for action with more choices and a global range of identities to choose from. However, at the same time, it offers insecurity and risk. Power might be taken away from the local and put in the hands of others such as large corporations and associations of international politicians. The risks of globalization also include the loss of traditions that some might feel are important. Environmental damage and warfare may also be a consequence of a globalized world. Develop your understanding of the pros and cons of globalization by carrying out Exercise 9.8.

Exercise 9.8

Using the internet, summarize the arguments that suggest that globalization is a positive force and those that suggest its effects are negative.

Unequal localization?

Zygmunt Bauman (1998) like Giddens sees the process of globalization as a 'time/space compression': the reduction in global distances and relationships. However, Bauman is critical of the effects of globalization at a local level.

Bauman suggests that the process of globalization for some leads to localization for others. In an age when global means having power (the ability to travel, purchase, sell and consume global products and ideas), those who lack the finance to become global, find themselves pushed more and more towards their local community, cut off from the increasingly global-looking world. In an age when being global matters, being localized is a form of inequality, a position of insecurity.

> Globalisation divides as much as it unites... Alongside the emerging planetary dimensions of business, finance, trade and information flow, a 'localising', space-fixing process is set in motion. Between them, the two closely interconnected processes sharply differentiate the existential conditions of whole populations and of various segments of each one of the populations. What appears as globalisation for some means localisation for others;

signaling a new freedom for some, upon many others it descends as an uninvited and cruel fate. (Bauman, 1998, p. 2)

All of us are, willy-nilly, by design or by default, on the move. We are on the move even if, physically, we stay put: immobility is not a realistic option in a world of permanent change. And yet the effects of that new condition are radically unequal. Some of us become fully and truly 'global'; some are fixed in their 'locality' – a predicament neither pleasurable nor endurable in the world in which in the 'globals' set the tone and compose the rules of the life-game. Being local in a globalised world is a sign of social deprivation and degradation. (Bauman, 1998, p. 2)

Globalization and the risk society

For Beck *et al.* (1994) the effect of globalization is to both create a *post-traditional social order* and to create a *risk society*. In other words, globalization might strip away traditions by exposing more global choices for lifestyle, yet at the same time it exposes us to more global risks, and to a heightened awareness of these risks, which leads to increased insecurity and anxiety in society.

Giddens (1994) suggests that the awareness of risks in society leads to a situation of *manufactured uncertainty*. By this, he means that we are becoming more and more aware that life involves risks, and that these risks have been created by the actions of people and governments – recession, nuclear power, skin cancer due to CFC gases, etc.

It is not the case that life is more risky than before, but rather that we are now aware of the involvement of humanity in creating these risks. The awareness of these global risks leads to what Giddens and Beck describe as a period of reflexive modernity. This age is characterized by the increased reflexivity of individuals themselves: the ability for people to think about society, their position in society and who they wish to be. This risk society thus encourages insecurity, but at the same time it opens up possibilities – it allows people to think about the globalized world they now live in, and to choose how they wish to act in this world.

Inequality and global risks

The inequality and powerlessness of the local, is an idea developed further by Ulrich Beck (1999). He suggests that we are now living in what he calls a world risk society, yet these risks are worse for some rather than others. In particular, in this global age, he suggests that 'pollution follows the poor'. While the West expands, and pursues even more wealth, the poor become even worse off: Western culture is imposed, debt is encouraged and health risks increase.

Beck cites the following statistics to show how globalization can mean increased risk (see Exercise 9.9):

- more than 2,400 million people live without sanitation;
- 1,200 million have no safe drinking water;
- similar numbers to the above have inadequate housing, health and education;
- more than 1,500 million are undernourished.

(A)

Exercise 9.9

Find examples in recent news coverage of how globalization creates risk. You can use these examples in your written work, as they will illustrate your understanding and analysis of the points you are making. There are many good examples in Africa and Latin America, as well as in some other parts of the world. Use the Internet/ newspapers and CD Rom, or you can investigate one particular state and look at the issues that Beck raises in the bullet points above, in relation to that state.

Beck argues that although all risks have been intensified – such is the global, interconnected nature of the ecological system – some are able to limit the risk, whereas others are in a more unequal situation – often dependent upon others for help and aid.

Beck suggests that this global risk society means that security is provided for some at the expense of others. These global risks include pollution, financial collapse and even the political destabilization of governments if they mismanage these risks. At their most extreme they might threaten the financial stability of once stable economic systems, or might cause whole populations to live in near-death situations.

Beck notes six key features of the global risk society:

1. Societies operate economic and political policies on the basis of two logics of distribution: the distribution of goods and the avoidance of the distribution of harms.

2. It makes no sense for governments to try and calculate the risks before they happen. In some cases – such as millions unemployed; these are things seen as separate from the decision-making of the individual nations and are left to a global market economy – there is no compensation for global recession.

3. Global risks, when they do strike, have a social explosiveness about their impact: they lead to rapid and profound political, social and cultural changes.

4. After the experience of global risks the institutions within nation states might collapse.

5. The effect of potential risks is discussed by politicians in terms of responsibility – and this becomes a worldwide political concern.

6. Due to the threat of risk, new political options are sought by governments – new forms of political participation and new forms of financial security, in the light of global insecurity.

These global risks are sometimes avoided by the wealthier societies, yet at other times global risks suddenly surprise the wealthier across the globe, causing problems in trade, markets, manufacturing and in finance. These risks thus give rise to a climate of global insecurity, but an insecurity that is often ignored by the wealthy until it is too late. The collapse of the housing market in the USA in late 2007, caused by an over-eagerness to provide mortgage loans to house-buyers who could not really afford them, for example, led to financial problems in banks and national economies all around the world.

New global politics?

The political implication of global risks is the rise of *a new global politics* that seeks to manage the insecurity that global risks cause. This earth politics seeks to find new ways to be political in the global age; it seeks new ways to manage the distribution of goods, and the avoidance of harms. For Beck, this earth politics has yet to develop fully – but is essential if we are to deal with the problems raised by globalization.

There is a new dialectic of global and local questions which do not fit into national politics. These 'glocal' questions, as we might call them, are already part of the political agenda – in the localities and regions, in governments and public spheres both national and international. But only in a transnational framework can they be properly posed, debated and resolved. (Beck, 1999, p. 15)

For Anthony Giddens (2001) this new global politics (a politics that is both globally shared and that deals with issues of globalization itself) is what he and others refer to as the *Third Way* in politics (see Chapter 6). Another thinker who shares this belief in the development of a new global politics is David Held (Held and Guibernau, 2001), who suggests that we are not witnessing the end of the state but rather increased activity of the state in the global sphere. Nation states are not over and they still command power within their territories, but seeing power and politics as *simply* and *solely* a product of decision-making within a set territory is too simplistic for the new global age. In particular, issues of fate and sovereignty have changed due to globalization. For Held, the idea that nation-states exclusively command their own separate fate without any consideration of the global is nonsense today. Instead, the focus of politics and the stage where it is played has moved – from the national to the international, but it is still very much the state that is the focus of this political activity.

Living in an unruly world?

A key theme provided by many sociologists when thinking about globalization is that of insecurity. Indeed, for some, this is a key characteristic of what we might call the 'postmodern condition' (see Chapter 5). For others, it is certainly true that society has changed – especially due to the impact of the process of globalization – and that this runaway or unruly world needs to be better understood.

As Herod *et al.* (1998) note:

> We live in unruly times and, increasingly, in unruly places and spaces. Throughout the globe at the end of the twentieth century a series of unruly and contradictory problematics are working themselves out across states, nations, economics, environments and bodies. (Herod *et al.*, 1998, p. 1)

Globalization itself is also seen as a contradiction – causing freedom and increased dependence; leading to insecurity, yet offering choices; creating risks and leading to new-style global politics. What is certain in this uncertain world is that society has profoundly changed – and that globalization is one of the key movements in the process.

PROTEST AND REVOLUTION

Giddens and Beck's notion of reflexive modernity suggest that people are thinking more about society, their position in society and who they wish to be. People have always engaged in protests against decisions made by rulers, but as business and commerce have become globalized, so have protests, through the creation of new social movements. But perhaps the most traditional and effective form of protest has been *political revolution*, in which one political system is overthrown, usually violently, and another put in its place.

Different political systems have been the subject of revolutions, and the systems that have replaced them have also varied. Often, revolutions overthrow colonial powers (e.g., the American War of Independence), monarchies (the French Revolution, the Russian Revolution) or military dictatorships (Nicaragua, Cuba). In the USA, colonial rule was replaced by a democratic republic, the French Revolution ended up with the return of a monarchy in the form of Napoleon, and the Russian Revolution led to a communist state, which itself was overturned in 1992. Despite this variation, revolutions do have features in common:

1. *Social and economic conditions*: clearly one of the conditions for a revolution is a large number of people who are economically deprived and feel exploited or oppressed. This was the case in Russia at the beginning of the twentieth century. In the UK at that time, working-class men had already been given the vote by Disraeli and his one-nation Toryism meant that people were receiving some degree of social welfare. Moreover, working people felt that they had a constitutional voice through trade unions and the newly formed Labour Party. This may be why mainstream socialism

in the UK has never been of the revolutionary kind. However, there is evidence to suggest that a people who are grossly deprived and oppressed are less likely to engage in revolution than when they begin to experience a slight improvement in their conditions. Severe deprivation leads to bitter resignation, whereas slight improvements in conditions lead to rising expectations and revolutionary fervour.

2. *Unresponsive governments*: the lack of success of revolutionary socialism in the UK at the end of the nineteenth and start of the twentieth centuries was less a function of the economic conditions of the people, but more a result of the perception that the state was prepared to change in order to benefit the working class. A government that is unwilling to reform in response to the calls of its own people is much more at risk of a revolution. The Czar in Russia was notoriously imperious, rejecting demands for social reform. When Marie-Antoinette, wife of the King of France, was told that thousands of French people had no bread to eat, she famously said 'Let them eat cake'.

3. *Radical intellectuals*: whereas Marx believed that revolutions in industrialized societies would result from a spontaneous uprising of the oppressed proletariat, all revolutions (including the one in Russia) have been led by small groups of radical intellectuals. In Russia, it was Lenin and the Bolsheviks, and the communist regime in the Soviet Union was later toppled largely as a result of the activities of university students and lecturers. Intellectuals have also had major parts to play in the pro-democracy movement in China, in the toppling of communist governments in Eastern Europe and in anti-colonial revolutions in South America.

4. *Legitimacy*: once a revolution has taken place and the existing system has been overthrown, the real task of the revolution begins. The overthrown leaders and their supporters will try to regain power, and measures must be put in place to defeat the counter-revolution. Marx referred to this stage, which he believed to be temporary, as the 'dictatorship of the proletariat', and argued that the revolution can only succeed if attempts to reverse it are ruthlessly suppressed. This has led in many cases to the killing of former leaders and violent suppression of any opposition to the revolution. However, the real task of any revolution is to change the hearts and minds of the people. Oppressed people may be unified by their common hatred of the oppressive regime, but once the regime has been disposed of, internal division and back-sliding can occur. A revolution can only succeed if it manages to undo the internalized oppression of its people, so that they genuinely believe in the principles of the new system, rather than turn on that as equally oppressive as the system that was originally overthrown.

Revolutions are often violent, but they consist of the oppressed majority using their superior numbers to overwhelm the controlling minority. People who are in the minority to begin with, but nevertheless wish to bring about the overthrow of a political system or regime, sometimes turn to *terrorism*.

Terrorism

Terrorism is the use of violence or the threat of violence in order to achieve political aims. The definition of terrorism used by the US State Department is 'politically motivated violence perpetrated against non-combatant targets by subnational groups of clandestine agents, usually intended to influence an audience' (Tilly, 2004).

Terrorist aims can be very specific; the IRA, for example, wanted British forces to leave Northern Ireland and for Ireland to become a single, united state. They can refer to social behaviour rather than obvious political questions; some animal rights activists, or anti-abortion campaigners, for example, occasionally threaten or carry out violence in order to prevent others from behaving in ways that they consider to be immoral. Or the aims can be political but general; it is not clear exactly what Al Qaeda hoped to gain by orchestrating the suicide bombings of the World Trade Center in 2001 apart from a general destabilization of Western democracies.

Bergesen and Lizardo (2004) list six ways in which terrorism has changed in recent times:

1. Terrorist organizations have tended to move away from a hierarchical system with a single command structure to a network form. Al Qaeda, for example, consists of independent cells, operating on their own and ignorant of each other's identity.
2. Terrorist organizations are less likely to openly claim responsibility for specific acts; very often no one will claim responsibility, or more than one organization will do so.
3. Terrorist demands used to be very specific; the releasing of named people from prison, for example. Nowadays, demands can be vague or even non-existent. For example, no demands were made by any group relating to the attacks in New York September 2001 or in London in July 2005.
4. Terrorist groups are increasingly linked to religious ideologies. This has been seen in the increase of terrorist attacks carried out by Islamist groups but also in other attacks, such as the release of poisonous gas in the Tokyo

underground by a religious group called Aum Shinrikyo. Previously, terrorist groups were more likely to be linked to class demands, for example, the German Red Army Faction.

5. Terrorist targets are increasingly spread around the world instead of being focused in Europe or in the Middle East. Apart from the attack in New York in 2001, there have been incidents in many other countries, such as Bali, Argentina and Kenya.

6. Terrorists have become more indiscriminate in their attacks and more willing to kill or injure civilians or bystanders.

These features of contemporary terrorism suggest that terrorism itself is becoming more globalized, and it may even be the case that many acts of terrorism are a response to changes in the global structure. As hegemonic empires such as the USA weaken they increasingly use military force to maintain their position, rather than relying on economic power and consent; this provokes terrorists to use force themselves.

Despite the fact that almost every society condemns acts of terrorism, Johnson (1981) suggests that those that perpetrate them try to argue that these acts of violence are legitimate political tactics, and are justified by the violent and oppressive acts of others. If terrorist organizations are compared to pressure groups that have adopted extreme tactics, then they would be outsider groups and relatively powerless to influence governments. They are weak organizations that use terror as a weapon against established regimes. Even if the terrorists do not succeed in persuading regimes to bow to their demands, then at least they have succeeded in drawing the world's attention to their conflict.

However, as Johnson points out, terrorist tactics can also be used by a government against its own people. *State terrorism* involves the use of (usually illegal) violence by a government or its agents against individuals or groups. This form of terrorism is present in authoritarian or totalitarian states, such as the former Soviet Union, North Korea, Nazi Germany, Iraq under Saddam Hussein etc. Despite being fundamentally in conflict with the principles of liberal democracy, it can be argued that state terrorism occurs even in countries such as the USA and the UK, albeit on a less widespread and systematic basis. For example, Margaret Thatcher's use of the Metropolitan Police force against striking miners in the 1980s, the detention and torture of suspects detained without trial at Guantanamo Bay by the US government etc.

A third point made by Johnson is that the principles that lead liberal democracies to reject terrorism also make them more vulnerable to terrorist attacks. Once these attacks take place it can be very difficult to identify and capture the perpetrators as terrorist organizations operate underground and with no clear links to any established state. The danger of identifying terrorists with an established state was clearly demonstrated in the USA's response to the bombing of the World Trade Center in 2001. Following this terrorist attack, the USA declared war on Afghanistan and then Iraq. Neither conflict was helpful in suppressing or reducing acts of terrorism. Governments under threat from terrorists are understandably reluctant to give in to the terrorist demands, but very often react to terrorist attacks by suspending or curtailing civil liberties in their own countries. This so-called war on terror is designed to protect the public by making it harder for terrorists to operate. However, it could be argued that the curtailments in civil liberties are more harmful to society than the initial attacks that provoked them. Furthermore, when specific acts of terror are somehow linked to particular groups of people, curtailment of civil liberties can lead to the targeting of specific groups which can be perceived as racist, thereby creating even more resentment. For example, Al Qaeda is linked to a form of fundamentalist Islamism which very few Muslims in the UK agree with. However, the activities of this terrorist group have led to Islamophobia and police discrimination in the UK, which has caused a great deal of resentment among the Muslim community and probably led to more young people being recruited to terrorist organizations.

Terrorist organizations have also moved into cyberspace to assist in achieving their political aims. The use of virtual communications has become a central strategy of terror groups, both in planning and executing violent actions and in waging ideological warfare. That is, terrorist groups not only seek to commit acts of violence but they also exercise 'soft power' through what is called 'cybercortical warfare'. The aim of such tactics is to influence the morale and will of those it sees as their enemies and to counterbalance the propaganda of established states to which they are opposed. To spread their views unmediated by governments and anti-terrorist forces, terrorist groups maintain a constant online presence (see Conway, 2006). They use this presence to publish their ideas, communicate anonymously between cells of the organisation and influence the international agenda. For example, they seek to counter the hostile global view of such groups through the use of alternative language and narratives, for example calling their activists 'freedom fighters' (see Reilly, 2006). However, it is difficult to assess the efficacy of terrorist groups' use of the Internet, partly because of the secretive nature of some of the communication and partly because those who visit the sites are likely to be already sympathetic, or accessing them as 'enemy combatants'. In a more proactive use of the internet, terrorist groups may also engage in cybercrime or cyberterrorism, attacking the communication technologies of states through hacking into protected sites to gather information or sabotage opponent websites.

Ⓐ

List as many examples as you can think of for each of the following:

1. international terrorist organizations
2. terrorist organization operating only within the UK
3. instances of state terrorism perpetrated by different governments (e.g., in Zimbabwe, the UK, the USA, etc.)
4. recent curtailments of civil liberties in the UK

War

Established regimes under attack from terrorists will always try to define and treat those terrorists as criminals, whereas the terrorists themselves tend to think of themselves as freedom fighters or soldiers in a war. War can be seen as arising out of the failure of politics to solve conflicts between groups of people, but it has not been a rare occurrence throughout the history of civilization. It is estimated that there have been about 14,500 major wars since 3600BC, killing around 4 billion people (Crump, 1999). The UK has fought in 25 separate wars since the Second World War ended in 1945, five of which have occurred within the life of the current Labour Government (Holsti, 2004).

Mary Kaldor (1999) has traced how the nature of war has changed over history:

- *Seventeenth and eighteenth centuries*: wars fought during this period tended to be waged by authoritarian dictatorships (monarchies) in order to consolidate borders or resolve dynastic conflicts. Soldiers were professional mercenaries and the key military tactics used were laying siege and defending citadels with the use of firearms and gunpowder. Armies were paid for by taxation and borrowing.
- *Nineteenth century*: with the advent of nation-states, wars reflected conflicts between nations. Armies were still professional, but conscription became necessary in order to make up the numbers. The advent of railways and telegraph made rapid mobilization possible.
- *Early twentieth century*: the First World War was so called because it involved conflicts between coalitions of states and empires, rather than individual nation-states. Wars were fought not simply as a result of national conflict but, as in the Spanish War, for ideological reasons as well. The scale of war increased dramatically, with the advent of mass armies and the enormous firepower of tanks and aircraft. Civilians began to be

seen as legitimate targets of war and a mobilization economy provided the funding.

▪ *Late twentieth century*: wars now tend to be fought between blocs and are mostly based on ideological conflict. The participants are smaller numbers of highly trained professionals, using highly technologically developed weapons, including nuclear weapons. The business of war is underpinned by a widespread military-industrial complex.

It may be that war in the twenty-first century will focus on information technology so that military power, defined by Giddens (1990) as 'control of the means of violence', will consist of the ability to damage the enemy's information infrastructure using computers rather than guns. Giddens argues that the industrialization of war has increased the ability of nation states to use violence and that this has led to new peace movements. Organized peace movements go back to the First World War, when it became clear that war was becoming increasingly destructive. The advent of nuclear weapons meant that war has become incalculably more dangerous for ordinary people and this has increased the prominence of peace movements.

Ⓐ
Exercise 9.12

What do you think a twenty-first-century 'information war' would consist of? What would you target if you wished to attack the information structure of a country, and how might you do it?

CONCLUSION

This chapter has examined the history and definitions of nationalism and nation states. Some argue that the advent of information technology and cheap transport has created a globalized world in which the concept of the nation has a much smaller role than before. It is true that conflicts in the twenty-first century tend to be between ideologically based blocs rather than individual nation states, but, on the other hand, new nation-states are continuing to be created in different areas of the world and seem to be an important aspect of people's sense of identity.

Exam focus

'Theories of globalization have exaggerated the loss of power of the nation-state.' Evaluate the arguments and evidence for this view.

First, attempt this question without looking back to any of the material in the chapter. This should provide you with a skeletal outline for a full response. Then, go over the material in the chapter, selecting which arguments and studies might be useful to build up the knowledge in your response (**K, U**). Next, choose where you are going to place those arguments and studies in your outline response and rewrite your answer (**I, A**). Read through your work and decide if there are any parts of it that need to be boosted (**An**) and re-read the chapter, looking for relevant information to include. Lastly, re-read your answer looking for evaluation points that you have included (**E**) and for each one add to it to build up your marks for evaluation. If necessary, rewrite your conclusion to ensure that you sum up the arguments in favour and against the view expressed in the question and decide which position is better supported by the evidence.

Important concepts

- nationalism • natural nationalism • the information society • national identity • imagined communities • myth of origin • globalization • internationalization • liberalization • universalization • westernization • deterritoriality • supra-territoriality • economic globalization • cultural globalization • political globalization • environmental globalization • the risk society • new global politics • protest, revolution, terrorism, war

Summary points

- From the late seventeenth to the late eighteenth centuries 'national' developed its modern political sense, referring to a population within a specific territory who are the *subjects* of those who rule the territory.

    o Weber identifies a number of problems when thinking about what a nation is. He defines a nation as a community which normally tends to produce a state of its own.

    o Gellner argues that it is not that nations create feelings of nationalism, but rather, that the ideology of nationalism creates the nations themselves.

- o In contrast, Shils argues that nationalism is a 'natural' feature of all human societies.
- o Bauman suggests that feelings of nationalism are very powerful and that nationalism is ultimately rational. He refers to nationality as an 'imagined community'. A key set of symbols used by nationalist ideologies to create this imagined community is the 'myth of origin'.

- There are several different definitions of the term **'globalization'**:

  - o *internationalization*
  - o *liberalization*
  - o *universalization*
  - o *Westernization*
  - o *deterritoriality* or *supra-territoriality*

- We can identify a number of types of globalization:

  - o *economic globalization*
  - o *cultural globalization*
  - o *political globalization*
  - o *environmental globalization*

- The process of globalization is experienced across the world in a highly contradictory fashion. It creates security and at the same time causes anxiety; it protects and it creates risks; it creates opportunity and it takes away autonomy; it encourages redistribution and it furthers inequality.

  - o Beck argues that the effect of globalization is to both create a *post-traditional social order* and to create a *risk society*.
  - o Giddens suggests that the awareness of risks in society leads to a situation of *manufactured uncertainty*. The awareness of these global risks leads to a period of 'reflexive modernity'.
  - o The political implication of global risks is the rise of *a new global politics* that seeks to manage the insecurity that global risks cause. Giddens refers to this new global politics as the *Third Way*.

- The notion of reflexive modernity suggests that people are thinking more about society, their position in society and who they wish to be. However, the most traditional and effective form of protest has been *political revolution*, in which one political system is overthrown, and another put in its place.

  - o Revolutions are often violent, but they consist of the oppressed majority using their superior numbers to overwhelm the controlling minority.
  - o People who are in the minority to begin with, but nevertheless wish to bring about the overthrow of a political system or regime, sometimes turn to *terrorism*.
  - o Terrorist tactics can also be used by a government against its own people.

- ○ Established regimes under attack from terrorists will always try to define and treat those terrorists as criminals, whereas the terrorists themselves tend to think of themselves as soldiers in a war.
- ○ War can be seen as arising out of the failure of politics to solve conflicts between groups of people, but it has been a common occurrence throughout history and its nature has changed over time with the development of new technologies.

Critical thinking

1. What should the role of a citizen be in a modern nation?
2. Do nations lead to nationalism or does nationalism lead to the creation of nations?
3. Why do people form nations?
4. Define the term globalization.
5. What are the advantages and disadvantages of globalization?
6. Do revolutions ever succeed?
7. What is the difference between a soldier fighting in a war and a terrorist?

References

Abbot, P. and Wallace, C. (1991) *Gender, Power and Sexuality* (London: Macmilllan).

Abbot, P. and Wallace, C. (1997) *An Introduction to Sociology: Feminist Perspectives* (2nd edn) (London and New York: Routledge).

Althusser, L. (1971) *Lenin and Philosophy* (New York: Monthly Review Press).

Amos, V. and Parmar, P. (1984) 'Challenging Imperial Feminism', *Feminist Review*, Vol. 17.

Anderson, B. (1991) *Imagined Communities: Reflections on the Origin and Spread of Nationalism* (revised edn) (London and New York: Verso).

Arblaster, A. (1994) *Democracy* (2nd edn) (Buckingham: Open University Press).

Arquilla, J. and Ronfeldt, D. F. (2001) *Networks and Netwars: The Future of Terror, Crime, and Militancy* (Santa Monica, CA: RAND).

Ashe, F., Finlayson, A., Lloyd, M., MacKenzie, I. and Martin, J. (1999) *Contemporary Social and Political Theory: An Introduction* (Buckingham: Open University Press).

Baudrillard, J. (1983) *Simulations* (New York: Semiotext(e)).

Bauman, Z. (1990) *Thinking Sociologically: An Introduction for Everyone* (Cambridge, MA: Basil Blackwell).

Bauman, Z. (1992) *Intimations of Postmodernity* (London: Routledge).

Bauman, Z. (1998) *Work, Consumerism and the New Poor* (Buckingham: Open University Press).

Bauman, Z. (1999) *In Search of Politics* (Cambridge: Polity Press).

Bauman, Z. (2000) *Liquid Modernity* (Cambridge: Polity Press).

Beck, U. (1999) *What Is Globalization?* (Cambridge: Polity Press).

Beck, U., Giddens, A. and Lash, S. (1994) *Reflexive Modernization: Politics, Traditions and Aesthetics in the Modern Social Order* (Stanford, CA: Stanford University Press).

Becker, H. (1963) *Outsiders: Studies in the Sociology of Deviance* (New York: Free Press).

Beer, S. (1985) *Diagnosing the System for Organization* (Chichester: Wiley).

Bennett, W. L. (2003) 'Communicating Global Activism: Strengths and Vulnerabilities of Networked Politics', *Information, Communication and Society* 6:2.

Bergeson, A. J. and Lizardo, O. (2004) 'International Terrorism and the World-system', *Sociological Theory* 22:1.

Berra, M. (2003) 'Information Communications Technology and Local Development', *Telematics and Informatics* 20:3.

Bimber, B. (2003) *Information and American Democracy: technology in the evolution of political power* (Cambridge: Cambridge University Press).

Bimber, B., Stohl, C. and Flanagin, A. J. (2009) 'Technological Change and the Shifting Nature of Political Organisation', in A. Chadwick and P. N. Howard (eds), *Routledge Handbook of Internet Politics* (Abingdon: Routledge).

Birch, A. H. (1993) *The Concepts and Theories of Modern Democracy* (London: Routledge).

Börzell, T. A. and Risse, T. (2003) 'Conceptualising the Domestic Impact of Europe', in K. Featherstone and C. M. Radaelli (eds), *The Politics of Europeanisation* (Oxford: Oxford University Press).

Brittan, S. (1975) *Second Thoughts on Full Employment Policy* (London: CPS).

Butler, D. and Stokes, D. (1969) *Political Change in Britain* (London: Macmillan).

Cabras, A. (2002) 'Beyond the Internet: Democracy on the Phone?', in M. J. Mazarr (ed.), *Information Technology and World Politics* (Basingstoke: Palgrave Macmillan).

Callinicos, A. (2001) *Against the Third Way* (Cambridge: Polity Press).

Callinicos, A (2003) *An Anti-Capitalist Manifesto* (Cambridge: Polity Press).

Callinicos, A. and Harman, C. (1987) *The Changing Working Class: Essays on Class Structure Today* (London: Bookmarks).

Castells, M. (2004) *The Power of Identity: The Information Age, Economy, Society and Culture Volume 2* (2nd edn) (Oxford: Blackwell).

Chadwick, A. (2006) *Internet Politics: States, Citizens and New Communication Technologies* (Oxford: Oxford University Press).

Churton, M. and Brown, A. (2009) *Theory and Method* (Basingstoke: Palgrave Macmillan).

Coglianese, C. (2004) 'Information Technology and Regulatory Policy: New Directions for Digital Government Research', *Social Science Computer Review* 22:1.

Cohen, N. (2001) 'Democracy is dead. Now what?' *New Statesman* 11 June.

Cohen, R. and Kennedy, P. (2007) *Global Sociology* (Basingstoke: Palgrave Macmillan).

Cohen, S. (1972) *Folk Devils and Moral Panics* (London: MacGibbon and Kee).

Cohen, S. (2002) *Folk Devils and Moral Panics: the Creation of theMods and Rockers* (3rd edn) (London: Routledge).

Conway, M. (2006) 'Cybercortical Warfare: Hizbollah's Strategy', in S. Oates, D. Owen and R. K. Gibson (eds), *The Internet and Politics: Citizens, Voters and Activists* (London: Routledge).

Cornfield, M. (2004) *Politics Moves Online: Campaigning and the Internet* (New York: Century Foundation Press).

Crewe, I. (1986) 'On the Death and Resurrection of Class Voting in Britain: Some Critical Comments on How Britain Votes', *Political Studies* XXXIV:4.

Crook, S., Pakulski, J. and Waters, M. (1992) *Postmodernization: Changes in Advanced Society* (London: Sage).

Crump, A. (1999) *The A–Z of World Development* (London: New Internationalist).

Dahl, R. A. (1961) *Who Governs? Democracy and Power in an American City* (New Haven, CT: Yale University Press).

Dahlberg, L. (2001) 'The Internet and Democratic Discourse: Exploring the Prospects of Online Deliberative Forums Extending the Public Sphere', *Information, Communication and Society* 4:1.

Delphy, C. (1984) *Close to Home: A Materialist Analysis of Women's Oppression* (Amherst, MA: University of Massachusetts).

Denver, D. (2006) 'A Matter of Duty?' *Sociology Review* 15:4

Diani, M. (2000) 'Social Movement Networks: Virtual and Real', *Information, Communication and Society* 3:3.

Dowding, K. (1996) *Power (Concepts in Social Thought)* (Minneapolis: University of Minnesota Press).

Downs, A. (1957) *An Economic Theory of Democracy* (New York: Harper and Brothers).

Dunleavy, P. and Husbands, C. (1985) *British Democracy at the Crossroads* (London: George Allen & Unwin).

Dunleavy, P. and O'Leary B. (1987) *Theories of the State* (London: Macmillan).

Durkheim, E. (1988) *Über die soziale Arbeitsteilung* (Frankfurt: Suhrkamp).

Eatwell R. and Wright, A. (eds) (1993) *Contemporary Political Ideologies* (London: Pinter).

Etzioni, A. (1995) *The Spirit of Community: Rights Responsibilities and the Communitarian Agenda* (London: Fontana Press).

Firestone, S. (1979) *The Dialectic of Sex: The Case for Feminist Revolution* (London: Women's Press).

Foucault, M. (1984) 'Space, Knowledge, and Power', in P. Rabinow (ed.), *The Foucault Reader* (New York: Pantheon).

Foucault, M. (1991 [1977]) *Discipline and Punish: The Birth of the Prison* (Harmondsworth: Penguin).

Friedrich, C. J. (1954) 'The Unique Character of Totalitarian Society', in C. J. Friedrich (ed.), *Totalitarianism: Proceedings of a Conference Held at the American Academy of Arts and Sciences, March 1953* (Cambridge, MA: Harvard University Press).

Fukuyama, F. (1992) *The End of History and the Last Man* (Harmondsworth: Penguin).

Furlong, A. and Cartmel, F. (1997) *Young People and Social Change: Individualization and Risk in Late Modernity* (Buckinghamshire: Open University Press).

Gamble, A. (2000) *Politics and Fate* (Cambridge: Polity Press).

Gane, M. (ed.) (1992) *The Radical Sociology of Durkheim and Mauss* (New York: Routledge).

Gellner, E. (1964) *Thought and Change* (London: Weidenfeld and Nicolson).

Gellner, E. (1983) *Nations and Nationalism* (Ithaca, NY: Cornell University Press).

Gibbins, J. (ed.) (1989) *Contemporary Political Culture: Politics in a Postmodern Age* (London: Sage).

Gibson, R. K., Lusoli, W. and Ward, S. J. (2005) 'Online Participation in the UK: Testing a Contextualized Model of Internet Effects', *British Journal of Politics and International Relations* 7:4.

Giddens, A. (1971) *Capitalism and Modern Social Theory: An Analysis of the Writings of Marx, Durkheim and Max Weber* (Cambridge: Cambridge University Press).

Giddens, A. (1972) *Politics and Sociology in the Thought of Max Weber* (London: Macmillan).

Giddens, A. (1981) *The Class Structure of the Advanced Societies* (London: Hutchinson).

Giddens, A. (1985) *A Contemporary Critique of Historical Materialism. Vol. 2. The Nation State and Violence* (Cambridge: Polity Press).

Giddens, A. (1986) *Durkheim* (London: Fontana Modern Masters).

Giddens, A. (1990) *The Consequences of Modernity* (Cambridge: Polity Press).

Giddens, A (1991) *Modernity and Self-Identity: Self and Society in the Late Modern Age* (Cambridge: Polity Press).

Giddens, A. (1993) *Sociology* (Cambridge: Polity Press).

Giddens, A. (1994) *Beyond Left and Right – the Future of Radical Politics* (Cambridge: Polity Press).

Giddens, A. (1998) *The Third Way: The Renewal of Social Democracy* (Cambridge: Polity Press).

Giddens, A. (1999) *Reith Lectures*, http://news.bbc.uk

Giddens, A. (2000) *The Third Way and Its Critics* (Cambridge: Polity Press).

Giddens, A. (ed.) (2001) *The Global Third Way Debate* (Cambridge: Polity Press).

Giddens, A. (2006) *Sociology* (Cambridge: Polity Press).

Goffman, E. (1969) *Behaviour in Public Places* (Harmondsworth: Penguin).

Goffman, E. (1974) *Frame Analysis: An Essay on the Organization of Experience* (New York: Harper & Row).

Goldthorpe, J. H., Lockwood, D., Bechhofer, F. and Platt, J. (1968) *The Affluent Worker: Attitudes and Behaviour* (Cambridge: Cambridge University Press).

Graf, J., Reeher, G., Malbin, J. and Panagopoulos, C. (2006) *Small Donors and Online Giving: A Study of Donors to the 2004 Presidential Campaigns* (Washington, DC: Institute of Politics).

Gramsci, A. (1971) *Selections from the Prison Notebooks* (London: Lawrence and Wishart).

Grant, W. (1985) 'Insider and Outsider Pressure Groups', *Social Studies Review*, September.

Habermas, J. (1987) *The Theory of Communicative Action (Vol. 2): Lifeworld and System – A Critique of Functionalist Reason* (Cambridge: Polity Press).

Habermas, J. (1988) *On the Logic of the Social Sciences* (Cambridge: Polity Press).

Habermas, J. (1991) *The Structural Transformation of the Public Sphere: An Inquiry into a category of Bourgeois Society* (trans. Thomas Burger with Frederick Lawrence) (Cambridge, MA: MIT Press).

Hakim, C. (1995) 'Five Feminist Myths about Women's Employment', *British Journal of Sociology* 46:3.

Hall, S. (1984) 'The State in Question', in G. McLennan, D. Held and S. Hall (eds), *The Idea of the Modern State* (Buckingham: Open University Press).

Hallsworth, S. (1994) 'Understanding New Social Movements', *Sociology Review* 4.

Hartmann, H. (1981) 'The Unhappy Marriage of Marxism and Feminism: Towards a More Progressive Union', in L.Sargent (ed.), *Women in Revolution: The Unhappy Marriage of Marxism and Feminism* (London: Pluto Press).

Heath, A. F., Jowell, R. and Curtice, J. (1985) *How Britain Votes* (Oxford: Pergamon).

Heaton, T. and Lawson, T. (2009) *Education and Training* (Basingstoke: Palgrave Macmillan).

Held, D. (ed.) (1993) *Prospects for Democracy: North, South, East, West* (Cambridge: Polity Press).

Held, D. and Guibernau, M. (2001) 'Globalization, cosmopolitanism, and democracy: an interview with David Held' *Constellations 9 (4)*.

Heller, A. and Feher, F. (1991 [1988]) *The Postmodern Political Condition* (Cambridge: Polity Press).

Herod, A., O'Tuathail, G. and Roberts, S. (eds) (1998) *An Unruly World? Globalization, Governance and Geography* (London: Routledge).

Himmelweit, H. T., Humphreys, P. and Jaeger, M. (1985) *How Voters Decide* (revised edn) (Buckingham: Open University Press).

Hobsbawm, E. J. (1992) *Nations and Nationalism since 1780. Programme, Myth, Reality* (2nd edn) (Cambridge: Cambridge University Press).

Holsti, K. J. (2004) *The State, War and the State of War* (Cambridge: Cambridge University Press).

House of Commons (2001a) *Research Paper 01/38, General Election results, 1 May 1997* (London: House of Commons).

House of Commons (2001b) *Research Paper 01/54, General Election results, 7 June 2001* (London: House of Commons).

House of Commons (2005) *Research Paper 05/33, General Election results 2005* (London: House of Commons).

Hunter, F. (1953) *Community Power Structure: A Study of Decision Makers* (Chapel Hill: University of North Carolina Press).

Hutchinson, J. and Smith, A. D. (eds) (1994) *Nationalism* (Oxford: Open University Press).

Inglehart, R. (1990) *Culture Shift in Advanced Industrial Society* (Princeton, NJ: Princeton University Press).

Jalonick, M. C. (2006) 'YouTube Catches Candidates in Compromising Positions', *USA Today* 22 August.

Jensen, C. S. (2000) 'Neofunctionalist Theories and the Development of European Social and Labour Market Policy', I 38:1.

Johnson, P. (1981) 'The Seven Deadly Sins of Terrorism', in B. Netanyahu (ed.), *International Terrorism* (New Brunswick, NJ: Transaction).

Jones, M. and Jones, E. (1999) *Mass Media* (London: Macmillan).

Kaldor, M. (1999) *New and Old Wars: Organized Violence in a Global Era* (Cambridge: Polity Press).

Kane, S. and Kirby, M. (2003) *Wealth, Poverty and Welfare* (Basingstoke, Palgrave).

Kidd, W. (2001) *Culture and Identity* (Basingstoke: Palgrave Macmillan).

Kirby, M. (1999) *Stratification and Differentiation* (London: Macmillan).

Klein, N. (2000) *No Logo* (London: Flamingo).

Kumar, K. (1978) *Prophecy and Progress: The Sociology of Industrial and Post-Industrial Society* (Harmondsworth: Penguin).

Lash, S. and Urry, J. (1987) *The End of Organised Capitalism*. University of Wisconsin Press.

Lash, S. and Urry, J. (1994) *Economies of Signs and Space (Theory, Culture & Society)* (London: Sage).

Lawson, T. and Heaton, T. (2009) *Crime and Deviance* (Basingstoke: Palgrave Macmillan).

Lindblom, C. E. (1977) *Politics and Markets* (New York: Basic Books).

Lukes, S. (1974) *Power: A Radical View* (London: Macmillan).

Lusoli, W. and Ward, S. J. (2006) 'Hunting Protestors: Mobilisation, Participation and Protest Online in the Countryside Alliance', in S. Oates, D. M. Owen and R. K. Gibson (eds), *The Internet and Politics: Citizens, Voters and Activists* (London: Routledge).

Lyotard J.-F. (1984) *The Postmodern Condition: A Report on Knowledge* (Manchester: University of Manchester Press).

MacDonald, R. and Coffield, F. (1991) *Risky Business? Youth and Enterprise Culture* (London: Falmer Press).

MacKenzie, I. (2005) *Politic Concepts: A Reader and Guide* (Edinburgh: Edinburgh University Press).

Mackintosh, M. and Mooney, G. (2000) 'Identity, Inequality and Social Class', in K. Woodward. (ed.), *Questioning Identity: Gender, Class and Ethnicity* (London: Routledge).

Majone, G. (2005) *Dilemmas of European Integration: The Ambiguities and Pitfalls of Integration by Stealth* (Oxford: Oxford University Press).

Mann, M. (1986) *The Sources of Social Power: A History of Power from the Beginning to A.D. 1760 (Vol. 1)* (New York: Cambridge University Press).

Marx, K. and Engels, F. (1969) [1848] 'The Manifesto of the Communist Party' in *Marx/Engels Selected Works, Volume One* (Moscow: Progress Publishers) pp. 98–137.

Marsh, D. (1983) *Pressure Politics: Interest Groups in Britain* (London: Junction).

Marshall, G., Newby, H., Rose, D. and and Vogler, C. (1988) *Social Class in Modern Britain* (London: Hutchinson).

Marx, K. (1954 [1852]) *The Eighteenth Brumaire of Louis Bonaparte* (Moscow: Progress).

Marx, K. (1963 [1845]) *Karl Marx: Early Writings* (trans. and ed. by T. B. Bottomore) (New York: McGraw-Hill).

Marx, K. and Engels, F. (1967 [1848]) *The Communist Manifesto* (New York: Penguin).

Marx, K. and Engels, F. (1976 [1845]) *The German Ideology* (Moscow: Progress).

McAllister Groves, J. (1995) 'Learning to Feel: The Neglected Sociology of Social Movements', *The Sociological Review* 43:3.

McLellan, D. (1995) *Ideology* (2nd edn) (Buckingham: Open University Press).

Michels, R. (1962 [1911]) *Political Parties* (New York: Free Press).

Mills, C. Wright (1956 [1970]) *The Power Elite* (New York: Oxford University Press).

Mills, C. Wright (1959) *The Sociological Imagination* (New York: Oxford University Press).

Mills, C. Wright (1963) *Power, Politics & People: The Collected Essays of C. Wright Mills* (New York: Oxford University Press).

Moravcsik, A. (2005) 'The European Constitutional Compromise and the Neo-functionalist Legacy', *Journal of European Public Policy* 12:2.

Nash, K. (2000) *Contemporary Political Sociology: Globalization, Politics and Power* (Oxford: Blackwell).

Offe, C. (1996) *Modernity and the State: East, West* (Cambridge, MA: MIT Press).

Ohmae, K. (1995) *The End of the Nation State: The Rise of Regional Economies* (London: Free Press).

Park, A. (1996) 'Teenagers and Their Politics', in R. Jowell, J. Curtice, A. Park, L. Brook and D. Ahrendt (eds), *British Social Attitudes Survey: 12th Report* (Aldershot: Dartmouth).

Parsons, T. (1960) *Structure and Process in Modern Societies* (Glencoe, IL: Free Press).

Parsons, T. (1967) *Sociological Theory and Modern Society* (New York: Free Press).

Pattie, C., Seyd, P. and Whiteley, P. (2004) *Citizenship in Britain: Values, Participation and Democracy* (Cambridge: Cambridge University Press).

Pearce, F. (1989) *The Radical Durkheim* (Winchester, MA: Unwin Hyman).

Pollack, M. (2002) *The Engines of Integration: Delegation, Agencies and Agenda-setting in the EU* (Oxford: Oxford University Press).

Reilly, P. (2006) 'Civil Society, the Internet and Terrorism', in S. Oates, D. Owen and R. K. Gibson (eds), *The Internet and Politics: Citizens, Voters and Activists* (London: Routledge).

Rheingold, H. (2002) *Smart Mobs: The Next Social Revolution* (London: Perseus).

Richardson, J. J. and Jordan, A. G. (1979) *Governing Under Pressure: the Policy Process in a Post-parliamentary Democracy* (Oxford: Martin Robertson).

Rocher, G. (1974) *Talcott Parsons and American Sociology* (London: Nelson).

Rodgers, J. (2003) *Spatialising International Politics: Analysing Activism on the Internet* (London: Routledge).

Rosamund, B. (2000) *Theories of Europen Integration* (Basingstoke: Palgrave Macmillan).

Rose, R. and McAllister, I. (1990) *The Loyalties of Voters: A Lifetime Learning Model* (London: Sage).

Ryan, A. (1999) 'Britain: recycling the Third Way', *Dissent* 46/2.

Sandholtz, W. and Stone Sweet, A. (1998) *European Integration and Supranational Governance* (Oxford: Oxford University Press).

Sarup, M. (1993) *Post-Structuralism and Postmodernism* (Hemel Hempstead: Harvester Wheatsheaf).

Saunders, P. (1990) *Social Class and Stratification* (London: Routledge).

Scholte, J. A. (2000) *Globalization: A Critical Introduction* (New York: Palgrave) p. 1.

Senior, M. and Viveash, B. (1998) *Health and Illness* (London: Macmillan).

Shils, E. (1957) 'Primordial, Personal, Sacred, and Civil Ties', *British Journal of Sociology* 8.

Smith, A. D. (1986) *The Ethnic Origins of Nations* (Oxford: Blackwell).

Steele, L. and Kidd, W. (2000) *The Family* (Basingstoke: Palgrave Macmillan).

Tilly, C. (2004) 'Terror, Terrorism, Terrorists', *Sociological Theory* 22:1.

Topf, R. (1989) 'Political Change and Political Culture in Britain, 1959–87', in J. Gibbins (ed.), *Contemporary Political Culture* (London: Sage).

UNDP (United Nations Development Programme) (1999) *Human Development Report: Globalization with a Human Face*.

Walby, S. (1986) *Patriarchy at Work* (Cambridge: Polity Press).

Walby, S. (1988) 'Gender Politics and Social Theory', *Sociology* 22:2.

Walby, S. (1990) *Theorising Patriarchy* (Oxford: Blackwell).

Walby, S. (1997) *Gender Transformations* (London: Routledge).

Waters, M. (1995) *Globalization* (London: Routledge).

Weber, M. (1948) 'Politics as a Vocation', in H. Gerth and C. W. Mills (eds), *Max Weber: Essays in Sociology* (London: Routledge).

Weber, M. (1968 [1921]) *Economy and Society: An Outline of Interpretive Sociology*, 2 vols (ed. By G. Ross and K. Wittich) (Berkeley, CA: University of California Press).

Weber, M. (1978) *Economy and Society: An Outline of Interpretive Sociology* (Berkeley, CA: University of California Press).

Westergaard, J. and Resler, H. (1976) *Class in a Capitalist Society: A Study of Contemporary Britain* (New York: Basic Books).

Williams, A. (2007) 'The Future President, on your friends list', *New York Times* 18 March.

Williams, R. (1976) *Keywords: A Vocabulary of Culture and Society* (London: Croom Helm).

Zweig, F. (1961) *The Worker in an Affluent Society* (London: Heinemann).

Index

Titles in the
Skills-Based Sociology *series*

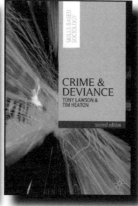

978-0-333-68763-5   978-0-230-21782-9   978-0-230-21781-2

*Designed to cover the key concepts, issues and
contemporary debates in Sociology*

978-0-333-96889-5   978-0-230-21792-8

To order visit www.palgrave.com